LEGALIZED INEQUALITIES

LEGALIZED INEQUALITIES

IMMIGRATION AND RACE IN THE
LOW-WAGE WORKPLACE

*Kati L. Griffith, Shannon Gleeson, Darlène Dubuisson,
and Patricia Campos-Medina*

The Russell Sage Foundation   NEW YORK

THE RUSSELL SAGE FOUNDATION

The Russell Sage Foundation, one of the oldest of America's general purpose foundations, was established in 1907 by Mrs. Margaret Olivia Sage for "the improvement of social and living conditions in the United States." The foundation seeks to fulfill this mandate by fostering the development and dissemination of knowledge about the country's political, social, and economic problems. While the foundation endeavors to assure the accuracy and objectivity of each book it publishes, the conclusions and interpretations in Russell Sage Foundation publications are those of the authors and not of the foundation, its trustees, or its staff. Publication by Russell Sage, therefore, does not imply foundation endorsement.

BOARD OF TRUSTEES
Jennifer Richeson, Chair

Marianne Bertrand	David Laibson	Thomas J. Sugrue
Cathy J. Cohen	David Leonhardt	Celeste Watkins-Hayes
James N. Druckman	Earl Lewis	Bruce Western
Jason Furman	Hazel Rose Markus	
Michael Jones-Correa	Tracey L. Meares	

ROR: https://ror.org/02yh9se80
DOI: https://doi.org/10.7758/rioz4023

LIBRARY OF CONGRESS CATALOGING IN PUBLICATION CONTROL NUMBERS:

LCCN 2024058835 (print) | LCCN 2024058836 (ebook)
ISBN 9780871545343 paperback | ISBN 9781610449403 ebook

Copyright © 2025 by Russell Sage Foundation. All rights reserved. Printed in the United States of America. No part of this publication may be reproduced, stored in a retrieval system, or transmitted in any form or by any means, electronic, mechanical, photocopying, recording, or otherwise, without the prior written permission of the publisher. Permission is not granted for large language model training. Reproduction by the United States Government in whole or in part is permitted for any purpose.

Cover art: *Dignidad trabajadora* by Orlando Hernandez. 37,36 cm by 56,44 cm, digital illustration created in Adobe Photoshop. © 2025 Orlando Hernandez. Reprinted with permission.

The paper used in this publication meets the minimum requirements of American National Standard for Information Sciences—Permanence of Paper for Printed Library Materials. ANSI Z39.48-1992.

Text design by Matthew T. Avery. Front matter DOI: https://doi.org/10.7758/rioz4023.8852

RUSSELL SAGE FOUNDATION
112 East 64th Street, New York, New York 10065
10 9 8 7 6 5 4 3 2 1

CONTENTS

List of Tables vii
About the Authors ix
Acknowledgments xi

1   Introduction *1*

PART 1 Underregulated Rights at Work 21

2   Worker Precarity in the Low-Wage Workplace *23*
3   Challenging Precarity in the Low-Wage Workplace: Barriers and Pathways *40*

PART 2 An Immigration Regime at Work 67

4   How the US Immigration Regime Shapes Worker Precarity *69*
5   The US Immigration Regime as Barrier and Pathway to Challenging Precarity *97*

PART 3 Racisms and Colonial Legacies at Work 113

6   How Racisms and Colonial Legacies Shape Worker Precarity *115*
7   Racisms and Colonial Legacies as Barriers and Pathways to Challenging Precarity *145*
8   Conclusion *163*

Methodological Appendix 185
Notes 193
References 213
Index 243

TABLES

Table 1.1 Regional Origin by Immigration Status, Gender, Location, and Education 8

Table 1.2 Average Age and Time in the United States (in Years) by Immigration Status and Regional Origin 9

Table 2.1 Job Type by Gender, Regional Origin, and Immigration Status 32

Table 3.1 Pathways to Challenging Bad Jobs: Wages Example 53

Table 4.1 Immigration Regime Mechanisms and the Nature of Worker Precarity 70

ABOUT THE AUTHORS

KATI L. GRIFFITH is the Jean McKelvey-Alice Grant Professor in the Department of Global, Labor and Work at the School of Industrial and Labor Relations at Cornell University.

SHANNON GLEESON is the Edmund Ezra Day Professor in the Department of Global, Labor and Work at the School of Industrial and Labor Relations and the Brooks School of Public Policy at Cornell University.

DARLÈNE DUBUISSON is assistant professor of Caribbean studies at the University of California, Berkeley.

PATRICIA CAMPOS-MEDINA is a Senior RTE Faculty and the executive director of the Worker Institute at the School of Industrial and Labor Relations at Cornell University.

ACKNOWLEDGMENTS

The idea for this book emerged from a great conversation over a not-so-great meal at a now-defunct restaurant in Ithaca, New York, in 2015. A law scholar and a sociologist, both interested in access to justice for low-wage immigrant workers, came together to launch this project. Fueled also by conversations with a multidisciplinary team at what was then the Institute for Social Sciences (Steven Alvarado, Matt Hall, and Jordan Matsudaira), Kati Griffith and Shannon Gleeson embarked on what would become a large-scale investigation into the nature of low-wage immigrant work.

This effort crucially relied on the expertise of two scholars who brought important disciplinary insights to the work and were rooted in the communities from which we were learning. Darlène Dubuisson, an anthropologist and Haitian studies scholar, joined the project, first as an interviewer, then as an invaluable intellectual partner. Then Patricia Campos-Medina, political scientist and longtime labor leader, contributed her decades of experience working closely with the Central American immigrant community. While working across canons and methods might seem like a challenge, it turned out to be one of our superpowers. We stripped ourselves of the conveniences of disciplinary jargon to find our common ground. We listened to each other and pushed ourselves to travel into new intellectual territory. It has been a long road to get here, and we have many people and institutions to thank.

First and foremost, we thank the workers who spent time with our research team. They often had to travel long distances after working long shifts to engage in an interview with us. They shared their often difficult and degrading experiences at work and narrated what, in their opinion, was driving the inequalities they faced. They shared their hopes for a better future for themselves, their families, and the country they left as well as the country they now called home. They talked about the impact of immigration policies on their everyday dealings with employers, the non-immigrant public, and government authorities, and also about racism as a palpable daily reality rather than a historical artifact in their lives. Their voices are the bedrock of this book, and we honor their time and contribution. Lawyers, union organizers, and other advocates also lent their voices to this project. They too are immensely busy and yet still managed to carve out time to meet with our team. We thank them for their willingness to share their expertise and for describing both the challenges and opportunities they faced in their immigrant worker advocacy.

Our team's interviewers were outstanding. They brought both their language skills and their cultural expertise to the process of recruiting and interviewing workers. They were thoughtful and resourceful, working around their own and respondents' busy schedules and complicated work and home lives. They were patient and persistent, even as we weaved our way through the unknowns of the COVID-19 pandemic. We thank Alicia Canas, Jhims Gerard, James Alaindy Gourdet, Kennys Lawson, Jessica Santos, Perry Tima, Lynne Turner, and Daphney Vastey, as well as our two coauthors, Darlène and Patricia, who conducted the bulk of the interviews.

We engaged dozens of scholars, including many undergraduates from Cornell's ILR School as well as Cornell Law students and other students across Cornell. They performed a wide spectrum of tasks, from the most tedious to the most analytically interesting, depending on the season of the project. They too contributed important insights, drawing sometimes on their own family backgrounds and community relationships. Some honed their analytical skills through the time-consuming but analytically critical process of transcribing and coding interviews, as well as drafting memos. All of their contributions are evident in the pages that follow, and we thank them for the time, effort, and talent that they brought to the project over the last ten years: Caro Achar, Gaëlle Alcindor, Kevin Alvarenga, Kevin Diaz, Dolores Eslava, Alexis Fintland, Mimi Goldberg, Juan Guevara,

Christopher Ioannou, Christina Jean-Louis, Sophonie Joseph, Ethan Lodge, Laura Martinez, Jennifer O'Brien, Nathan Pflaum, Alexa Salazar, Valerie Silva, Jesusla Sinfort, Catherine St. Hilaire, Vivian Vázquez, and Lesly Zhicay.

The project would not have been possible without funding support from a number of entities. Cornell's Institute for Social Sciences funded the early days of the project and provided the time and space for exchange with immigration colleagues across the campus and the country. The Russell Sage Foundation also funded key elements of the project, as did the Cornell Center for the Social Sciences, the Cornell Center for the Study of Inequality, the Cornell Population Center, and the Mario Einaudi Center for International Studies. An American Bar Foundation (ABF)/JPB Foundation Access to Justice Faculty Scholarship gave Shannon time to dedicate to the project and provided a key forum for feedback as the project developed. We thank Deans Kevin Hallock and Alex Colvin for the ILR School's financial support throughout the project, and Cornell's Worker Institute for supporting our collaboration. We acknowledge Cornell's Pierce Memorial Fund for also supporting a book workshop that brought together experts in the field to comment on the full manuscript.

Indeed, the project benefited from insightful collegial feedback from many sources. We presented parts of the book at Iowa School of Law, UC Davis School of Law, Texas A&M Law School, Southwestern Law School, Princeton University, CUNY Graduate Center, New School for Social Research, the American Bar Foundation, the American Sociological Association, the Labor and Employment Relations Association, the Law & Society Association, and countless Cornell convenings, including those at the Cornell Institute for the Social Sciences, the ILR Alumni Association, Cornell's ILR School, and Cornell's Center for Innovative Hospitality Labor and Employment Relations. In each forum, colleagues pushed us to further hone our argument and to consider implications for both scholarly debate and practical applications. Cornell's "Making Time to Write" series, through the Provost's Office for Faculty Development and Diversity, provided indispensable support and encouragement for the long slog of book writing.

In the final stage of the project an insightful group of scholars read parts of the book and provided line edits as well as broader substantive comments that helped push the book to another level. We thank Leisy Abrego, Ming Hsu Chen, Andrew Elmore, Jennifer Gordon, François Pierre-Louis, César Rosado-Marzán, and Chris Tilly for their time digging into the manuscript. Participants at our April 2023 book workshop engaged in daylong discussions and workshops to help us improve the book. These colleagues generously gave of their time and talent, and each made an imprint on the final revision of the book. We are indebted to Briana Beltran, Anne Marie Brady, Ginny Doellgast, Miranda Hallett, Tamara Lee, Risa Lieberwitz, Jamila Michener, Gali Racabi, Ben Rissing, and Maite Tapia for these contributions. Also shaping our thinking were conversations over the years with many others: Charlotte Alexander, Janice Fine, Jessie Hahn, Michael Iadevaia, Tricia Kakalec, Mark Pedulla, Leticia Saucedo, Josh Stehlick, Shoba Wadhia, and Steve Yale-Loehr. We also thank our thoughtful colleagues in Cornell ILR's Global Labor and Work Department.

Earlier analyses of this research can be found in our previous publications in the *Handbook on Social Policy and Employment* (forthcoming), the *Annual Review of Law and Social Science*, *Law & Social Inquiry*, *Denver Law Review*, *Southwestern Law Review*, *ILR Review*, *Comparative Labor Law and Policy Journal*, and chapter 6 of *Race, Gender, and Contemporary International Labor Migration Regimes: 21st-Century Coolies?*

The project would not have been possible without the excellent administrative assistance we have received from staff colleagues at Cornell: Rhonda Clouse, Claire Concepcion, Armando Flores, Jonathan Long, Megan Pillar, Christine Schmidt, Anne Sieverding, Lori Sonken, and Anneliese Truame. We also thank Cornell ILR's Communications Team, especially Mary Catt and Julie Greco, and Cornell ILR's Catherwood Librarians, especially Aliqae Geraci, for supporting our research.

We appreciate Suzanne Nichols and Russell Sage Foundation Press for believing in this project and helping us bring it to fruition. Suzanne's keen eye and insightful comments encouraged us to strengthen the book in a number of ways. The three anonymous reviewers provided detailed and hard-hitting suggestions that improved the organization, flow, and impact of the book.

Finally, each author would like to extend a personal note of gratitude.

Kati Griffith

Robert and Jack, age three when I started and age twelve when I finished, inspired me to keep going with this project. When I told them stories about specific injustices and indignities that our interviewees faced, they would often ask why? That question drove me to do better, as did their steadfast belief in tolerating nothing less than equality, freedom, and respect for all. Leslie, my co-conspirator for twenty-seven years of life, kept me grounded, laughing, and well fed. She is also a no-holds-barred editor and precise analytical thinker whom I consulted throughout the project. The words "thank you" are not enough to express my deep gratitude to her.

Shannon Gleeson

The solitary days and long nights of writing were made infinitely easier by my steadfast companions: Chahta, Sequoia, Cypress, and even Paco. My two-legged friends and family members—spread across California, Florida, Texas, and New York—always offered encouragement, even when it was not always clear where I was going or what I was doing, and why. Sofya Aptekar and Els de Graauw provided a place to lay my head whenever I came to town. The littles in my life have kept me honest about when it is time to quit and go play. My hot room and grittycize crews have provided routines for body and soul that have been indispensable, especially during the dark season of the pandemic. Jaclyn Kelley-Widmer has doubled as both writing partner and running mate. And Gabriel, always the hours.

Darlène Dubuisson

When I began working on this project in 2016 as an interviewer, I lived in Brooklyn, New York, in an area affectionately known as "Little Haiti." At that time, I was in the troughs of my PhD studies, grappling with managing my upcoming fieldwork in Haiti while caring for a toddler. My early experiences on the project—trekking across New York City to interview Haitian immigrants in their homes and workplaces and often at the Starbucks in the Target on

Flatbush—taught me the importance of flexibility, improvisation, and humor in qualitative research. I am grateful for this experience, as it helped shape me into the researcher I am today. I am also thankful to my son, Kingston Lennan, for being by my side and inspiring me to strive for professional and personal success. I appreciate all those who opened their lives to me and helped with recruitment through their personal and familial networks. Lastly, I am eternally grateful to Kate and Shannon for inviting me to collaborate on this book and helping guide my path as a scholar.

Patricia Campos-Medina

My journey as a scholar of immigrant worker precarity officially began in 2012 when I entered the graduate program at Rutgers University–Newark wanting to explore the dynamics of race, migration, and precarity for Central American workers. After two decades as a union leader, I felt I needed to put into a theoretical framework of analysis all the stories my family members and countless workers had shared while I supported their efforts to organize low-wage workplaces. I brought this lived experience to academia and to my partnership with Shannon and Kate, who suggested—over a glass of wine at the Statler Hotel lobby after a Worker Institute retreat in 2017—that I join their research team as a field researcher on this project. We carried this project through a global pandemic, with workers who were considered essential yet lacked basic health protections. They demonstrated courage to show up to work, to fight to protect their families and their future. I am indebted to all the workers for trusting me with their stories and for believing in my commitment to amplifying their voices through this research. I am also grateful to my field research team, Jhims Gerard, Perry Tima, and Daphney Vastey, who became my partners in capturing, understanding, and elevating the Haitian American experience in New York and New Jersey. I also want to thank the countless community organizations that validated our research team by making introductions to community leaders. Specifically, I want to thank Reverend Charlie Wirene of the HUUB, Blanca Molina of CEUS, Carmen Salavarrieta of Angels for Action, Diana Mejia of Winds of the Spirit, and Chia Chia Wang of American Friends Service

Committee. I also want to thank my husband Bob and sons Diego and Enrique for their love and patience as I spent countless weekends in the field or on Zoom calls talking to workers. Finally, thank you, Shannon and Kate, for your generosity of spirit in helping me become a better scholar of the immigrant experience in the American workplace.

INTRODUCTION 1

Beyond the unlivable wages and lack of upward mobility, low-wage work in the United States can be full of danger and degrading treatment. Through over three hundred conversations with immigrant workers of color in the New York City metropolitan area and over fifty of their advocates, we documented this reality and traced the government's role in fueling it. To do so, we asked workers about their experiences at work and focused on three institutional orders to contextualize their experiences: the underregulated workers' rights system, the immigration regime, and the intractable legacies of legal racism and xenophobia in the United States. We heard extraordinary and pervasive stories of poor working conditions. For example, a worker at a popular sandwich chain described almost freezing to death in a food freezer. A home health aide was sent to the hospital after a bloody attack by a struggling Alzheimer's patient. A construction worker, donning no safety gear, broke his back after falling from a roof at a job site. A Black warehouse worker was routinely denied a lunch break, in contrast to his White counterparts. Workers told us they often felt unable to change conditions like these.

Indeed, immigrants and people of color are overrepresented in "bad jobs" that are rife with bad wages, bad schedules, bad benefits, and bad treatment.[1] One-third of all immigrants in the United States are classified as low-income (under 200 percent of the federal poverty line),[2] and Black and Hispanic individuals overall are similarly overrepresented in poverty statistics.[3] Degraded workplaces are notorious for not complying with health and safety protections, failing to meet minimum pay requirements, and fostering many

https://doi.org/10.7758/rioz4023.1322

forms of discrimination and harassment.[4] Workers in low-wage jobs also face myriad forms of disrespect—which are rarely prohibited by law—as they interact with customers, patients, coworkers, and supervisors.[5]

For the workers we talked to, there are many barriers to fighting for better conditions and few pathways to get there. In the aftermath of a bad experience, workers have a choice to make. If they feel their employer has violated their rights, they must decide whether to engage with a hard-to-access legal framework that perpetuates, rather than mitigates, inequality.[6] Though *many* federal, state, and local laws protect employees, the threshold for a formal legal violation is exceedingly high.[7] Some workers are not legally classified as "employees" and thus do not have rights under labor and employment laws. Even when they are employees who know their rights and how to exercise them, they risk a lot when they come forward, whether alone or in concert. They risk losing their job and not being able to pay the bills. They risk further racial or sexual harassment. If they are the nearly one in five workers in the United States who are foreign-born, they may also fear immigration status repercussions for themselves or their family members, or even deportation.[8] These barriers debilitate a workers' rights enforcement system that relies on workers, or their advocates, to come forward to identify and expose wage, discrimination, and safety issues, through either an individual complaint to the government or a collective one.

Worker organizing efforts can seem out of reach. Formidable barriers often block the path for organized labor groups to win additional rights and benefits, including labor unions and other worker organizations. Private contractual agreements between employers and employees that would provide protections that go beyond legally required minimums, including union collective bargaining agreements, are rare in the low-wage workplace. Our interviews with workers did not, however, emphasize only the challenges. They also reminded us that workers sometimes defy the odds and push back against bad conditions, both through subtle actions that maintain their dignity and through overt actions that confront their employers in a public forum.

Analytical Approach

THE STATE

This book illuminates how government regulation (and underregulation) degrades workplace conditions as well as workers' ability to contest them. We interpret government action and inaction broadly to include statutory frameworks, enforcement systems, and other implementation processes. We also include both the punitive arms of governance and the everyday mundane aspects of government bureaucracies.[9] Through enacting, enforcing, administering, and interpreting laws, or by deciding not to do so, the government feeds poor working conditions and disempowers workers.[10]

The three parts of this book disaggregate and interrogate three key policy arenas through which this occurs: (1) the underregulation of workers' rights, (2) an immigration regime that disempowers workers; and (3) failure to counteract racialized labor hierarchies and colonial legacies. We examine these three domains successively in three pairs of chapters that focus on how the government fuels precarious working conditions and shapes barriers and pathways to change. Throughout, we highlight instances of workers resisting despite the odds—sometimes individually and sometimes collectively, sometimes quietly and sometimes loudly.

First, the government underregulates relations between employers and workers, granting employers wide latitude to unilaterally set the contours of low-wage work. The ease with which employers can terminate a worker in the United States makes it harder for workers to bargain for better jobs or to hold their employer accountable for even the most egregious workers' rights violations. Workers have legal rights to engage in collective action, but these protections are weak and labor unions have struggled to counter employer power in many sectors.

Second, the government promotes an immigration regime that weakens immigrant workers' bargaining power and strengthens employer dominion over working conditions. The immigration enforcement and administration machinery deepens the vulnerabilities of an already weak workers' rights system. It deputizes employers as immigration enforcement agents and criminalizes the everyday lives of noncitizen immigrants. And its policies and practices foster unstable temporary statuses and anti-immigrant sentiment.

Third, the government insufficiently redresses (formerly legal and still entrenched) racialized labor hierarchies that trace back to periods of enslavement and colonialism.[11] Drawing on the work of critical race theorists, and through our interviews, we illustrate how racial inequities pervade the labor market, sometimes explicitly, sometimes implicitly.[12] Despite formal prohibitions against racial discrimination in labor and immigration policy, racialized labor hierarchies have dictated, both then and now, which kinds of workers are deserving of fair and humane treatment, and which workers are not.

These three domains are intricately connected and in practice have never operated independently of one another. However, the legal apparatus that governs each arena is often formally siloed, relying on a distinct institutional framework. By reviewing each domain in succession, we are able to unpack the ways in which government action or inaction translates into workers' experiences. As we separate and isolate these mechanisms to understand them better, we also reveal how they combine in the work lives of low-wage immigrant workers of color. Rather than understand class, immigration status, race, and national origin as demographic categories, we engage them as systems of power that mark how workers characterize their experiences.

To be sure, there are many stratifying factors shaping immigrant workers' lives; we focus on the three most salient in our interviews. We also acknowledge the existence of other axes of difference and inequality that stratification scholars have documented. For example, gender and patriarchy are also inextricably linked to class, immigration, and exclusions based on race and national origin. As such, our analysis points throughout the book to the gendered experiences of workers and builds on the insights of many feminist scholars, including Catharine MacKinnon, who refers to gender itself as "an inequality of power."[13]

WORKER (DIS-)EMPOWERMENT

We define "worker empowerment" expansively in the tradition of Frances Fox Piven and other social theorists whose work focuses on the lives of the working poor and popular protest.[14] Worker power, we contend, is the ability of a worker to change the status quo at the workplace level, even incrementally, and/or a worker's ability to voice their complaints and demand fair and dignified treatment. Worker power includes the ability of workers, along with their organizations, to act together to gain contractual and political rights that go beyond existing legal minimums—what some would refer to as "associational power."[15] It also includes workers' agency to demand (aggressively and subtly) better wages, safer workplaces, and environments free of sexual and racial harassment, even if these demands go unmet. These manifestations of worker power may operate separately or in tandem.

Our analysis of worker power builds on existing definitions of power, which see power as the ability to make someone (in this case, an employer or their representative) do something they would not otherwise do.[16] Scholars typically theorize power relations between employers and workers at the political, sectorial, and workplace levels of labor and economic policy.[17] We incorporate these multilayered definitions of power into our analysis. Worker power goes beyond trying to obtain tangible and measurable changes to wages and working conditions. It is a worker's ability, despite the challenges, to find some dignity even in degraded low-wage workplaces plagued by disrespect and bias.[18] In a structural environment that gives workers few practical tools for demanding change, such acts to change the status quo demonstrate that workers are not passive victims. Thus, while a worker's ability to call out disrespect is challenging to measure through surveys or other quantitative means, it should not be overlooked. As the book will reveal, workers often found quiet and creative ways to demand dignity in the workplace. Although exerting power did not always lead to structural change, workers often found ways to resist while preserving their tenuous jobs in an unstable employment environment.[19] Achieving a personal sense of dignity is empowerment for some workers, even if such empowerment often does not result in changes to material conditions.[20]

HISTORICAL ROOTS

At the center of our analysis is that the labor, immigration, and race policy arenas have long shaped low-wage worker experiences, and that historical inequalities continue to matter today. Historical processes are critical for understanding why xenophobia and racism persist in the workplace. Indeed, Avidit Acharya and her colleagues find that "institutions of the past continue to sway attitudes of the present."[21] Both governments and employers have used racial hierarchies that privilege Whiteness to justify and advance immense power differentials between the owners of wealth and their laborers. During the period of the transatlantic slave trade, governments promoted a labor hierarchy that legitimized the unfree labor of Black Africans. For more than three hundred years, enslaved Black Africans enriched White slave owners, who legally profited from unfree labor throughout the Americas. White settler colonialism in its many forms also institutionalized racial inequality in the Americas, dispossessing Indigenous communities of land and many other resources.[22] The slave trade created and upheld legal racial hierarchies for decades upon decades. Through various periods of empire, ruling governments maintained a racial caste system to justify exclusions and mistreatment of colonial subjects. Many of these communities still have not recovered from the economic, social, and political devastations of empire in the United States and across the globe and are migrating to search for better.

Even as colonial administrations fade, racial-ethnic hierarchies, power relationships, and migration processes from the colonial period continue to reverberate in contemporary times.[23] White supremacy fundamentally marked the foundation of labor and employment law and immigration law in the United States.[24] Migrant labor regimes, for instance, draw on existing racial hierarchies to determine which migrants are displaced in search of work, and how those migrants are subjugated at work.[25] Contemporary civil rights protections cannot offset deeply ingrained racial and ethnic inequities.[26] While race-neutral in writing, contemporary laws are not race-neutral in practice and their consequences continue to reverberate in low-wage workplaces today, across all categories of immigrant workers.[27]

Thus, at the heart of our approach is the recognition that unbridled capital accumulation combines with the creation and maintenance of national borders and the lasting marks of legalized racism to shape the experiences of low-wage workers of color.

Research Strategy

Our methodological approach is largely inductive. We rely on interviews with individual workers and their advocates to describe key aspects of the nature of low-wage immigrant work, identify the policy arenas that shape it, and explore the potential for worker empowerment (for more details, see the methodological appendix). In seeing, through our interviews, how three different forms of government action or inaction play out in the lived experiences of workers, we build on work that implores scholars to center workers' voices in analyses of workers' experiences.[28] Unlike studies based on random sampling models and large datasets that can identify the causal factors driving wages and working conditions, our inductive interview strategy illuminates how government policies disempower workers and unpacks this "disempowerment" as an active process rather than a static state.[29] By permitting us to focus on how law operates in practice, this approach reveals the dialectic ways in which the government fosters precarity for low-wage workers and highlights the agency with which workers respond. This bottom-up approach draws on workers' own characterizations of how they perceive the dynamics in their workplace.

Thus, the voices of over three hundred low-wage immigrant workers of color in the New York City metropolitan area between 2016 and 2021 lay the cornerstone of our study. We recruited volunteer participants through legal services providers and other worker advocacy groups, as well as through interviewee referrals (see the methodological appendix). To illustrate the impact of immigration status on low-wage immigrant work experiences we interviewed workers with three different immigration statuses: 82 workers (27 percent) had no immigration status ("undocumented" or "unauthorized"); 130 (43 percent) had temporary protected status (TPS, "temporary"); and 89 (30 percent) had either gained lawful permanent residency or become naturalized as citizens ("permanent") (see table 1.1).[30]

To unravel how race and regional origin shape immigrants' work experiences we set out to talk to both Haitians and Central Americans who had arrived during different periods. The many waves of Haitian migrants to the United States have included intellectual and political elites as well as those fleeing violence, natural disaster, political

Table 1.1 *Regional Origin by Immigration Status, Gender, Location, and Education*

	Haitian	Central American	Other	Total
Total	138	151	12[a]	301
Immigration status				
Undocumented	27	48	7	82
Temporary	50	78	2	130
Permanent	61	25	3	89
Gender				
Men	64	68	4	136
Women	74	83	8	165
Location				
New York City	83	4	3	90
Long Island	1	51	7	59
New Jersey	52	95	2	149
Other	2	1	0	3
Education				
Less than high school	31	76	3	110
High school	40	23	4	67
College or more	63	45	4	112
Did not say	4	7	1	12

Source: Authors' tabulation.
[a]Peru (5), Colombia (2), Guinea (2), Ecuador (1), Jamaica (1), and Mexico (1).

corruption, and, of course, economic deprivation.[31] In the Central American region, ongoing military interventions and capital extraction have displaced thousands of Central Americans since before the civil wars of the 1980s through to the political and economic instability of today.[32] Although each Central American country has a distinct history and present circumstances, we talk about Central Americans as a group given their overlapping histories of colonialism, the similar ways in which they are racialized within the United States, and their collective immigrant advocacy efforts.[33]

On the whole, we spoke to 138 (46 percent) immigrants from Haiti, 151 (50 percent) from Central America, and 12 (4 percent) from other countries, for a total of 301 workers. We focused on Haitian and Central American communities because of their shared representation in the low-wage labor market and their distinct histories of race relations in their countries of origin and the United States. Sampling across these two groups allows us to analyze the data comparatively in order

Table 1.2 *Average Age and Time in the United States (in Years) by Immigration Status and Regional Origin*

	Age	Time in the United States
Undocumented		
All	35.2	9.3
Central American	31.5	11.2
Haitian	39.1	4.1
Other	44.0	14.3
Temporary		
All	44.3	17.9
Central American	43.3	19.6
Haitian	44.7	15.3
Other	57.5	20.0
Permanent (lawful permanent resident or citizen)		
All	42.0	15.9
Central American	42.3	20.6
Haitian	42.2	13.9
Other	37.0	15.2

Source: Authors' tabulation.

to see commonalities and differences in how low-wage immigrant workers of color talk about racialization and other conditions at work. Given both the nature of our interview approach and the occupational segregation in this hyperdiverse region, respondents were not necessarily employed alongside each other. Although workers described their experiences with their coworkers, our data do not systematically speak to tensions *between* our two communities of focus: Haitian and Central American workers.

Undocumented respondents were overall younger and more recently arrived. Across all categories, Haitian respondents had been in the country for fewer years. However, the distinctions between temporary and permanent respondents are more nuanced (see table 1.2). Revealing the settled nature—and prolonged liminality—of the TPS community, the average temporary worker was forty-four years old and had been in the country for almost eighteen years, whereas permanent workers were slightly younger, at forty-two, with sixteen years in the country.[34] Given the different migration histories of our two main national- and regional-origin groups, our distribution by status for Haitians and Central Americans was distinct.[35]

Our approach to respondent selection yielded a sampling of a wide spectrum of low-wage jobs and industries, and the workers with whom we spoke often had complex job histories.[36] We talked to informal care workers and certified home health aides, all mostly women. We also talked to (mostly male) day laborers and workers on more formalized construction crews. Other workers were in jobs ranging from restaurant work, cleaning, light manufacturing, and retail. The variation in jobs, immigration statuses, race, and regional origin helped us uncover both similar narratives among low-wage workers and key areas of differentiation in worker experience. Because the period of interviews spanned three presidential administrations and a global pandemic, we were also able to identify consistent elements of the specific conditions of low-wage work experiences that these major events might have exacerbated.

We spoke with workers across the New York City metropolitan area according to the settlement patterns of each immigrant community with which we engaged: New York City, Long Island, New York, and New Jersey. In a region with some of the strongest labor laws in the country and some of the densest concentrations of immigrant and labor advocates, we offer our findings as a conservative baseline of the challenges that immigrant workers of color face in the United States.[37] Indeed, the New York–New Jersey–Pennsylvania region has 12.1 percent private-sector union membership (13.0 percent coverage), or twice the national average of 6.0 percent (6.8 percent coverage).[38] Our research shows how three dimensions of government action or inaction drive precarity for low-wage immigrant workers of color even in contexts where we might least expect this impact. As such, these insights span far beyond this region and these two immigrant communities.

Besides interviewing Haitian and Central American workers, we also spoke with fifty of their advocates engaged in policy advocacy, organizing, and legal services provision in organizations working on the ground in the New York City region as well as groups advocating at the state and national levels. Through conversations with these key informants, we were able to discern the common challenges facing immigrant workers and learn their strategies for navigating challenges at work and the responses from employers and their representatives. Advocates often confirmed workers' accounts, yet their perspectives were an important complement to the worker interviews because they were often directly mediating the relationship between employers and workers.

We paired these interviews with a careful analysis of the legal and policy landscape for workers' rights and immigration regulation at work. We considered not just how workers intersected with the contemporary labor and employment law and immigration law regimes, but also how they intersected with the racism and xenophobia that have persisted since the period of transatlantic slavery and colonialism. Although an array of public documents spell out employers' obligations to their workers, it is only through talking with workers that we can discern how they experience the ways in which their employers navigate these obligations. We did not talk systematically to a sample of employers, but rather relied on the narratives of workers and their advocates to identify employer interests and concerns. Additionally, we drew on several exchanges with employer-side legal counsel and business associations in convenings focused on management practices in low-wage service industries.

Book Outline

This section provides a roadmap for the book and highlights our key analytical interventions and insights.

UNDERREGULATED RIGHTS AT WORK

Part 1 illuminates how the government's failure to advance labor and employment laws that provide robust rights for workers and their organizations ("workers' rights") feeds dangerous, illegal, biased, and disrespectful working conditions (chapter 2). It also makes it hard for employees to demand more dignity and their employer's basic legal compliance with workers' rights (chapter 3).

In the United States an at-will employment regime permits employers to define the contours of low-wage work without government intervention on behalf of the poor.[39] Only a few laws and regulations protect against sudden job loss, and the requirements for obtaining these protections are steep. On paper, employers cannot fire someone because of a protected status, such as race, national origin, or sex, including sexual orientation, gender identity, or gender expression. They cannot fire an employee for bringing labor and employment law claims against them, and they cannot fire an employee for participating in some forms of collective activity with their coworkers. These protections are important exceptions to at-will employment, but they are also woefully under-enforced and hard to prove in many cases.[40] As a result, an "employer decides all" norm is allowed to prevail.[41] US underregulation contrasts with many systems across the globe that allow firings only for a legally recognized reason.

Labor relations scholars have long called for reregulating the labor market in the United States.[42] Yet labor unions and other worker organizations fight an uphill battle in the current legal and business contexts and have not been able to sufficiently turn the tide in the United States.[43] Unions in the private sector have been under strain and in decline for decades. In 2022, they represented just 6 percent of the private-sector workforce. Pro-worker legislative attempts have failed in the US Congress decade after decade.[44] Gendered and racialized exclusions persist from the New Deal era, such as exclusions of domestic and agricultural workers under the 1935 National Labor Relations Act. Except for the few states where the political context is favorable and resources are available, state governments have not filled the gap.

New business models have also intensified power imbalances in the low-wage workplace. With extensive misclassification of workers as independent contractors rather than employees, many workers do not have the rights that workers with "employee" status do. Lead companies today commonly also use intermediary companies, like staffing agencies, franchisees, and subcontractors, in ways that shield them from regulation. These business intermediaries are sometimes thinly resourced and disproportionately incentivized to cut labor costs to generate profit.[45] Legally speaking, joint employer liability is possible if both businesses (the lead and the intermediary) sufficiently influence wages and working conditions.[46] Yet this is far from how it appears to workers, who are typically confused about whether they have one or two employers. This intermediary structure in turn shields lead companies from liability and their duty to bargain with workers, further complicating workers' ability to mobilize to enforce their rights.

In chapter 2, we document the common challenges faced by Haitians and Central American immigrants of various legal statuses, such as unsafe work, meager pay, and myriad indignities, across a wide array of low-wage industries. On balance, the overarching challenges of unpaid, unsafe, and degraded work were universal across low-wage job experiences, even if they manifested in distinct ways across industries, gender identities, national origins, and immigration statuses.

Chapter 3 describes the common barriers encountered by workers and their limited opportunities to push for change. In the face of indignities and injustice, workers sometimes reported not knowing their rights or how to assert them. They also reported feeling like they had no power to change things, staying quiet for fear of losing their job, and facing employer retribution if they spoke up. By confusing subcontracted and gig workers about their employment status, some business models made it even more complicated for them to improve their wages and working conditions. Nonetheless, some workers did occasionally engage in informal resistance and mobilization, even as other workers avoided resisting employer actions altogether. A rare few workers pursued formal legal claims, sometimes joining up with worker organizations, to contest their workplace conditions.

AN IMMIGRATION REGIME AT WORK

The immigration regime magnifies unequal power relations between employers and low-wage immigrant workers through a variety of mechanisms. It gives employers a role in immigration enforcement at work, criminalizes immigrant workers, promotes unstable temporary statuses, and amplifies anti-immigrant sentiment through policy and practice. Part 2 shows how the US immigration regime fosters precarious working conditions for immigrants (chapter 4) and inhibits their ability to denounce abuse (chapter 5). We focus on three broad categories of immigration status—undocumented, temporary, and permanent—to examine the distinct work experiences of workers in each category and the common narratives across all three.

Compared to workers who have authorization to work in the United States, the immigration regime puts undocumented workers in a particularly vulnerable position. Beyond outright exclusion under immigration laws, employers' role in immigration enforcement subordinates undocumented workers' rights and constructs barriers to change. The Immigration Reform and Control Act (IRCA) of 1986 delegated immigration status screening to employers. Along with making undocumented workers fearful about speaking up about abuses of workers' rights, IRCA also led courts to muddy the waters between workers' rights and their immigration status. Workers are often excluded from basic protections because they do not believe that they have rights as workers, or because courts reduce the legal remedies available to them owing to their undocumented immigration status.[47]

The immigration regime also advances policies and practices that equate low-wage immigration with criminal behavior. A decade after IRCA, the 1996 Illegal Immigration Reform and Immigrant Responsibility Act (IIRAIRA) and the Antiterrorism and Effective Death Penalty Act (AEDPA) criminalized immigrants through the creation of new mechanisms for detention and deportation.[48] This legislation also allowed local police forces to work with federal immigration agencies.[49] These actions amplified low-wage undocumented workers' exposure to a criminal justice system that disproportionately polices communities of color. Through criminalizing immigrant workers and empowering employers as agents of immigration enforcement, the immigration regime worsened an already insecure and underregulated low-wage environment for undocumented workers.

Yet beyond the binary between undocumented and documented, we also find that the immigration regime poses a unique set of challenges for workers with temporary immigration status. Temporary statuses promote instability and insecurity for workers too. In this study, we focus on workers with temporary protected status, a relief program that grants temporary work authorization to workers from designated countries and also grants them temporary reprieves from deportation. If the government extends their TPS relief, workers from Haiti and many Central American countries (including El Salvador, Honduras, and Nicaragua) must submit paperwork to renew their status and work authorization. As for guest workers and individuals with other temporary statuses, TPS does not provide workers with a path to permanent residency.

Some workers with TPS who said it was better than undocumented status also recounted the ways in which their status had burdened their relationships with their employers and with potential employers. Employers are subject to IRCA sanctions if they do not properly verify employees' work authorization. Workers with TPS reported that many employers hesitated to employ them, or that they let these employees with TPS go too quickly if their physical proof of renewal was delayed.[50] Employers have no legal obligation to do otherwise under at-will employment provisions, and immigration status discrimination protections do not reach these workers. Some workers with temporary status even reported feeling more precarious than undocumented workers at times, especially when politicians proposed the wholesale termination of the TPS program. Despite the benefits TPS offered, these workers became a known deportation target once they agreed to register their presence and location with immigration authorities.[51] Thus, through a variety of mechanisms, the immigration regime fosters a unique form of precarity for workers with temporary status.

The immigration regime even multiplied workplace precarity for immigrants with more permanent statuses such as lawful permanent residency and naturalized citizenship. Even though these workers were more secure in their own immigration status, their fears for their loved ones and neighbors who might have been deportable made them apprehensive about inviting retaliation if they were to come forward to challenge their employers. Their interviews also conveyed that their more stable status did not make them immune to race and national-origin discrimination. Indeed, racism and xenophobia have persisted, in both past and present, despite workers' permanent immigration status.

Together, chapters 4 and 5 zero in on the distinct instantiations of the immigration regime's disempowerment of workers with undocumented, temporary, or permanent status. Historically, US immigration regulation has layered an additional "precarity multiplier" at the workplace on top of the underregulated workers' rights regime experienced by all low-wage workers.[52] To this day immigration policies are framed as "race-neutral," but they create hierarchies by immigration status and are built on the racial inequities of the past, as our respondents confirmed.

RACISM AND COLONIAL LEGACIES AT WORK

Alongside the contemporary workers' rights and immigration regimes, slavery and racist colonial pasts *and* presents disempower workers of color—across immigration statuses—in the low-wage workplace. The government does little to interrupt persistent and damaging legacies of racism at work. The Civil Rights Act of 1964 and the civil rights laws that followed made some progress by outlawing racist practices at work, but they are still largely inadequate to address the root causes of the many manifestations of racism and xenophobia in workplaces.[53] While the relationship between race and power may go largely unnoticed in discussions of low-wage White workers, it becomes very apparent when we consider the lived experiences of low-wage immigrants of color. Part 3 provides insight into immigrant workers' racialized experiences and the ways they connect to the government's failure to address the injustices that continue to flow from long legacies of legalized racism.

In chapter 6, we argue that the legacies of slavery and multiple waves of colonialism and contemporary US imperialism continue to influence working conditions for low-wage immigrants of color. These dynamics shade the forms of degradation at work and how immigrant workers of color interpret and respond to them. Chapter 7 details how workers weigh the costs and opportunities associated with coming forward to demand better working conditions. Anti-Black and anti-Latino sentiment at work and beyond poses a series of challenges to those considering whether to come forward to challenge bad jobs, either individually or in concert with coworkers. Nonetheless, we also highlight the seeds of both individual and collective resistance being sown by workers.

The wide variety of racist and demeaning treatment at work recounted by Haitians and Central Americans reflect some commonalities, but also some key differences. These two groups have distinct relationships to their countries of origin. For Haitians, centuries of the transatlantic slave trade across the globe and with the United States fostered anti-Blackness and anti-Haitian sentiment. The Haitian

Revolution, which led to the first Black-led republic, also had lasting impacts on the experiences of Haitian immigrant workers in the United States. The contemporary realities of poverty and inequality in Haiti continue to drive Haitian migration to neighboring countries, including north to the United States. Political repression during a three-decade dictatorship—with several US-backed interventions—as well as corruption and crumbling infrastructure have worsened the effects of a series of natural disasters, including the 2010 earthquake and the humanitarian crisis that followed.[54] All these factors, past and present, are integrated into how Haitians view working conditions in the United States and how they balance the pros and cons of challenging employer power in the workplace.

Like Haitians, many Central American migrants are also leaving a country with a long and sordid legacy with colonial powers and imperialist US policies. This history is often ignored in the two-dimensional media coverage of the harrowing journeys north of Central American migrants. Behind Mexico, three of the four top countries of origin of undocumented immigrants in the United States are Central American.[55] The colonial caste system that Spain implemented throughout Latin America pushed Black and Indigenous workers to the bottom of a hierarchy that equated Whiteness with power and privilege.[56] Fueled by US interests and interventions, many Central American countries suffered brutal civil wars in the 1980s, and political violence and economic instability continue to drive out migrants.[57] Their experience in their country of origin also frames how migrants evaluate and respond to workplace abuse. These historical and contemporary realities inform how Central American workers view their treatment at work and also how employers, coworkers, and customers view the Central American workers they encounter in low-wage jobs.

The Haitians and Central Americans we spoke to shared different experiences of being racialized at work by customers, supervisors, coworkers, and patients. Haitians talked about anti-Black bias, as well as anti-Haitian bias based on Haiti's long-disadvantaged position in the global order following its successful slave rebellion and push for independence. Haitians are one of the largest groups of Black immigrants in the United States; at 16 percent, they are behind only Jamaicans (17 percent).[58] Many reported having endured anti-Black bias from coworkers, supervisors, patients, and customers and often invoked slavery when describing these experiences. In contrast, Central Americans recounted the erasure of their national origin under the homogenizing and degrading rubric of Latinidad.[59] Central American respondents told us that their supervisors and the public they interfaced with at their jobs often assumed they were Mexican and associated them with criminalizing tropes of Latinos. The Spanish language became a unifying feature for Central Americans that linked them to other Latino populations, while also obscuring their particular ethnic and national-origin histories.

Conclusion

Our study suggests taking a three-pronged approach to tackling the widespread injustice in the low-wage workplace: (1) reregulating the low-wage workplace to advance workers' rights, (2) reforming an immigration regulatory system that unduly privileges employer interests over workers' rights, and (3) addressing the roots of racial injustice in labor relations and immigration policy. This approach opens avenues for future research, legal reforms, and organizational strategies.

We offer a series of specific reforms that could further empower low-wage workers, including the need for "just cause" dismissal protections, broader definitions of rights-bearing employees, and other supports to allow workers to engage in a range of collective actions. We must reregulate the low-wage economy to incentivize employer compliance and create real penalties when they fail to do so. At present, violating workers' rights is most often viewed by employers as just the "cost of doing business."

Further, we must sound the alarm against the proliferation of the politically popular temporary statuses and call for a universal pathway to citizenship, despite the deadlock in Congress. At the very least, we must remove employers' role in immigration law enforcement. Three decades of employer verification requirements have shown little to no deterrent effect on unauthorized work. Meanwhile, employers' role in immigration enforcement has enhanced their power over workers and fostered precarity and employment insecurity even for workers with temporary work authorization.[60] Additionally, it is imperative that we revise discrimination protections to capture the wide variety of ways in which racial and national-origin biases continue to disadvantage workers of color throughout the country. Existing protections are exceedingly transactional and individualized and do little to address enduring forms of racism, xenophobia, and other factors driving bias.

Because seemingly separate policy arenas—labor and employment standards, immigration law, and historical policies that legitimized racist labor hierarchies—interact to drive inequality, we must put these policy debates and related advocacy and organizing efforts in conversation with each other, despite the enormity of the task ahead. Advancement on all fronts is necessary; proceeding on one alone is insufficient. In the concluding chapter, we offer some beginning steps to this end and advance the fundamental principle woven throughout the book. Scholars, advocates, and policymakers must center workers' voices and wrestle with these three sites of worker disempowerment fueled by government actions and inactions to promote a more comprehensive view of justice in the low-wage workplace.

PART 1
UNDERREGULATED RIGHTS AT WORK

The United States underregulates a variety of workers' rights from wage and hour standards to health and safety in the workplace, to protections from discrimination. That is, the government enacts few protections for workers and their organizations, insufficiently enforces the protections that are in place, and allows business models that evade regulation to proliferate. This underregulation exacerbates enormous economic power differentials between employers and low-wage workers. Chapter 2 illuminates workers' experiences of underregulation and degrading work conditions across the low-wage workforce. Chapter 3 then outlines the enormous barriers they must confront when pushing for change and reveals that, against all odds, some workers do come forward.

There is no universal experience of underregulation; workers' experiences differ according to factors such as their gender, immigration status, and race. Part 1 establishes a critical baseline for understanding how the underregulation embedded in labor and employment law shakes the foundation for workers' rights in the United States. The labor and employment law regime that first emerged in the New Deal era was built on racist and sexist foundations. In the 1930s, Black workers dominated in the South—Black men were agricultural workers and Black women were domestic laborers—yet they were excluded from the baseline wage and worker organizing protections provided by the 1938 Fair Labor Standards Act (FLSA) and the 1935 National Labor Relations Act (NLRA). The racist and sexist origins of these exclusions of a disproportionate segment of workers of color have been widely documented.[1] Workers with insecure immigration

https://doi.org/10.7758/rioz4023.7653

status also face formidable barriers, as discussed in part 2.[2] Civil rights–era protections that prohibit employment discrimination insufficiently protect workers of color and often demand a high evidentiary burden. These regulatory failures foment power differences in workplace experiences by race, sex, and national origin.

Part 1 establishes the common policy structures for all low-wage workers across our diverse sample. In doing so, these chapters document the pervasiveness of bad working conditions and illuminate how low-wage workers sometimes resist despite the odds.

WORKER PRECARITY IN THE LOW-WAGE WORKPLACE 2

Capitalism drives a race to the bottom in search of ever-increasing profit in a globalized world. Out of this reality has emerged a regulatory regime that disempowers workers and fuels unsafe, poorly paid, degraded labor in the United States. Employers define most aspects of the low-wage work experience, such as wages, safety protocols, and conditions of hiring and firing. Many of the worker protections that are hallmarks of the modern labor and employment regime were put in place during the New Deal era, but since then gaps in these legislative efforts have increasingly widened, intensifying worker disempowerment. Compared to wages in other advanced industrial democracies, US wages are low. About one-third of the US workforce—52 million workers—earn less than $15 per hour.[1] While only 1.1 million workers earn at or below the federal minimum wage of $7.25 per hour,[2] this legal standard is far out of step with the costs of living today and drives wage suppression.[3] Social provision in the United States is also notably scarce or hard to access. As Françoise Carré and Chris Tilly argue in their comparative study of the retail sector, the market intersects with governmental regulatory choices.[4] Compared to France, for example, compensation, hours, and mobility opportunities are lower in the United States because this competitive sector is underregulated. The market drives a lot of precarious working conditions, but governmental regulatory interventions (or failures to intervene) delineate the choices that companies can make within market realities.

A legal framework that enables weak enforcement mechanisms gives employers massive control over the nature of low-wage work. The government has mandated certain labor standards, such as the

https://doi.org/10.7758/rioz4023.7204

minimum wage, some collective activity, and freedom from some forms of discrimination. However, these rights are inadequately enforced. Compared to the mid-1970s, when private union contracts covered one-quarter of all workers, private-sector unionization rates hover in the single digits today. Union power is even weaker in low-wage jobs. For example, unions have 2.5 percent coverage in accommodation and food services, further compounding worker disempowerment.[5] Historically, unions were one of the only institutions that could counterbalance employers' power and successfully demand improved treatment and mechanisms of accountability.[6] Although important efforts at union revitalization are being made and new forms of worker organizing are afoot, they have not come close to organizing the vast majority of the low-wage labor market. Underregulation is further accentuated by companies' use of independent contractor models and intermediary companies, such as staffing agencies, in ways that blur where companies' labor and employment law responsibilities lie, if they have any at all.

The workers we interviewed reported a wide variety of precarious conditions at work, including the unequal ways in which their wages were set and their need sometimes to fight for on-time payments, a fair schedule, and regular breaks. Some workers told of dangerous working conditions, the severity and nature of which varied widely by industry. Workers also described what they perceived as discrimination and harassment, abuses that are often hard to prove but that define workers' experiences. For many, the most salient aspect of their work experience was that they were often made to feel degraded and demeaned. Workers had a deep desire to be treated with dignity and respect, regardless of what the letter of the law allowed.

Government Action and Inaction

The government's inaction in the sphere of labor and employment law fosters worker precarity and blocks worker mobilization, but not, importantly, as a mere artifact of a "free" market. Rather, businesses have secured the upper hand in employer-employee relations. Indeed, this employer advantage derives from past bursts of unified business mobilization.[7] Such mobilizing bouts, which have most often occurred in times of economic crisis, can have lasting reverberations.[8] They institutionalize corporate priorities, such as employer advantages in the workplace, including administrative processes,[9] and even in global governance structures.[10] This institutionalized advantage, not the revered free market tips the scales toward employers even during times when labor might otherwise have market-based leverage. US employers, for instance, continue to benefit from, among other things, their collective actions to push back against efforts to regulate the workplace (1965–1975) and to defeat labor law reform efforts.[11]

LIGHT LEGISLATIVE INTERVENTION

In the United States, few pieces of legislation have been enacted to empower low-wage workers. US labor and employment law provides a baseline of substantive rights to workers, but only to those who fit the varying and sometimes hotly contested definitions of "employee." Some state laws are more generous, but federal law sets the baseline for workers' rights. Compared to Western European democracies, these legislative interventions are paltry. They do not protect workers from most unjustified firings at will, and they provide only a narrow set of protections. Under US law, there are some limits on an employer's ability to fire someone because of their protected status under the law, or because they are engaging in union organizing or have made a wage complaint against the employer. In general, however, protections against retaliatory firings are not as broad as "for cause" protections; they are also under-enforced and hard to prove in many cases.[12] The lack of constraints on employers' ability to fire at will enables employers to retain significant control over their workers, who could lose their jobs on a whim.

Beyond protections from termination, the substantive rights of workers related to working conditions are also paltry under US law. For example, the Fair Labor Standards Act (FLSA) requires employers to pay employees a minimum wage for the first forty hours of work each week and an overtime premium for hours worked above forty. The FLSA does not provide rights to vacation, holiday, severance, or sick pay. It does not mandate meal or rest periods. It does not provide for premium pay for weekend or holiday work. It is a basic minimum wage and overtime statute, with some child labor restrictions.[13] The

Occupational Safety and Health Act of 1970 establishes employers' responsibility to keep their workers safe and healthy but allows many dangers to go unregulated.[14] The National Labor Relations Act prohibits retaliation against workers engaged in "concerted" activity seeking better wages and working conditions. However, the NLRA has weak penalties for lawbreaking employers and provides insufficient support for labor's use of strikes and boycotts to pressure employers.[15] The NLRA also systematically excludes agricultural and domestic workers, both job categories traditionally filled by workers of color. Further, federal civil rights laws restrict employers from engaging in some forms of discrimination, but the scope of what counts as discrimination is too narrowly defined.[16] All told, this legal landscape amounts to relatively light legislative interventions on behalf of worker rights.

LIGHT ENFORCEMENT

In addition to these light legislative interventions on behalf of workers, workers' rights are under-enforced, in part because legal violations can be hard to prove.[17] Even beyond that, however, insufficient funding for enforcement efforts, the complexity of the enforcement process, and the lack of widespread worker organizing feed an environment of under-enforcement. Federal, state, and local governments have not provided enough resources to support the agencies charged with enforcing worker rights. For example, the Wage and Hour Division of the US Department of Labor (DOL) is charged with enforcing the FLSA, which covers 135 million workers in 7.3 million business establishments. As of December 2021, it had only 757 investigators across the entire country.[18] Insufficient enforcement resources tie the hands of the individuals charged with workplace health and safety as well. Government oversight for enforcement of safety and health regulations is typically sparse and usually is not undertaken until *after* an accident is reported.[19]

The fragmented and labyrinthian enforcement machinery is also hard for workers to access. Different laws are enforced by different agencies. Even within large agencies, like the US Department of Labor, there are subdivisions that vary in their enforcement authority.

A glance at the complexity of DOL's organizational chart reveals over twenty offices and agencies.[20] States and localities have passed additional laws and created agencies to enforce them as well. Standards themselves vary by industry (and state) and can be very detailed, as is the case in the Occupational Safety and Health Administration (OSHA) workplace safety space.[21] Specialization in US regulation may itself be a problem.[22] This potpourri of laws and enforcement agencies makes it very difficult for low-wage workers to know where to turn for help when they feel their rights have been violated in the workplace.[23] They often need to work with "brokers" if they are to have a chance of navigating this thicket.[24] We return to the barriers and opportunities that workers face in challenging bad working conditions in the next chapter.

HEAVY CHALLENGES TO WORKER ORGANIZING

Beyond basic legal minimums, successful worker organizing activity is key to demanding good jobs and employer compliance with basic rights. But current frameworks make worker organizing in the United States exceedingly difficult. Since the COVID-19 pandemic, there has been an upsurge in labor activity in the United States, with ongoing campaigns against Starbucks and Amazon, among others.[25] High-profile consumer-focused campaigns and grassroots efforts, however, are not a sufficient counterweight to weak laws and weak enforcement. The private sector in the United States is "nearly union-free, to a degree not seen in a century."[26] In part, economic shifts away from a union-strong manufacturing sector to a service sector, as well as geographic shifts in production to less union-friendly locations, account for declines in union density in the private sector.[27] Beyond economic shifts, the federal law protecting private-sector unionization has progressively become a weaker intervention in labor relations, with little teeth to substantially alter employer behavior.[28] Moreover, political and judicial assaults on union power have also played a significant role. The US Supreme Court, for instance, has tipped the scales in favor of employer interests over the collective rights of employees. While public-sector unions have fared better than private-sector unions, they too are under assault. Supreme

Court cases like *Janus v. AFSCME* have made it ever more difficult for unions to fund their organizing, representation, and advocacy efforts.[29] Beyond the courts, Congress has been hostile to unions in the decades since the New Deal period. The Taft–Hartley amendments in the late 1940s shifted the balance toward deeper protection of companies' ability to achieve profit maximization at the expense of collective action protections.[30]

The decline in union representation feeds chronic underregulation of workers' rights. Unions are a "core equalizing institution," argues Jake Rosenfeld.[31] When successful, they can secure contractual rights for employees beyond the statutory minimums. Collective bargaining agreements can provide "for cause" protections that do not exist in US legislation. They can provide higher wages, increased benefits, and other protections that flow only from contractual rights in the United States. Unions can also provide the vigilance needed to hold employers accountable in an environment of light enforcement. They can play a role in ensuring that basic rights under the FLSA, the NLRA, Title VII of the Civil Rights Act, and the Occupational Safety and Health Act are followed. They also help push for better working conditions and wages at the workplace and in the policy sphere. The decline of private-sector unionization is key to understanding sharp increases in income inequality and the degraded working conditions in the United States.[32]

The reality of the contemporary low-wage workplace is that most workers never interact with a union or other organization that can help them make the connections necessary to ensure that their rights as workers are enforced and advanced beyond what the law requires. Community groups and worker centers play a crucial role in encouraging enforcement of basic labor standards[33] and in pushing for workers' rights policy initiatives at the state and local levels.[34] As unionization rates continue to fall, and governments fail to become "robust, active, and strategic enforcers," these worker centers are one of the last lines of defense for workers.[35] Generating new standards alone does little to actually improve conditions on the ground in the absence of meaningful enforcement mechanisms.[36] Organizations help to make "rights real."[37] A key ingredient is deep sustained investment in collaborative enforcement between government and worker groups.[38] Yet worker centers face formidable obstacles. Their funding streams are insecure,[39] and political forces are waging a campaign against them to weaken their momentum.[40]

HEAVY PROLIFERATION OF BUSINESS MODELS THAT EVADE REGULATION

Some of the ways in which businesses organize their operations can intensify underregulation of low-wage work. While some businesses ship manufacturing abroad to cut costs, a whole range of industries utilize a combination of technological innovations and business models to come out ahead by avoiding employer responsibilities. Some of these practices have become endemic to particular industries, such as franchised restaurants, subcontracted construction teams, and warehouse work that relies on temp agencies. Labor scholar David Weil developed the concept of "fissuring" to highlight how layered business models feed low standards in the low-wage workplace by making regulation—and unionization—harder. In the fissured business model, lead businesses do not directly employ the workers who drive their profits. In other words, legally, these workers no longer appear to be their direct "employees"—a legal category that invokes worker rights in the workplace. Employers have "shed" these functions by engaging third parties—often franchisees, subcontractors, independent contractors, or temporary staffing agencies—to carry them out. These intermediary companies are typically thinly resourced, and they cut labor costs in order to gain a marginal profit. This fissuring "spills over to the wage-setting decisions of other businesses and to the labor markets in which they compete for workers."[41] Moreover, this structure can lead to more wage and hour violations, as well as injuries, as intermediary businesses try to squeeze their workforce to stay afloat in an increasingly competitive business environment.[42]

As Weil argues, these business models allow businesses to "have it both ways." They can "benefit from work executed in strict compliance with central corporate objectives and not be required to treat the workers who do it as their employees with the obligations that relationship holds."[43] Some lead companies retain sufficient control to constitute a joint employer relationship with the intermediary company, which can make them ultimately responsible for labor and employment law violations.[44] Lead companies sometimes build a lot of control into their business relationships to protect their brand or profits. Even if they remain involved at arm's length, however, they may exert significant influence, such as through monitoring mechanisms, software algorithms, and contracts with franchisees. Nonetheless, courts have been slow to expand lead company responsibility for workers' rights. A federal appeals court, for instance, did not consider the McDonald's franchise to be a joint employer with its franchisee even though it provided the software to the franchisee that miscalculated overtime and led to the wage violation at issue.[45]

The full extent of fissured business models and independent contracting is hard to measure, but such models are undoubtedly a key force shaping the low-wage workplace. Consulting multiple data sources is necessary to fully understand how "alternative work arrangements" interact with workplace inequality.[46] The Bureau of Labor Statistics (BLS) conducts the Contingent Worker Survey (CWS) to track some forms of alternative work arrangements, including temporary help, on-call employment, contract work, and independent contracting. It estimates that in 2023 there were "10.6 million independent contractors (6.9 percent of total employment), 2.6 million on-call workers (1.7 percent of total employment), 1.4 million temporary help agency workers (0.9 percent of total employment), and 933,000 workers provided by contract firms (0.6 percent of total employment)."[47] This estimate, Weil explains, is undoubtedly an undercount owing to widespread misunderstanding among respondents about what their actual employment status is or about the controls that a lead company may have on the intermediary company they work for directly. Moreover, it is possible for a worker to have a traditional employer who is an intermediary for another lead company. This type of fissured arrangement would also not be picked up by the CWS. Rather than rely on a household survey, we need to interrogate contracting relationships between business entities and other factors. Weil, for instance, draws from a variety of sources to project, conservatively, that close to 19 percent of workers in the private sector work in an industry governed by fissured arrangements. This number "could easily double" if we were to "consider the additional fissured workers in occupations and in industries with mixed use of practices."[48]

Taken together, all these ways in which workers' rights are severely underregulated—owing to government inaction in the labor and employment law sphere—breed worker precarity.

The Many Forms of Worker Precarity in the Low-Wage Workplace

We synthesize the ways in which the underregulation of low-wage work creates common challenges across workers' multiple job histories. Our interviews with Haitian and Central American workers across three statuses revealed complex work histories. This was unsurprising, as high turnover rates are endemic to low-wage industries, such as the service sector.[49] Workers across all immigration statuses toiled in manufacturing, warehouses, care work, retail, food service, construction, and residential services such as cleaning and landscaping. Levels of formality differed in the 888 jobs that workers talked about (see table 2.1). Sometimes workers were able to move up the chain; in other circumstances they moved around laterally. Care work, for instance, encompasses both live-in domestic workers, who are often paid in cash, and home health aides (HHAs), who are typically formally employed (usually by agencies) and often must be certified. Workers across many different types of jobs explained what they valued and what they struggled with at work.

Common problems across different kinds of low-wage jobs include underpayment and an unsafe workplace. Being paid overtime premiums, for example, seemed elusive to some low-wage immigrant workers who labored well over forty hours per week. Indeed, workers complained of not even getting paid for all of their hours. They described job quality in terms not only of wages and benefits but also of control over the scheduling and execution of work, which mattered to them as well.[50] Workers valued features of their job that are difficult to measure—their dignity, feeling empowered, and their autonomy on the job.[51] They also complained of degrading treatment, such as receiving the dirtiest and most physically demanding job assignments. Some jobs, to be sure, had unique challenges, such as the safety risks in construction and the widespread use of just-in-time scheduling in retail.[52] In the section that follows, we consider the common challenges we found across our interviews with workers.

Table 2.1 *Job Type by Gender, Regional Origin, and Immigration Status*

	Total	Gender		National Origin			Immigration Status		
		Male	Female	Haitian	Central American	Other	Undocumented	Temporary	Permanent
Administrative/clerical	74	30	44	34	40	0	0	16	58
Manufacturing/warehouse	158	66	92	57	100	1	70	43	45
Care work[a]	134	14	120	77	45	12	15	71	48
Retail	76	27	49	26	47	3	8	40	28
Food service[b]	158	70	88	41	109	8	43	78	37
Residential service[c]	96	52	44	10	86	0	28	44	24
Construction[d]	86	83	3	9	74	3	38	40	8
Other	106	67	39	58	46	2	16	63	27
Total jobs	888	409	479	312	547	29	218	395	275
Total respondents	301	136	165	138	151	12	82	130	89

Source: Authors' tabulation.

Note: These counts represent the total number of job types that respondents discussed over the course of the interview.

[a] Care work includes both formal positions (such as home health aides and nurse's assistants) and informal positions (such as nannies and babysitters).

[b] Food service includes work in restaurants, both fast-food and fast-casual and fine dining, and also includes both back-of-the-house and front-of-the-house positions.

[c] Residential service refers to positions, such as landscaper and cleaner, that require interfacing with residential customers.

[d] Construction includes formal jobs at companies, jobs obtained through subcontractors, and informal jobs, such as work as day laborers.

UNDERPAYMENT OF WAGES AND OVERTIME COMPENSATION

Wage rates in low-wage work are predictably low, but even worse, workers reported not being paid the legal minimums for all of the time they spent working. Underpayment of wages and overtime compensation is perhaps one of the most common dimensions of precarious low-wage work. Consistent with other surveys of low-wage workers, workers discussed not being paid at least the minimum wage for all the hours they worked and not being paid an overtime premium for hours they worked above forty in a workweek.[53] An oft-cited three-city survey of low-wage workers similarly finds that more than 20 percent of workers were paid less than the minimum wage in the prior week. Even more strikingly, 77 percent of workers missed out on a legally required overtime premium when they worked over forty hours in a week.[54]

Some have dubbed this phenomenon "wage theft" to raise awareness about the severity of the problem. Some employers underpay workers in extraordinary ways, but there are also a host of other seemingly benign practices that steal bits of workers' time and wages.[55] César Rosado Marzán defines twenty-one different ways in which wage theft occurs based on his ethnographic work with a Chicago worker center.[56] Common mechanisms across different kinds of low-wage work include not being paid for all of the hours worked, such as when an employer asks an employee to keep working even after they have "punched out" of the system that tracks work hours. Late payment and no payment for the last week of work are also very common. Direct deductions as well as failure to reimburse workers for required materials or trainings can also bring their wages below legal minimums. Regardless of an employer's intention, these oversights have real consequences for workers living at or near the poverty line.

Some mechanisms of wage theft are more common in specific low-wage industries. This is the case, for example, in industries where tipping is customary. For restaurant workers, tip levels become a major factor in determining whether employers are liable to make up the difference.[57] Federal laws allow employers to count some tips that employees receive toward their minimum wage and overtime obligations, but they can do so only if the tips bring the wages up to those full wage rates. In restaurants, the federal minimum is a meager

$2.13 per hour, as of 2024; the assumption is that workers can make up the difference with tips. Workers cannot, however, always rely on tips to bring them to the minimum wage. Moreover, reliance on tips has been shown to generate a whole host of inequities, including rampant sexual harassment.[58] Employers commonly fail to make up the difference during weeks when tips are low, leaving workers earning less than the legal minimum.

Myrlande, a Haitian restaurant worker with permanent status, is a case in point.[59] Even including the meager tips she made, Myrlande regularly made less than $3.00 per hour for her six days of work at the restaurant. She eventually left because "the manager lady was disrespectful and treated us all very poorly," but it took a while for her to leave. Myrlande admitted that, like other workers we heard from, she simply "had no other options at the time."

Industries that commonly pay workers on a commission basis provide another example. Like the laws governing tipped workers, employers can generally pay their workers on a commission basis as long as, at the end of the day, the worker is being paid at least the minimum rates required by law for all hours worked. Diana, a Nicaraguan office cleaner with permanent status, experienced this form of commission-based wage theft firsthand.[60] She talked about how hard the work was and how incredibly exploited she felt. Commission arrangements, at first blush, may sound like a good option for some workers. The idea is that, by working faster, you make more than you would working at a set hourly wage. But that was not Diana's experience. She would have preferred to receive the straight minimum wage per hour worked, given the relative ease of tracking and predictability. Instead, she was paid for each office she completed, an arrangement that she deemed to be an unfair ruse. Payment on commission can make wage and hour calculations more challenging for workers. As Diana put it, "They try to trick you," because it is hard to know how much you are making per hour when paid on this basis.

DANGERS ON THE JOB

Beyond wages, all categories of workers discussed the dangers they faced at their jobs. Our interviews suggested that workplace safety protections are chronically under-enforced. Indeed, low-wage workers across job types often risk injury and illness to varying degrees. Some industries are notorious for their hazardous workplaces, which in turn become normalized as part of the job.[61] For example, Carmen, a Nicaraguan temporary worker, commented that, when she was working in hazardous workplaces, she did not think they posed problems at the time because the conditions were so common across the many low-wage jobs she worked.[62] Construction workers regularly face hazards such as falling, being struck, slipping in trenches, and even being electrocuted.[63] The immigrants we interviewed who worked in dangerous work environments faced different types of hazards. For example, Harold, a Haitian driver for an international delivery company who had permanent status, talked about the constant threat of back injuries from lifting boxes, the imperative to attend to customers first, and frequently missed or delayed breaks.[64] Ultimately, he "left before [he] got injured."

Workers in the restaurant industry talked about hazards in the kitchens of fast-food and fast-casual restaurants, such as hot fryers and greasy floors. One Haitian permanent worker, Marcello, described how a simple stocking job in a freezer at a sandwich chain almost killed him.[65] "My shift was nine to five, sometimes seven p.m. I would find myself in that freezer [at] midnight, still working. At times I would work a full twenty-four hours. . . . You are in a freezer all day. I would go completely numb. . . . My knees would ache, and [I] feel all the aches now." Beyond navigating the hazards at work, others, like Benjamin, a Haitian permanent worker, described having to go to work sick.[66] Sick pay is not federally mandated, and few states and cities have filled the gap. As a result, many low-wage workers must choose between losing critical pay or endangering their own health and that of their customers and coworkers.[67] These concerns were especially heightened during the COVID-19 pandemic.

Domestic and care work jobs also pose dangers that often go unrecognized by regulators, in part owing to the isolated nature of the work.[68] We interviewed many home health aides, who in the Northeast are overwhelmingly Caribbean women who rely on an agency to place them at a job site. These workers often felt that the agency prioritized the patients (the clients) over workers' well-being and dignity. This presented them with the impossible choice of whether to endure the persistent hazards or lose income that they and their families relied on. Clara, a Haitian temporary worker, explained, "Well, even if the [patient] does something to you, when you tell the coordinator... the coordinator doesn't want you! They don't want you! It's the patient that they want. . . . They don't want you. It's the patient that they want."[69]

Mistreatment by patients and isolation come with the job.[70] Many HHAs, like Maxime, a Haitian temporary worker, conceded this reality.[71] They told stories of physical assault, unhealthy living conditions, and few opportunities to escape the physical toll of their work. For example, Victoria, a Haitian temporary worker, talked about getting bitten by a client.[72] Paula, a Haitian permanent worker, showed us an arm covered in scratches.[73] Though HHAs should technically be able to complain to their placement coordinator, many coordinators never intervened. Some coordinators would even purposely place workers with particularly difficult patients rather than refuse these patients service or refer them to better equipped support providers. Fabiola, a Haitian temporary worker, was placed with two difficult patients. One struck her during an Alzheimer's outburst over an improperly cooked steak, and the other forced her to sleep in freezing conditions.[74] Both incidents sent her to the emergency room. In both cases, Fabiola viewed the coordinator as well as the agency as negligent. Yet it was Fabiola who was ultimately fired from the agency, owing to her health problems, which no doubt were worsened by the physical toll of the job, she noted. By that point, exhausted from the abuse, she was happy to leave. Fabiola, like other low-wage workers, quite reasonably blamed her private employer. She and other workers were subject, nonetheless, to the broader context of lax governmental protections, weak unions, and underfunded enforcement resources.

Independent contractors, who are highly underregulated, felt a unique form of vulnerability. Since they did not appear to have an employer, or any other entity responsible for their safety, they often did not know where to turn when they were harmed at work. Nelson, an undocumented Salvadoran laborer who sought work at a popular day labor site outside a home improvement store, was beaten up by security guards.[75] Another time fellow workers attacked him at the corner. In neither case did he have access to a specific employer that carried workers' compensation insurance, nor was this small informal job site a targeted jurisdiction for an OSHA investigation.

DISCRIMINATION, HARASSMENT, AND DEMEANING TREATMENT

While lost wages are trackable, and job hazards are often blatant for all to see, a third, less tangible category of unchecked worker precarity left a profound impression on the workers we interviewed. Haitian and Central American workers across statuses and industries discussed what they viewed as discrimination and harassment based on their race, national origin, and sex or gender. Others stopped short of identifying a formally prohibited abuse as such, but they would recount having received demeaning, undignified treatment that might or might not have risen to the level of a provable legal violation. Women especially found themselves constantly having to repel sexist behavior. Women workers spoke of intrusive "flirtations" or belittlements they had to endure as part of their work. Ruth, a Salvadoran undocumented worker, talked about the sexist comments she endured from male workers when she started work as the only woman in a kitchen cabinet assembly facility.[76] It was worth it to her to stay despite the treatment and isolation because of the job's stability and higher pay. As the company hired more women and she befriended some of the workers, Ruth reported that conditions improved. Workers of all genders described having to endure a broad spectrum of racialized treatment by employers and supervisors as well as coworkers, ranging from overt racist remarks to everyday degradation, such as having their intelligence questioned. Service workers also described being abused by their patients, customers, and the broader public with whom they interacted at work.

These manifestations of racism and sexism—and sometimes homophobia and other forms of prejudice—remind us that job quality is far more than simply a matter of wages, benefits, promotions, and safety. All of these are basic minimum standards for worker well-being, even survival, but as Arne Kalleberg explains, workers also value autonomy and other "intrinsic rewards" beyond material remuneration.[77] Workers care about dignity and respect, and they want their contributions to be sufficiently noticed and appreciated.[78] Neera, a Haitian undocumented worker, left a job at a hair salon where her manager constantly yelled at her.[79] "They don't respect people. . . . They didn't respect our rights at all. I didn't like how they were treating me, so that is why I left that job," she explained. Others, like Myrlande, the Haitian permanent worker mentioned earlier, described her lack of payment in and of itself as a sign of disrespect. Magdala, a Haitian temporary worker, shared the challenges and indignities of working with patients who suffered from dementia and spoke of how much she valued being treated kindly and respectfully.[80] Conversely, workers recounted experiences of racist humiliation, while others told of demeaning sexual behavior and comments.

These experiences are difficult to operationalize in labor force surveys, are hard to capture in a single indicator, and can vary depending on the type of industry. This is the challenge of empirically capturing bias and discrimination.[81] Moreover, workers do not always identify whether they felt that the humiliation was gendered,[82] racist, xenophobic, or some combination thereof.[83] Despite extensive case law, the quotidian experience of discrimination rarely rises to the level of an actionable offense.[84] Yet, workers' accounts of their experiences at work deepen our understanding of these abuses. Service jobs, for instance, often expose low-wage workers to a variety of forms of harassment by customers. Guillermino, a Honduran temporary worker, detailed how patrons would shout racial slurs at him as he quietly drove the bus.[85] Diana, a Nicaraguan permanent worker mentioned earlier, told us that, in her work as a restaurant server, drunk customers would make sexual comments about her and sometimes touch her inappropriately right in front of her supervisor, who did nothing about it. Though the nature of discrimination, harassment, and undignified treatment varied, such treatment was a consistent theme among the low-wage workers we interviewed.

In part 3, we return to this discussion by situating contemporary manifestations of racism and xenophobia within long histories of labor systems that explicitly privileged White workers over workers of color. The government has done little to counteract persistent racism and xenophobia at work.

Conclusion

Extreme power inequality between employers and workers, sanctioned by the government, allows for pervasive precarity across the low-wage workforce, even in relatively labor-friendly contexts like the New York City metropolitan area. Details vary across industry depending, for instance, on whether a job is public-facing or on the level of isolation a worker endures. The nature of harassment may differ for workers who interface mostly with customers and patients. That said, workers across all differences in our sample commonly reported wage theft, danger, discrimination, harassment, and demeaning treatment. Immigrant workers with no documents, those with temporary authorization documents, and those with permanent status all shared these common conditions of precarity. Similarly, though the precise nature of the wage theft, workplace hazards, and harassment they experienced was not uniform, Haitians and Central Americans alike were subject to the common forms of workplace precarity discussed here.

We have set out some of the baseline working conditions of low-wage work in an underregulated low-wage economy. These conditions are a "best-case scenario" given that workers in the New York City metropolitan area have more legislative support, enforcement initiatives, and union involvement compared to the federal baseline for workers elsewhere. Nevertheless, these workers spoke about myriad ways in which they were degraded at work. In chapter 3, after describing the baseline barriers faced by workers pushing for improvements at work—whether on their own or as a group, and whether informally or formally through unions or government channels—we introduce various pathways to worker empowerment.

3 CHALLENGING PRECARITY IN THE LOW-WAGE WORKPLACE: BARRIERS AND PATHWAYS

One might wonder whether low-wage workers can ever push to improve their workplace experiences. We asked the workers we interviewed to reflect on how they navigated challenging conditions at work such as nonpayment of wages, unsafe tasks, discrimination, sexual harassment, and a range of other demeaning experiences. While most respondents described a whole host of reasons for *not* taking action, some workers did find ways to challenge poor working conditions. We draw from interviews with Haitian and Central American workers across three different immigration statuses (undocumented, temporary, and permanent statuses) to lay out the barriers and pathways to resisting poor treatment in the workplace.

This chapter first lays out the barriers. Workers most often reported not pressing for change in the workplace either because they did not have the power to make changes or because they strategically understood that they could face job loss or other forms of retribution if they spoke up. Even in the context of poor wages and degrading working conditions, workers are rarely able to join a labor union organizing effort or engage with a worker organization. Legal challenges to employer behavior are also the exception rather than the norm. Indeed, on the whole, very few individuals file formal claims against their employer.[1] Research confirms that except for claims that emerge from injuries that result in hospitalization, only one-quarter of aggrieved workers, at most, ever formally complain.[2] And fewer than half of injured workers who triggered the workers' compensation system through their hospital intake forms filed a formal claim against their employer.[3]

https://doi.org/10.7758/rioz4023.3143

Second, the chapter highlights the stories of workers who did push back against employers or otherwise found ways to avoid feeling powerless at work. In some cases individual workers strategized on their own, and in other cases collectives of workers put forth their demands. Some workers accepted the harsh realities of low-wage work and focused on the dignity of their hard work. Others challenged their employers informally through oral grievances on the job or with the help of a worker organization. Workers turned to formal legal processes in only a few cases. Their efforts sometimes gained traction, but often did not. These observations are in line with Charlotte Alexander and Arthi Prasad's findings that workers' attempts to make a claim to improve their working conditions are not always immediately or ultimately successful.[4]

Much of the literature on workers' rights mobilization focuses on formal claims. Our study illustrates the value of also looking at the various forms of resistance that do not invoke formal legal processes. While the letter of the law empowered some workers to come forward, this was not always the case. Some worker demands were beyond the reach of any law handed down by a specific jurisdiction. Yet workers' sense of justice and dignity led them to make their demands anyway, and they sometimes won. Others simply knew in their gut that the indignities they were enduring, such as egregious sexual harassment, were wrong.

Barriers to Challenging Workplace Precarity

It is exceedingly difficult for low-wage workers to push back when they experience indignities, injuries, unpaid wages, and other poor conditions of employment. Workers commonly described feeling like they had no power to do anything about poor treatment. Stefano, an undocumented Haitian supermarket worker, was not given his legally entitled breaks at work and accepted this as just the "reality" of low-wage work.[5] He lamented that "there is nothing I can do, or anywhere I can go . . . so I just accept it as it is." Given that employers often have a large pool of low-wage laborers to turn to if things go awry with one worker, some workers expressed loyalty and thankfulness, even when talking about employers that were mistreating the workforce. Along these same lines, Inari, an undocumented Honduran bakery worker, was "appreciative" of the opportunity to work and thus was "not going to make trouble with the people who helped you when you needed it."[6] These dynamics reflect the same patterns of employer paternalism and worker feelings of loyalty that Kathleen Sexsmith finds among farmworkers in upstate New York.[7] In other cases, workers may stay on—having few to no options to leave—but enact quiet forms of resistance to recoup their dignity and personal sense of power.

Employers can dictate the terms of the working relationship and are often effectively immune from worker resistance. Employers have manipulated "weak labor laws"[8] and worked with the "union avoidance industry" to reduce the power and potential of the US labor movement to represent workers' interests.[9] Here we focus on four formidable barriers to formal and informal pushbacks. First, employers have wide freedom to fire workers, with few restraints. This hands-off system makes pushing back risky for workers and allows employers to fire employees at will, with only a narrow set of exceptions. The limits on firing that do exist can be hard to enforce, leaving workers afraid that they risk retaliation if they speak up about poor wages and working conditions. Second, US labor and employment law's reliance on workers themselves to enforce these laws through public complaints fosters additional barriers. Workers first need to know their rights, then know how to enforce them, and then they need to be willing to put their jobs at risk. Third, the proliferation of multilayered or informal contract-based business relationships can erect giant barriers for workers. Some business models, for instance, make it difficult for workers to ascertain which business entity should be the target of their grievances and who is ultimately responsible for their wages and working conditions. Fourth, when workers do resist, they often face opaque and seemingly futile assistance from human resource offices, supervisors, or union representatives. We turn to these barriers next.

FEW LEGAL RESTRAINTS ON EMPLOYERS: THE AT-WILL LEGAL SYSTEM

The at-will employment system in the United States deters worker claims. Indeed, various workers we interviewed felt that they could not speak up. Ana, a Haitian worker with lawful permanent residency who worked at a food processing plant, explained that workers did not feel that they could "vindicate [their rights] because they were afraid they will lose their jobs" by speaking up.[10] Assuming that she would have lost her job in retail if she demanded that she receive the full minimum wage, Martha also did not want to rock the boat. A Guatemalan woman in her late twenties who arrived as a child and was now a citizen, Martha reasoned, "I couldn't really fight it because it was the only job that I could work around my schedule at that time."[11] Workers felt easily replaceable, they told us, and thus did not want to risk pushing back against employers. Lina, a Haitian permanent worker employed in a restaurant, shared that she did not complain about getting paid below the minimum wage, never receiving overtime pay, and not being allowed to take needed bathroom breaks because she "felt they would find another person" to replace her.[12]

It was exceedingly common for workers to miss their meal or rest breaks, to work unpaid overtime hours, or simply to receive checks that came up short or were late. At first blush, losing a "bad job" full of indignities and legal violations might seem like not that bad an outcome. Under the at-will system, workers who are not subject to an employment contract can leave at any time. Many of the workers we interviewed, however, did not feel confident about finding a new job and so felt that leaving was not a viable choice. Workers "[did] not speak up" when there were health and safety concerns with their placements, said Cherline, a Haitian permanent worker, because they did not want to "lose their jobs" and did not "know if they would find another job."[13] Jonas, a Haitian worker who was a lawful permanent resident and worked for a moving company, also explained that he would consider complaining about poor treatment and legal violations at his job only after securing employment somewhere else.[14]

Given employers' at-will freedom to terminate the employment relationship on a whim, pushing back while still being employed was largely considered too risky and likely to result in immediate job loss. This fear of job loss was particularly consequential for low-wage workers who were living paycheck to paycheck. As expressed by Irina, a Haitian worker with lawful permanent resident status who worked in packing and receiving, "If you go and complain, they will fire you. And you have bills to pay. If they fire you, you won't be able to pay your bills. So you are left to bear it as it is."[15] Heloise, a Haitian home health aide with temporary protected status, emphasized the particular burden that women carried, especially those with transnational families.[16] She explained, "I think [what] women really deal with . . . is just the fact that we're women and we trying to work. We are single parents, we have to provide for our children. . . . We have families, we have to help them out, they [are] not here." For migrant workers like Heloise, the consequences of job loss reverberated both here and abroad.

THE GOVERNMENT'S FIRE ALARM ENFORCEMENT SYSTEM

Along with the at-will baseline, the government's reliance on workers as rights enforcers creates additional barriers. The United States has a "fire alarm" system that requires workers themselves to pull the fire alarm in order to expose employers' legal violations through nonpayment of wages, unsafe working conditions, and discrimination. This system contrasts with systems based on government audits and surprise inspections of workplaces. Legal scholars have dubbed US workers "private attorneys general" who enforce labor and employment laws on behalf of themselves as well as the government.[17] While this may sound like a rational law enforcement scheme, relying as it does on workers' firsthand knowledge, it does not sufficiently factor in barriers to workers' power to play the role of enforcer. It does not sufficiently acknowledge how difficult it is for many workers to step into the role of a "private attorney general" and pursue a formal claim against their employer through a court or government agency process. Low-wage workers have a lot to lose if they do step forward.

Two key elements of the fire alarm enforcement system are often missing in the low-wage workplace: workers knowing what their rights are, and workers knowing where to go when they make the difficult decision to stand up for those rights.

What Rights Do I Have as a Worker? It is difficult to know whether an employer is breaking the law if a worker does not know what their rights are as employees. The workers we interviewed were confused about a range of standards, including their rights to sick days and breaks, two areas of law that vary considerably state to state. As labor educators have long known, education is a necessary, even if not sufficient, ingredient of worker "claims-making."[18] Julian, who was an undocumented Haitian with a law degree from Haiti and was working as a package handler in the United States, was well aware of the importance of rights knowledge.[19] He explained that, as a newcomer, "I don't know all of the laws of this country." He predicted that if he did know the workers' rights laws better, he would be interested in learning more about unions, as he did not "want people to violate" his rights. Julian explained that he felt targeted by his Dominican supervisors because he was Haitian. He did not complain because he did not know the laws and because his mother-in-law told him, "When you are a man, you don't complain when you are at work.... Hold your stuff in your heart.... Just take the bullets." Julian's comment highlights the impact of gender on workers' understandings of their rights and responsibilities. Norms of masculinity can make men reluctant to demand better and safer conditions.[20]

Women who are pregnant and balancing the challenges of motherhood also face a distinct set of structural factors. Rosalinda, a Salvadoran temporary worker who lost her job at a supermarket after having a baby, similarly noted that lack of rights knowledge disadvantaged her in the workplace.[21] She lamented that she "did not know anything" about her right to disability benefits and pregnancy discrimination protections. "No one explained anything to me about these rights," she said. Rosalinda did not know "that you have the right to come back after you have the baby." She mistakenly thought companies were allowed to fire women who had children because these women needed a short break from work.

But knowing one's rights is not enough; workers also need to know how to go about enforcing those rights. Jeremias, an undocumented Haitian worker, described the dangerous conditions and long hours in a variety of warehouse and food-processing jobs he had held.[22] "[Employers] abuse you because there are no places you can go and complain." For workers like him, the impunity was inevitable. Similarly, Sylvanie, a Haitian lawful permanent resident who worked as a nursing home attendant, explained that employees unfairly had to choose between taking their required break and taking care of patients.[23] "When are you supposed to take a break?" she implored.

"By the time you take a break in a nursing home, and [especially] if you oversee a floor, then who is going to be there in case something happens?" Instead, workers did not take breaks so that they could get the work done. "You eat while you walk. If you get a chance to sit, then you can grab some water.... If any nurse tells you they take the whole thirty minutes [for a break], then it's a lie. There is no way you can every day." Sylvanie felt that workers needed to know how to access their rights without losing their job or compromising patient care. Indeed, employers would often put the onus on workers to comply with a break schedule, with little regard for the impact of the workload they had assigned on employees' ability to take those breaks.

Where Do I Go to Enforce My Rights? To claim formal rights, workers need to not only know what their rights are but how to deploy them—who to call, and where to go. If she had known where to go to complain, said Benita, a Haitian fast-food worker with permanent status, she would have reported not getting paid for all of her hours and chronically having her scheduled breaks cut short.[24] "The reason I didn't is because I didn't know. If I knew, I would have gone," she insisted.

But which government agencies are relevant for workers like Benita? Can workers get a lawyer and make complaints against their employer in court? Who can help workers navigate the government's fire alarm enforcement system? Most workers, and probably most Americans, do not know how to answer those questions. Inability to access the system is clearly a barrier to an enforcement regime that gives workers the responsibility to come forward as the complainants.[25]

Workers explained that they simply had no idea where to go to initiate the process—a revelation in the New York metro area, encompassing states with some of the most worker-friendly rules on the books. These workers did not have what Alexander and Prasad refer to as "procedural legal knowledge."[26] Saskay, an undocumented Haitian who braided hair at a beauty salon, knew her employer was violating the law.[27] She suffered ongoing verbal abuse and minimum wage violations and was aware of the protections covering her. However, she explained simply, "I don't know where to complain." When we asked workers experiencing unpaid wages about the US Department of Labor, the agency in charge of enforcing wage law, they commonly responded that they had never heard anything about it. Some workers attributed their lack of awareness to being new to the country. "I had only been here for a year," said Tiana, a Haitian fast-food restaurant worker with lawful permanent residency.[28] "I did not know the system or how it worked. There were a lot of things that I didn't know." Confusion about where to go to enforce wage rights, however, was not confined to new arrivals. Longer-term residents were not necessarily better informed. Irina had been in the United States for almost ten years and had lawful permanent residency when we spoke to her. She had suffered wage violations and was made to go to work sick or be fired. "I didn't know about [the Department of Labor] at all. If I had known about this and where to go, I would have reported this. I would have spoken up and even sued them because they don't respect people."

In some legal arenas, like wage and hour laws and antidiscrimination laws, employers are required to post information where workers can plainly see it. Employers are not required, however, to post information about workers' rights to engage in collective efforts with coworkers and with unions. And even when employers do make rights information available, they often communicate in English, not in the dominant language of most of their workers. Indeed, some workers' struggles with English posed yet another barrier to learning about their rights and being able to complain about poor treatment. For example, when asked why she did not complain about harassment and inadequate pay in her restaurant job, Wilda, a Haitian with lawful permanent residency, pointed to her language abilities.[29] She explained, "I never used to do this because I didn't have enough English to advocate in this way." Similarly, Alejandro, a Salvadoran with TPS who was working at a medical supplies store, explained why he never complained about persistent racial harassment and dangerous working conditions.[30] "I stayed quiet because I didn't know what to say in English," he said.

In some cases, the disjointed nature of federal and state government agencies, each with mandates over different aspects of worker rights, posed a primary barrier for workers. Michael Piore and Andrew Schrank critique the fragmented and specialized nature of US enforcement agencies, describing them as "distributed across dozens of different agencies at multiple levels of government, each with a relatively narrow jurisdiction."[31] Given this fragmentation, even the workers who did find their way to one of the labor and employment law enforcement agencies faced barriers to getting all of their claims addressed. For example, Carmen, a Nicaraguan with TPS we met in the last chapter, described the obstacles that she and her coworkers at a fast-food hamburger chain faced when they reached out to the government for help. She described their problems with getting paid and the hateful insults her manager often hurled at Indian and Hispanic workers. When a group of workers called the Department of Labor about the poor treatment, the agency responded only to the issues in its purview, the wage issues. "The only problem that was resolved," a disappointed Carmen reported, "was the unpaid overtime." Clearly, these workers had run up against a problem of agency jurisdiction.

Carmen's story reflects the inadequacy of a system that requires a worker to navigate multiple unlinked agencies to seek a solution.[32] Ostensibly, agencies could refer cases to each other, but here the agencies in charge of enforcing employment discrimination were not made aware of the complaints of racial harassment.

BUSINESS MODELS AS BARRIERS: INTERMEDIARY BUSINESSES AND CONTRACT WORKERS

Nonstandard work arrangements have long been described as a factor in increasing worker precarity. We reiterate their importance here with a focus on how they confound workers' ability to mobilize their rights.[33] These business arrangements make it difficult for workers to know who their employer is, or whether they are formal "employees" with a right to make demands. Low-wage employers often use intermediary businesses to contract workers, or they will declare workers "independent contractors" in an effort to shield themselves from responsibility, liability, and union-organizing drives.[34] This is not new. Since before the New Deal, businesses, with maximizing profit as their central goal, have restructured in the face of regulation in an attempt to find a loophole that absolves them of responsibility for workers' labor and employment law rights.[35]

Who Is My Employer? Intermediary Companies as Buffers Immigrants seeking work often turned to temporary staffing agencies, which have become a popular mechanism to find jobs in industries ranging from health care to manufacturing. These agencies dispatch workers to external worksites and act as intermediaries—and a convenient buffer—between the workers and the actual entity responsible for their pay, treatment, and other benefits. Even though both the intermediary company and the lead company may be their employers, this is not how it appears to workers on the ground. Like most workers in his position, Paul, the undocumented Haitian working in food manufacturing whom we met in the last chapter, concluded that he worked solely for the intermediary company. The company where he was placed to work, he thought, was not responsible for his wages and working conditions. He and other workers were regularly paid late. Paul had called the temporary staffing agency that placed him at the factory several times and was still awaiting a response when we talked to him. Even though the managers at the manufacturing facility where he worked might have been able to put pressure on the agency to pay him and his coworkers on time, Paul did not see them as responsible for his pay in any way.

Intermediary companies can even get in the way of workers lodging a challenge. Even though Samuel, an undocumented Haitian who regularly worked loading and unloading boxes from trucks at a warehouse, worked alongside workers employed directly by the warehouse, he saw his employer as the temporary staffing agency that had placed him there and signed his checks.[36] The warehouse was unionized, but Samuel, whose work was similar to the work of the unionized workforce, was not a union member because he was considered to have a separate employer (the agency). When asked why he did not push back against the warehouse company when he experienced degrading and unjust treatment on the job, he noted that he could not do that. "You cannot speak to a union" about such mistreatment, he said, "because you are not employed. The union is there for employed workers."

Even though Samuel worked alongside unionized warehouse employees, doing similar work, he saw himself as being in a different category because he had landed the job, and completed his hiring paperwork, through the temp agency. Because the company classified him as a temp, it did not occur to Samuel that under the law he might have had two employers, or joint employers. "You are a contracted [worker]," he said, so "you can't really speak to anyone" at the company about your problems: "I work with the agency, not them.

So I can't go to them for vindication or claims because I don't work for them directly." The agency, however, was a dead end for Samuel. With no real power to change the working conditions at the warehouse, the agency was unable to resolve Samuel's issues. Change in this kind of scenario is possible only if the lead firm is recognized as a joint employer and the workers are aware of that fact.

Some workers, however, intuited that they might have two employers, joint employers, which were both responsible for ensuring proper compliance with labor and employment laws. For example, Leslie, an undocumented Guatemalan, was placed by a temp agency to work as a packer of chocolates on another company's assembly line.[37] She assumed that the chocolate company had some obligation to her as a worker since it was directing her work. At one point she was not paid for sick days that employees had a right to under state law. When Leslie confronted the chocolate company, its representative said that, since she was not the company's employee, she needed to take the issue up with the temporary staffing agency to make sure she was paid correctly under the law. She did take it up with the agency but was never paid fully for the sick days.

Am I an Employee? Independent Contractor Misclassification and Other Contract Work For independent contractors, day laborers, and other kinds of under-the-table informal workers, there was no one to complain to because they were not employees and had no employer. In their view, they were not part of the formal workforce and thus were not "employees" under the law with rights to claim or reclaim. In low-wage work, companies all too commonly misclassify workers as "independent contractors" rather than "employees."[38] Workers, however, often do not know they are being misclassified, or if they do, they're uncertain about how to go about making that case. Regardless of the legal reality of their status as employees, our interviews convey that workers' conclusions that they were not rights-bearing employees inhibited their ability to push back against precarious working conditions.

Juano's experience exemplifies how unconventional job relationships block pathways to resistance.[39] Juano, an undocumented Haitian immigrant, found a job stocking packages for an international package delivery company through informal channels. One day when he was stocking packages, his fingernail was ripped off, a routine but incredibly painful injury that he was left on his own to deal with. He did not feel like it was the company's concern, or that it would care enough to help, because he was not the company's direct employee and had obtained the job informally. For this injured worker, informal employment deprived him of "access to certain privileges."

For Heloise, the Haitian independent contractor with TPS, her legal status did not give her control over her own working conditions or a sense of safety from predatory individuals. If anything, that status made her more vulnerable to sexual harassment throughout the course of her sales position, a challenge that men in sales jobs do not face in the same way. Indeed, Heloise asserted, "the most dangerous work I have ever done was as an independent contractor." One of her jobs with an energy supply company required her to walk around neighborhoods in the dark, going house to house, trying to sell energy plans. On a few occasions during her canvassing, she was subjected to lewd comments and threatened by men in some of the houses she approached. She constantly felt unsafe walking at night, but a condition of her contract was that she do this work during the evening hours, when most people would be home from work. Working alongside someone else could have provided more security at night, but as an independent contractor with no official supervisor, she had no way to request this arrangement, and it would have fallen to her to hire a coworker to accompany her. Though technically Heloise was self-employed and free to do whatever she liked, she was boxed in with few choices.

Pushing back against employers without the help of a government agency or other advocate is a difficult prospect. Workers described wide variation in how employers responded to their internal complaints. All told, the picture they painted was one of opaque and futile internal complaint processes.

OPAQUE AND FUTILE INTERNAL COMPLAINT PROCESSES

Workers discussed not only the barriers within government entities to resolving complaints but also barriers to accessing relief via internal union processes, supervisors, or human resource (HR) offices. The strain on unions that makes it difficult for some to connect fully with their membership was evident in the accounts of frustrated respondents. Workers sometimes did not know who their union representative was, let alone how to contact them if they wanted to complain about an indignity or injustice. Linda, a Haitian unionized home health aide with lawful permanent residency, said that her job "is supposed to have [a union], but I never see them."[40] As a result, workers with a problem had to "figure it out on our own," Linda lamented. Similarly, Eva, a Salvadoran with TPS who worked as an office cleaner, lost her union benefits when the company was sold to a non-unionized company.[41] The impact was devastating. Now, Eva reported, she had "no idea at all" where to go with problems, adding, "I am not informed."

As protections have evolved over the decades, companies have created systems to manage complaints before they become a legal liability.[42] These internal dispute processes, which rely on supervisors and HR departments to field worker concerns, have added a roadblock at times. Some workers reported that these employer representatives had given them the runaround, without resolving the problem. Salvador, a Salvadoran with TPS and a cleaning job, said that it was common for his employer to "steal workers' wages."[43] When workers confronted various management personnel, each would point their finger at someone else. For example, workers would be told that they needed to talk to "the secretary," who told them they needed to speak with "central administration," who told them the secretary handled such issues. Workers found these supposed internal complaint processes to be nothing more than a brick wall, and sometimes they simply gave up and accepted the wage theft. Rocio was a Haitian immigrant whose mother had petitioned for her lawful permanent residency before she arrived in the United States more than a decade earlier.[44] In her previous warehouse position, Rocio sometimes needed to sit down when lifting pallets to avoid swelling and hypertension episodes. She could not get an accommodation after many requests and eventually had to resign. "When you're poor, that's how it is. If I left the job to go home, I won't have anything. . . . If I were to fall dead on my face, that would be just that." When we spoke to Rocio, she was unemployed and could not get a call back from the temporary staffing agency for a new placement.

Table 3.1 *Pathways to Challenging Bad Jobs: Wages Example*

	Demands for Legal Minimums		Demands Beyond Legal Minimums	No Explicit Demand
	Internal Informal Process	External Formal Process	Negotiation and Bargaining	Quiet Resistance
Individual	Demand on manager to pay overtime	Overtime claim to the Department of Labor or the court system	Salary negotiation	Individual slowdown
Collective	Demand on manager to pay overtime	Overtime claim to the Department of Labor or the court system	Salary negotiation (multiple workers, worker centers, union collective bargaining agreement)	Coordinated slowdown

Source: Authors' compilation.

In spite of the many barriers to confronting workplace injustices, our interviews also revealed myriad creative ways in which workers fought against feelings of powerlessness at work. We turn to these stories next.

Many Pathways to Resistance

Workers can find ways to demand better workplace conditions and avoid feeling powerless despite the giant barriers in their path. Much of the literature focuses on the visible organizing campaigns launched by advocacy groups and unions or the process of making formal claims through courts and executive agencies.[45] We identify at least four main types of resistance from our interviews: formal claims, informal claims, requests for more than the legal minimums, and quiet resistance (see table 3.1). Our interviews suggest that workers do sometimes have agency despite vast power differentials, and that they are persistent, courageous, and creative.

Workers sometimes developed resistance strategies on their own, and other times in collaboration with collectives or receptive supervisors. Indeed, collectives can help workers both constitutively, by empowering them to step forward, and instrumentally, by providing them with the practical resources necessary to make change.[46] Coworkers, labor unions, and community organizations that work with low-wage workers facilitate worker empowerment.[47] Moreover, receptive supervisors and "high-road" managerial practices can make a difference for workers.[48] Despite the barriers, some workers found ways to communicate effectively with receptive supervisors and to creatively convince supervisors, even when they were initially hesitant, to be more responsive. Yet we can also see in the interviews that many efforts to push back against workplace indignities and injustices do indeed "fail." Raymundo's experience is a case in point.[49] In the wake of Hurricane Sandy, this Honduran TPS worker was part of a crew that was brought in for mold mitigation. Because of the enormous demand for this work, he was pressured to work additional hours and not always given the proper safety equipment. On one occasion, a health inspector arrived and told him not to proceed because of the danger to his lungs. Raymundo followed this advice and stopped working. In response, his employer fired him. He was never able to get his job back.

With lax enforcement, minimal sanctions, and low levels of complaints, many low-wage employers roll the dice and assume that their violations of labor and employment laws will go unnoticed.[50] Thus, worker pushbacks, even if infrequent and sometimes unsuccessful, are a key mechanism for regulating employers. As Alessandra, a Honduran fast-food worker with lawful permanent residency, put it, "If one stays quiet, they [management] do what they want with the majority."[51] Though in the minority, workers engaged in making claims against their employers become a critical element of labor standards enforcement, especially in contexts where unions or other collectives are not present and in industries where strategic enforcement efforts are not present.

VINDICATING LEGAL RIGHTS FORMALLY

Despite the associated challenges, workers did sometimes seek help from government regulators. Formal complaints, which are the apex of the dispute pyramid in traditional formulations of legal mobilization, were the exception, rather than the norm.[52] Nonetheless, among our sample, there was a group of workers who talked about interfacing with government agencies. Not all such encounters led to satisfying resolutions, and in fact many of them only made workers more resolute that claims-making was a waste of their time.[53]

However, some workers did contact government officials on their own in an effort to challenge employer abuses. For example, Walder, a Guatemalan construction worker who had achieved citizenship, approached the Wage and Hour Division of the Department of Labor for help when he was not paid.[54] He lost his job but won his back wages. He shared that he had learned English, picked up the fast-paced rhythm of cleaning work, and educated himself about his rights all "on his own." He would read everything he could find on worker rights, "because I did not want them mistreating me." Some workers, not knowing anything about the Department of Labor or which government office enforced laws pertaining to wages and hours, went directly to the police, the one government agency they did know about, to challenge an employer's wage theft. For example, Johanne, a Haitian worker with TPS, got into a dispute with his manager at a masonry job and threatened to call the police when the manager refused to pay him.[55] This bold risk paid off. When the police arrived and Johanne told his story, the boss agreed to pay.

Some workers took on employers directly, either as "lone wolves" or in collective ad hoc actions with their coworkers. Still others turned to various kinds of brokers to gather information about their rights and orient them to government procedures for filing a claim.[56] Lawyers were a key resource for some workers, such as Wilda, the Haitian nursing assistant with permanent status.[57] She recounted that after she fell at work and was transported to a hospital, employer representatives "informed me that I was responsible for all the hospital bills. That they would not pay anything. It was not until I hired a lawyer [that they] cover[ed] the bill. It took a lot of fighting before they agreed." Thereafter, her employer gave her the cold shoulder, despite the "no fault" premise of the workers' compensation system that Wilda rightfully accessed. She was eventually pushed out: "They put me in a position where I also grew to hate working there by how they treated me. I had no other choice but to leave."

Labor unions were another key broker for low-wage workers in our sample. To be sure, the unionized workers we spoke to were sometimes unhappy with their union or had a limited understanding of how union resources could support them or even what they were. Yet some workers—like Javier, an English-speaking Haitian naturalized citizen who was college educated and had worked in jobs ranging from fast food to banking and other state jobs—did sometimes turn to their union as a first line of defense.[58] Javier saw immense value in his union. When he worked for the state, he and his coworkers "would address . . . management the minute the issue arose. And also we would speak among ourselves and speak with the union representative at the time. That's one of the reasons why I became involved with the union. I became very much involved." Mateo, an undocumented Guatemalan, similarly credited his union at a manufacturing job for teaching workers their rights and how to complain about employer misconduct.[59] "They helped us . . . to file a claim or to complain," he said, "because they [also] taught us . . . to know our rights." Fabiola, the Haitian naturalized citizen in home health care we met earlier, concurred that unions helped workers learn about their rights. She also appreciated that employees who got hurt at work were "entitled to workers' comp."

In addition to unions, which represent a significant minority of workers in the New York metropolitan area, a range of other community organizations helped shepherd formal claims. Though community groups that provide resources and services to low-income communities are certainly not a panacea, some workers did learn about their rights through them, and how to access government agencies. Even English as a Second Language (ESL) classes and other community convenings often created spaces for educating and informing workers about legal assistance and government resources. Indeed, for some like Wilmer, a Salvadoran factory and construction worker with TPS, learning English was key to pushing back.[60] He explained, "When someone learns a little bit of English, then they can start to defend themselves at work." Community groups also provided critical referrals to other resources, as they did for Wilda, the Haitian nursing assistant we described earlier. She was able to engage with a lawyer thanks to a referral she received. Others were given information by a community group about how to access the government's complicated bureaucracy.

Oscar, an undocumented Salvadoran, worked at a bakery where he was paid for only eight of the ten to eleven hours he worked each day.[61] He had learned about the US Department of Labor from his ESL class. It took a while, but eight months later the government sent him a check for the $1,700 he was owed.

Worker centers were another key broker for workers who came forward with complaints. Worker centers have gained scholars' attention for the number of services they provide for marginalized low-wage workers.[62] They also often face political backlash from employer groups. Worker centers "have improved wages and working conditions for their participants through a combination of policy advocacy, collaborations with worker rights enforcement agencies, service provision, and pressure on employers."[63] These community groups help create the "co-enforcement" mechanisms that are essential in a context of rampant under-enforcement of worker rights.[64] Glenda, a Salvadoran with TPS who had worked various low-wage jobs, explained how she managed to recover her unpaid wages as a cashier.[65] With the help of an organizer from a long-standing and well-known worker center, she was able to file a complaint with the DOL for the $270 she was owed, a claim that took four months to resolve. With the support of the worker center, she explained, "I went to the [DOL], and they solved my problem, talked to the [boss], and he paid me the hours that he owed."

Worker centers not only assisted the workers we talked to with filing complaints but also helped them complain to authorities if a workplace issue was not resolved. One worker center that focused on day laborers—who are often hired informally for short-term construction and service jobs—used this strategy to help a number of respondents get paid.[66] Because day laborers so commonly experience wage theft, the main function of these centers is to oversee the otherwise unregulated transaction between a contractor and a day laborer. This worker center logged license plate numbers and copied driver's license information for each contractor so that, as Mateo explained, the contractor could not "mess with you" because the worker center staff would "send the lawyer to court" if that happened. Similarly, Dario, an undocumented Honduran, told us that day labor center staff educated him and other workers about their rights and sent demand letters on their behalf to contractors that had stiffed day laborers by withholding pay.[67] Worker center letters would demand payment of unpaid wages and notify the employer that a lawsuit was imminent if it failed to pay the wages owed. This letter was sometimes all it took for an employer to pay up.

VINDICATING LEGAL RIGHTS INFORMALLY

Workers used a variety of informal strategies outside of government bureaucracies to demand better wages, safe conditions, and solutions to discrimination in the workplace. These strategies were often overlapping and not mutually exclusive. Many of the workers who were well aware of legal frameworks when we asked about their knowledge of workplace rights chose not to pursue external complaints against their employers. Instead, they engaged in their own informal and internal strategies of nudging and/or refusing to accept illegal wage payments and bad working conditions. Sometimes they did so with the help of collectives; at other times they worked creatively alone to engage management in resolving the problem.

Labor and management scholars have argued that worker-friendly human resource practices are often win-win solutions that can stave off high turnover and low performance.[68] Indeed, some workers enjoyed more collaborative relationships with their supervisors; a worker with such a relationship could creatively find openings with their receptive manager to address issues. It is clear, however, that such relationships were not the norm.

Some workers sought out opportunities to push back "softly" and inconspicuously, without getting fired. Workers often knew which supervisors were more receptive than others and would seek out openings with these supervisors. Kaitlyn, a Guatemalan lawful permanent resident employed by an office cleaning company, regularly communicated her issues to a friendly supervisor who filtered her complaints up the chain of command.[69] "I've had some little problems that have actually improved talking with a supervisor," she explained. Similarly, Luna, an undocumented Haitian worker at a plastic bag packing center, managed to press her supervisor to review camera footage of the shop floor to resolve a dispute.[70] "Well, if you send a complaint, he can sometimes look at the camera to see who is at fault. If he sees they've done you wrong, he goes and speaks to the person for you. Or he calls both of us in the office, speaks to us, and makes us hug it out to kill it." While worker surveillance can be a form of domination at work, Luna turned the tables and managed to use it to her advantage.[71]

With reluctant supervisors, persistence at times paid off. Alessandra, described earlier in this chapter, said that she frequently was not getting enough hours at the fast-food chain where she worked. Complaining to their supervisor, however, was a constant chore for her and her coworkers. "It happens a lot. A new person comes in, they cut their hours, [but] not everyone, just those employees that don't stand up and defend themselves." Like other workers in our sample, Ana, a Haitian lawful permanent resident also described earlier, realized that to get paid for all the hours she worked as a home health aide, she had to be persistent. She knew that if she let her guard down, her employer would shave off hours of pay. Ana repeatedly called her employer's office to make sure she was paid for all the hours she worked.

Repeatedly nudging his supervisor was an ultimately successful strategy for Bruno, a Guatemalan naturalized citizen who has had many workplace safety concerns.[72] While working at a fast-food deli chain, he had a simple request: a new glove to help him avoid burns when handling hot bread on sandwiches. Technically he was given a glove, but it was "very broken," and he was still repeatedly getting burned. Providing an intact glove was an obvious responsibility of the employer, at a negligible cost, but Bruno nevertheless had to repeatedly complain before he got a replacement. Reflecting on the ordeal, Bruno was confused. "I don't know what happened. Eventually they put out a new glove, but it really took a lot to get it. Perhaps they were just negligent."

Like making workplace safety complaints, seeking relief from experiences of discrimination in the workplace sometimes required stamina. Guillermo, a Honduran warehouse worker with TPS, had proof, from pay stubs, that the White workers were paid $2.50 more per hour than workers of color.[73] He repeatedly pointed out to management that the workers were all doing the same work but receiving different pay. His complaints were long ignored, but he did not give up and ultimately management addressed his complaints.

Other workers were more direct and confrontational, simply refusing to take no for an answer from a supervisor or to put up with bad behavior. Nancy, an undocumented Salvadoran, recounted that an angry boss at a laundromat job repeatedly failed to pay her on a Sunday.[74] The boss finally caved in and returned with a check after Nancy stridently followed her to her car demanding to be paid. Chances are that she would not have been paid without exerting pressure on her boss. Joel, a Haitian lawful permanent resident, also refused to accept his employer's blasé response to a safety concern at work.[75] At a well-known pizza chain where he worked, the air conditioner broke one sweltering summer day. When his boss told him to just "open the door, so there could be a little breeze," Joel pushed back, saying, "The people can't stay, the store has to close." The employer was "finally forced to say yes" to closing the store early so that the workers could go home.

Getting creative, some workers used humor to challenge harassment at the workplace. Adalie, a Haitian home health aide with TPS, would jokingly snap back at a patient she cared for who regularly commented on her weight.[76] Indignant, she would turn the tables: "Do you see me, sir? Look at John, your body is so flat like a pancake! He said, 'Oh, my body flat like a pancake?' I say yes. Instead of being mad, I turn it around. He call me 'big butt,' I call him 'small butt.' But we laughed about it. And that was it." Using humor to challenge harassment was a difficult balance, since workers relied on endearing themselves to employers and supervisors who could be fickle in their tolerance for humor. Sometimes workers were able to stand up for themselves while not crossing a line that would have provoked employer retaliation. Other times they lost their jobs.

Formal human resource departments are typically found in larger and better-resourced firms. Navigating these departments, which are charged with ensuring that the employer and workers comply with labor and employment law, can be a labyrinthian process. Workers at establishments with an HR department offered understandings about when it is or is not worth going the HR route to lodge a complaint or seek restitution. Dara, a Haitian worker with TPS who worked for a major big-box store, frequently went to HR to resolve her concerns.[77] Gerald, a Haitian lawful permanent resident, found that his interactions with HR varied job to job.[78] When he was once laid off from his emergency medical technician job, he considered filing an internal HR complaint. In the end, he decided it was more work to approach HR than to simply get another job. In contrast,

Gerald did choose to file an internal complaint at his new job against a supervisor who was verbally abusing him. At one point another supervisor witnessed this treatment and suggested that Gerald file a complaint through HR. He did so, and just before mediation the supervisor apologized for his actions. Gerald felt like this apology was sufficient acknowledgment of wrongful action and "ended the process" with HR. That said, he told the supervisor that he now "expected him to treat everyone equally." Thankfully, he did not "receive this kind of treatment again" at that workplace.

Workers did not speak up only when a specific law had been broken or an actionable right had been identified. They sometimes demanded wages and benefits beyond the legally required minimum standards, or they simply called for greater respect. Union collective bargaining agreements provided one tool for registering such demands, but even in their absence, workers did not always limit themselves to the statutory minimums.

BEYOND LEGAL REQUIREMENTS:
DEMANDING DIGNITY AND RESPECT

Labor scholars consistently find that workers do not care only about poor pay and bad working conditions.[79] Worker dignity is a powerful frame for labor organizing campaigns[80] and can color workers' perceptions of their allies in the workplace.[81] Sometimes workers engage in "quiet revolt" to subvert unfair policies and abuse.[82] Indeed, good jobs are not simply about material benefits; workers' sense of respect and autonomy is paramount.[83]

These qualities fall largely outside of the arena of formal protection provided by labor and employment laws. Rather than using the law as a reference, workers at times judged their workplace as good or bad based on incidents of respect or disrespect. For example, Nadine, a Haitian with TPS who worked for an assisted living agency, asked to not be sent back to a particular job because of poor treatment from her patient.[84] The agency sent her back anyway, as it was completely within its legal right to do. Yet Nadine pushed back against the agency supervisor, who immediately took a disrespectful tone with Nadine. "So, he yell[ed] at me. And I'm like, 'Excuse me, I am not your child, do not raise your voice at me. . . . I don't care if I'm losing this job or not. Don't yell at me, don't raise your voice at me. Respect me, and I respect you... I'm not your child.' And that's it." For Nadine, the primary transgression to be addressed was her supervisor's infantilizing treatment, which prompted her to stand up to him. Doing so demanded a fair amount of courage, but it paid off when the supervisor eventually relented.

This same desire for respect helped drive other workers who believed they deserved more than what the law or their contract required. Mario, a Salvadoran with TPS, asked for a raise he knew his employer at a distribution center was not required to give him.[85] Otherwise, he liked his job, but it did not pay well enough. When Mario asked for the raise, his boss said no. Then Mario threatened to leave. The boss said okay and dared Mario to leave if he remained so unhappy. "So I went to look for applications," he explained. He ultimately went on to drive a truck for a moving company and made $2 more per hour at that job. As Mario and others discussed in this chapter show us, workers are not entirely powerless or unable to exercise agency. The massive barriers that structure the low-wage workplace are not absolute. And sometimes leaving a job leads to better conditions.

Workers pushed back individually but also sometimes spontaneously teamed up with their coworkers to demand more. Sofia, a Salvadoran naturalized citizen, rallied her coworkers at a food processing factory to demand health insurance.[86] She was threatened, and the company tried to fire her, charging that she was the group's ringleader. In the end, surprisingly, the collective effort prevailed and workers won health insurance coverage. Similarly, workers at a fast-casual restaurant formed an informal committee in solidarity with Marcello, a Haitian lawful permanent resident.[87] The collective offered Marcello support when he was fired, and it demanded his reinstatement. "They were the ones that fought to have me come back," Marcello explained. "My boss called me to come back. I told them I did not want to because of how I was treated."

These ad hoc collective efforts were not always successful. Zach, an undocumented Guatemalan restaurant worker, and his coworkers wanted a day off, which their boss repeatedly denied, as it was not required by law.[88] They also demanded paid holidays, to which the boss replied that doing so was impossible, given the demand for new projects. The groups were deflated after coming forward together and being told no repeatedly amid threats of termination. Ultimately, Zach felt that there was no use talking with the boss again.

Beyond informal collectives, unions also sometimes serve as a vehicle for demanding workplace conditions that exceed the legally required minimum standards. Through collective bargaining agreements, unions often achieve wages and benefits that are higher than what statutory law requires. These agreements also provide a built-in claims-making structure for resolving workplace disputes. Grievance procedures—a means of internal dispute resolution—are commonly included in collective bargaining agreements.[89] Moreover, appointed stewards can meet with a worker to proffer advice on next steps and can accompany workers to meetings. In other words, unions can sometimes provide backup where workers have been left to fend for themselves, often in front of teams of intimidating managers and HR professionals.

Workers sometimes acknowledged the benefit of unions as a means for demanding additional rights. Fabiola, a naturalized Haitian whom we met earlier and who became a middle school teacher, highlighted that unions can offset the huge power imbalances created by the at-will legal regime that allows employers to fire them without cause. She explained that "without the union, we would not have received a pay raise, and our job would not be secured. Management would have replaced us all at will." The teachers' union had made benefits accessible, including health insurance, tuition reimbursements, training, workplace safety protections, and a uniform allowance. German, a Costa Rican lawful permanent resident who had worked in food service, cleaning, and a variety of factory jobs, appreciated the sense of security his union provided.[90] He explained that, "with the union, one feels a bit more protected, like, that workers are more respected." As a union steward at his food processing job, he also credited the union with checking employer abuse and providing a relatively decent wage of $16 per hour, even though he worked only part-time.

Not all workers were able to explicitly challenge their employer through internal or external channels. While difficult to measure given their subtlety, "quieter" efforts should also be recognized as creative ways in which workers are pushing back against feelings of powerlessness at work.

ENGAGING IN QUIET RESISTANCE

Workers have a range of reactions to workplace abuse, notions of justice, and feelings about the possibility of restitution. For some workers, the primary goal, in the face of degradation and exploitation, was to slow down or to quietly refuse. This strategy of "feet dragging"[91] has long been documented by labor ethnographers as a "weapon of the weak."[92] In the contemporary context, this has also been referred to as "quiet quitting," which many have noted is a throwback to a well-established tool in the labor movement. Quiet quitting is "the idea of putting in just enough effort to not get fired, but without going above and beyond."[93] Unlike workers who are actively reclaiming their rights, these workers simply set a boundary and stick to it. This unwillingness to do more for less rarely leads to a tangible change in wages and working conditions. Yet it provides workers with a sense of power and control over their environment.

Other workers tried to reduce the litany of indignities coming at them by adopting the opposite strategy: excelling at all costs in an attempt to "be their best." This form of resistance was a way to preserve workers' sense of dignity and reclaim their power. Unlike dragging their feet, these workers sought a form of self-preservation and a model work ethic that gave them pride in their work. For example, Tiana, a Haitian lawful permanent resident described earlier, admitted that she was not happy with her work conditions in her job as a cashier at a fast-food restaurant, and she indeed complained to her family and others at home. But ultimately her dissatisfaction motivated her to "work harder, make more of an effort." Some workers even described this "carefully staged compliant behavior" as a form of strategic resistance that would make their worth clear to management.[94]

Workers described a variety of strategies they used to avoid feeling like powerless victims. While some may interpret them as naive demobilization and conformity, the effort it takes to push back was more taxing for some workers than just doing whatever it took to stave off the constant criticism and demands to work harder. Indeed, some critics have characterized the valorization of work as vocation, and the love of work, as a capitalist tool of control.[95] Moreover, as Kristin Bumiller argues, the inherent victimization that claims-making requires is dehumanizing and should be carefully understood as only one form of worker resistance.[96] Sandrine, a Haitian home attendant with TPS, said that she would rather see herself as capable and competent.[97] "I know some people who ask for help. Me, I think I'm strong enough. I just keep going." Wilda, the Haitian lawful permanent resident we met earlier, turned to her family for encouragement when she came home from her restaurant job feeling like she was treated like she "was nothing" in her workplace and did not belong there. Wilda's mother urged her "to not have these people steal your joy, don't let them take away who you are. Do what you need to do and move on. You went there to get paid, close your eyes, and make your money." The challenge this poses for worker organizing efforts and for a worker-led claims-driven regulatory regime is obvious, but as an individual coping mechanism, Wilda's mother's advice may be wise.

Conclusion

The US labor and employment regulatory regime poses formidable barriers for low-wage workers. It makes employees fearful about coming forward with demands or complaints, even when they face extreme exploitation on the job. It weakens the ability of collectives, such as labor unions, worker centers, and civil society groups, to serve as a counterweight to employers. It facilitates top-down supervisory and human resource models that can easily squelch worker voices and collective activity. It allows companies to pursue business models that separate them from the workers who provide labor for their pursuits, thus insulating them from employer liability and unionization.

Workers' stories, however, reveal that such barriers do not always rob them completely of their agency. Workers are not always disempowered, and sometimes they push back. They are creative, in multiple ways. Some are successful and some are not, but it is noteworthy that workers find avenues for maintaining their dignity and asking for better treatment, whether through internal channels or external claims processes.

Reducing the barriers to workers' complaints and collective activity would go a long way toward improving conditions for low-wage workers. Adjusting the at-will employment system, addressing the limits of the fire-alarm enforcement approach, and finding other ways to honor diverse employee voices would be good steps forward.

Workers, for instance, should at minimum be made aware of their rights in the workplace and how they can act on them. Labor education is a necessary, but not sufficient, factor in improving worker lives. Ching Kwan Lee finds in her study of worker organizing in China that nonprofit labor organizations pour significant resources into providing "legal advice and education," but that while "these grassroots organizations may empower workers individually and foster their collective capacity," they reach "only a tiny minority among the teeming millions of migrant workers."[98] Indeed, if all barriers were removed, there would still be many workers who do not push back against injustices. Nevertheless, the removal of these barriers would put more workers in a position to push back against workplace injustice, either individually or collectively.

The immigration regime and the persistent failure to address racism and xenophobia compound the precarities and barriers that all low-wage workers face, but sometimes they provide opportunities for organizing across difference. We turn to these dynamics next.

PART 2
AN IMMIGRATION REGIME AT WORK

The United States regulates immigration in ways that exacerbate poor job quality and harden barriers to improving those conditions. In the contemporary immigration regime, workers are stratified according to type of employment authorization under US immigration laws. Here we focus on unauthorized (or undocumented), temporarily authorized, and permanently authorized workers. Each category, which we refer to as a "status," frames distinct power relations between employers and workers. Chapter 4 details how the US immigration regime—including its administrative, enforcement, and legislative arms—multiplies worker precarity. In chapter 5 we see that, like labor and employment law, the immigration regime disempowers low-wage immigrant workers, though some workers find pathways forward.

Part 2 focuses not only on how current immigration status categories mark low-wage work experiences but also on how the immigration system systematically disadvantages immigrant workers of color. Like the contemporary labor and employment law regime, the regulatory framework surrounding immigration is built on a racialized labor hierarchy that legitimizes worker disempowerment. Employers, with the help of government interventions, often build labor hierarchies based on proximity to Whiteness. Racialized hierarchies have been embedded in, and continue to operate within, presumptively "race-neutral" contemporary systems of employer-employee relations, immigration, and capital accumulation.[1] Operating sometimes implicitly and sometimes explicitly, these legal structures shape notions of which workers deserve dignified work.

https://doi.org/10.7758/rioz4023.5131

Part 2 both sets a baseline for contemporary immigration policy's framing of the experiences of all low-wage immigrant workers and shows how experiences with US immigration policy differ between individuals in the three immigration status categories. It also highlights the persistence of racism and xenophobia despite improvements in status under immigration laws.

HOW THE US IMMIGRATION REGIME SHAPES WORKER PRECARITY

4

A punitive and chaotic immigration regime fuels worker precarity in the low-wage immigrant workplace in the United States. The interaction between workers' rights and the immigration regime is too often overlooked in studies of low-wage work.[1] Underregulation of employer-employee relations through labor and employment laws and regulation of immigration are often thought of as distinct legal arenas, but both are central to understanding the power dynamics in the low-wage immigrant workplace.[2] Throughout the last series of failed efforts in Congress at comprehensive immigration reform, a few scholars have engaged the deep connection between immigration policy and workers' rights and the impact of immigration policy on collective action.[3] Noting the significance of this political moment, Michael Wishnie has argued that comprehensive immigration law reform could have been "the most important labor and employment law reform" in decades.[4]

Our interviews illuminate how three different immigration statuses impact workers' experiences in US workplaces. Several scholars, such as Ming Hsu Chen, remind us that immigration status is a "spectrum" rather than a documented-undocumented binary.[5] We identify common immigration-regime-related themes emerging from our worker interviews and categorize these narratives across the three statuses of unauthorized, temporary, and permanent. This process reveals that immigration status hierarchies do shape the nature of work and manifest in distinct ways across a complex regulatory arena.

https://doi.org/10.7758/rioz4023.6571

Table 4.1 *Immigration Regime Mechanisms and the Nature of Worker Precarity*

	Undocumented Worker	Temporary Worker	Permanent Worker
Main Immigration Regime Mechanisms	Uncertainty Crimmigration Immployment	Uncertainty Crimmigration spillover Immployment Slow bureaucracy	Uncertainty Crimmigration spillover
Nature of Worker Precarity	Bottom of the barrel	Better, but some employment insecurity "Bad" jobs persist	Better "Bad" jobs persist

Source: Authors' compilation.

Among these various facets of the immigration regime (see table 4.1), interviews with unauthorized respondents exposed the most salient dynamics as the criminalization of immigrants and of worksite enforcement policies and practices. These two areas of law have become so intertwined that scholars have dubbed their intersections "crimmigration"[6] and "immployment" law.[7] Together, these legal structures, and the ways in which workers interpret them, fuel what we refer to as "bottom-of-the-barrel" conditions. They also encourage employers and members of the public who engage with low-wage workers to view undocumented workers as expendable and exploitable.

For temporary workers who rely on employment authorization documents (EADs, more commonly known as "work permits"), delays in processing EAD renewals, coupled with employers' obligation to verify those documents, are a primary contributor to workplace precarity. While temporary immigration status is an improvement over undocumented status, it does not automatically bring workers dignity and security in the low-wage workplace. Immigration officials *and* employers subject workers with temporary immigration status to surveillance throughout their tenuous period of authorization. Some workers accept precarious working conditions at least in part because they do not want to jeopardize their temporary relief from the threat of deportation or their temporary work authorization.

Finally, the experiences of permanently authorized workers (those with lawful permanent status or naturalized citizenship) reflect the critical security provided by this legal status, but also the disadvantages that persist for racialized immigrant workers. Workers with permanent work authorization chronicled how their status improved their work conditions and opportunities for mobility in ways not available to their undocumented and temporary counterparts. Nonetheless, they still felt the impact of exclusionary immigration measures in the lives of their undocumented and temporary families and communities. They were also not immune to the xenophobic and racist rhetoric that animates so many contemporary immigration debates. A more secure immigration status also did not neutralize the power of profit-seeking employers, which get to define almost all the rules of the game. These worker narratives further revealed that racism and xenophobia do not simply fade away as immigration statuses improve. Indeed, worker experiences take place within a larger historical context of racialized labor hierarchies, a topic we take up in part 3.

The Undocumented Worker Experience

Undocumented workers can be found in nearly all the mainstream establishments we regularly frequent and behind the production of much of what we consume every day. In 2022, 4.8 percent of US workers were undocumented immigrants, a share that was almost surely an undercount.[8] Even though their overall portion of private-sector workers is relatively low, undocumented workers fill a far higher share of low-wage jobs, ranging from farming (22 percent), construction (15 percent), and many service-sector occupations.[9] These shares are even higher in key immigrant destinations and specific ethnic niches. Undocumented workers are often employed in multiple positions, which is difficult to measure, especially when the jobs are informal. The 82 undocumented workers we spoke to shared their experiences at 218 jobs (see table 2.1).

Two fundamental aspects of the US immigration regime disadvantage these workers: the criminalization of immigrant workers and the subordination of their rights as workers.

CRIMINALIZING IMMIGRANT WORKERS

Immigration policies construct undocumented workers as criminals rather than as laborers trying to put food on the table and thrive in the community. They provide a powerful symbol for US employers and the public that pervades the lives of immigrants in low-wage jobs. This criminalization is more than simply rhetoric. The US government has amplified immigration consequences for less serious criminal convictions, expanded the criminal prosecution of fraudulent documents to gain employment, and fostered cooperation between local police and immigration officials. These law enforcement practices dominate media coverage, which can frame public perceptions of undocumented immigrants as criminals, often in racialized and gendered ways.[10] Further fueling stereotypes of immigrants as outsiders and criminal lawbreakers have been bombastic programs like the Trump-era "Office for Victims of Immigrant Crimes"[11] and the federal government's long-standing emphasis on aggressively enforcing immigration law.[12]

By requiring immigrants to provide documents at the point of hire, the Immigration Reform and Control Act (IRCA) of 1986 enhanced undocumented immigrants' exposure to criminal convictions and "the criminalizing of work."[13] After IRCA, the use of fraudulent documents expanded. Additionally, during the Clinton administration in the 1990s federal policies took a decisive turn toward criminalizing undocumented immigrants by further penalizing unauthorized entry, prioritizing antiterrorism measures, and expanding immigration enforcement mechanisms at the state and local levels. The buildup on the two-thousand-mile US southern border began in earnest during that period. And in 1996 two major federal laws criminalized unauthorized reentry into the United States: the Illegal Immigration Reform and Immigrant Responsibility Act (IIRAIRA) and the Antiterrorism and Effective Death Penalty Act (AEDPA). As a result, circular and seasonal labor migration, which had been par for the course, was increasingly viewed as criminal activity.[14] The terrorist attacks of September 11, 2001, led to the addition of yet another layer of surveillance that criminalized immigrant communities.[15] These measures included the removal of pathways to attaining a driver's license and other forms of identification that could ease police interactions, which are disproportionately concentrated in communities of color. Throughout the "war on terror" and the "war on drugs" era, federal officials gained new powers to detain immigrants in the interior of the country with the help of now-deputized local law enforcement accomplices. Many states have also followed with their own spate of enforcement mandates, which are popular with GOP voters.[16] These state policies have in turn become templates for further federal reforms.

SUBORDINATING IMMIGRANT WORKERS

The immigration regime not only criminalizes undocumented immigrants but also interferes with protections for undocumented workers and fosters clandestine work arrangements. By giving employers a decisive role in verifying the work authorization of their hires, IRCA devolved immigration enforcement to nonstate actors in the private sector.[17] This is a trend that persists even beyond the United States.[18] Taken together, employer sanctions have operated as "employer swords," feeding employer power and subordinating immigrant worker protections. The minimal implementation of employer sanctions has also made the risk of hiring undocumented workers simply the "cost of doing business" for many employers.[19]

While eligible undocumented employees have labor and employment law rights, those protections are inhibited by their immigration status. Prior to IRCA, the Supreme Court declared in its 1984 *Sure-Tan Inc. v. National Labor Relations Board* decision that undocumented immigration status is not a reason to exclude workers from their private-sector labor law rights as "employees," which permit them to engage in concerted action with their fellow workers.[20] Despite *Sure-Tan*'s proclamation that its holding was meant to avoid creating a "subclass" of easily exploitable workers, the Court's subsequent 2002 decision in *Hoffman Plastics* (after the passage of the 1986 IRCA) did just that. The *Hoffman* Court left *Sure-Tan*'s precedent regarding undocumented workers' rights intact but made it more difficult for advocates and regulatory agencies to enforce those rights in practice. *Hoffman* concluded that undocumented employees who were illegally fired for union organizing could neither be reinstated in their job nor receive the standard backpay remedy owed for being illegally fired.[21]

This Supreme Court decision and its aftermath compounded the existing fragility of the "gloves-off economy."[22] Moreover, it made undocumented workers among the most vulnerable to employer exploitation.[23] Labor law scholars have roundly critiqued this decision and shown that a worker does not really have full "rights" if there are no effective remedies that can deter employers from continued violations of those rights.[24]

While the scope of *Hoffman* was fairly narrow, the landmark decision opened the door for even broader challenges to undocumented worker rights. The focus of *Hoffman* was on the question of collective action, yet many employer attorneys have argued that its impacts go beyond the National Labor Relations Act and into regulatory arenas related to workplace safety, minimum wages, and discrimination protections. Thus, *Hoffman* has created an added tool for employers to challenge efforts to uphold worker rights. IRCA and the *Hoffman* decision have made workers more fearful and compliant and have also become a legal tool for deterring (or at least slowing) attempts to improve worker conditions, a theme we return to in the next chapter. Some states, such as California and New York, have created explicit protections for undocumented workers against immigration retaliation, as have some localities.[25] Their reach is limited, however, and to date no such protections exist nationwide.

WORKERS IN THE SHADOWS OF LOW-WAGE WORK

Given the criminalization of the undocumented immigrant community and the subordination of their rights as workers, it is not particularly surprising that undocumented workers operate "in the shadows" of low-wage work.[26] Undocumented workers' lack of work authorization creates significant barriers to entry into the formal labor market. Federal documentation verification programs, such as E-Verify, intensify these barriers.[27] Public contractors must use E-Verify. Also, many states now require private employers to use E-Verify and an increasing number of private employers use it voluntarily. Meanwhile, undocumented workers who remain in the United States continue to work, as evidenced by their substantial labor force participation. Undocumented workers are pushed into "the shadows" and sometimes into the informal cash economy or unregulated temp agencies. They have more restricted access to "good jobs" with higher wages and more humane working conditions. Accordingly, two dominant work-in-the-shadows themes emerged from the narratives of undocumented work told by our interviewees: the precarity of working when employers are unable to verify an immigrant's eligibility to work, and working at the bottom of the barrel.

Working While Unverifiable Undocumented workers described the precarity of unauthorized work as they shared their covert, though well-known and widespread, strategies to circumvent immigration status verification requirements. Workers often worked for cash "under the table" for employers that evaded the verification process, or they worked under someone else's (often borrowed) name. Some unauthorized immigrants used false identity cards to gain employment in the formal low-wage economy, and others found work through intermediaries such as temp agencies.

Informal and off-the-books work is ubiquitous and can amplify worker vulnerability. For instance, working informally can make it harder for a worker to determine whether they are being paid for all of their work, as they often do not receive a pay stub that shows how many hours they logged or what was deducted. Indeed, employers commonly use cash to avoid paying workers for overtime hours and to facilitate illegal deductions, such as for the tools and materials needed for the work project.[28] Michael, an undocumented Haitian immigrant who had worked in restaurants and warehouses, explained the inevitability of informal arrangements given his lack of work authorization documentation.[29] "When you don't have papers, you work under the table. It is the [way to avoid the] legal status of your work. They pay you in an envelope—dependent on the time and days you work—you are off the books." Given the immigration enforcement regime, some workers (and employers) are happy to avoid taxes and the added layer of government surveillance. Staying under the radar is what allows undocumented workers to earn a livelihood, and indeed some workers prefer to avoid taxes and like cash payment arrangements. Yet the informal nature of this arrangement is a key mechanism driving their labor precarity.

Using a "borrowed identity" to get a job is risky and can invoke a felony penalty in many jurisdictions. Respondents worked "on the books" with a borrowed identity in order to be paid more, but they acknowledged the risk in doing so. Indeed, immigration laws explicitly forbid workers from using fraudulent documents to gain employment.[30] Weighing the risk against the relative safety of staying "off the books" and under the radar by working in their own name, some preferred this option. As Michael shared, his current job "off the books" was "a bit better" than his last clandestine arrangement because "now I at least work in my name." For Michael, being able to work in his own name brought autonomy and a sense of security that was worth the trade-off of lower wages.

To find their way into jobs, undocumented immigrant workers often work with different types of labor brokers; taking this route, however, introduces an additional layer of precarity. As respondents confirmed, many brokers may be legally sanctioned businesses, but these contracted "agencies" create yet another layer of vulnerability for the workers they supply to bigger companies. All over the globe labor brokers open doors to work, charge a hefty price for doing so, and further reduce employer responsibility when things go wrong.[31] Their need to verify their immigration status led many of our New York City–based workers to work through temp agencies, which often had more lax hiring practices. These brokers coordinated the labor needs of the companies that retained them while simultaneously shielding them from employment verification responsibilities. These staffing agencies are notoriously underregulated compared to the lead companies that contract them, and they often target undocumented workers.[32] All low-wage workers face challenges when they work as misclassified independent contractors or directly for an intermediary rather than the entity where they work. Yet their lack of immigration status makes undocumented immigrant workers even more vulnerable. Nonetheless, these workers often felt that they had no choice but to engage in these arrangements and to tolerate the conditions that came with the job, given the immigration policy context.

Working at the Bottom Once hired, undocumented workers often face bad work conditions. The broader context of criminalization and subordination of undocumented workers' rights further degrades their labor experiences in the United States across a range of industries.[33] In a common narrative, worker interviewees described poor working conditions, such as low pay and degrading treatment, and employers that cut corners on health and safety. They recounted humiliating experiences of racial discrimination, and women reported pernicious sexual harassment. These experiences were particularly common for undocumented respondents. Consistent with the analysis of Jorge Durand and his colleagues, undocumented immigrants typically experience a "double disadvantage" generated "by virtue of working in the secondary sector and receiving an additional economic penalty because they are undocumented."[34] Though not the sole source of this precarity, undocumented status intensifies bad working conditions. It also amplifies racial and gendered injustice in the workplace, a subject that part 3 delves into further. For unauthorized workers, these injustices were piled onto lingering traumas from their origin country and from their often violent clandestine journeys, which had left them not only traumatized but indebted.

Undocumented workers described their immigration status as synonymous with workplace abuse. Seeking a better livelihood, they had often undertaken harrowing, dangerous, and deadly treks north. As of this writing, news stories continue to confirm the regularly recurring tragedies encountered by these migrants, such as the forty-six people found dead in a trailer in San Antonio in the summer of 2022.[35] Ultimately, the reality that migrants encountered in affluent regions such as the New York metropolitan area rarely matched their aspirations. Randy, a Salvadoran trucker who was now a naturalized citizen, reflected on his long journey.[36] "It was difficult at first," he explained. "When someone first comes to this country, they don't know anything, they think they will make money, but that's a lie." Randy first worked a grueling, fast-paced job washing dishes. "It was ugly," he admitted. Conditions improved when he later received temporary protected status and then permanent immigration status, which gave him access to a commercial license and an opportunity to own his own truck and business. He felt that his work was now better because of his "better status." His wife and daughter also felt better knowing that he was no longer at risk of deportation. Many challenges do still persist once workers like Randy become documented, but for the most part they are able to avoid the particularly acute degradation that undocumented workers experience.

Beyond the already well-documented material inequality along immigration status, undocumented workers described a litany of degrading tasks they were repeatedly asked to perform and the feelings of indignity those tasks provoked. For example, Marco talked about his first job in the United States cleaning toilets at a fancy supermarket in Beverly Hills, the first in a long line of degrading jobs he would hold.[37] He described in detail the "bitterly terrible" work of cleaning toilets all day and, beyond the physical toll, this work's "psychological impact" on him as a skilled craftsman. A trained furniture maker when he arrived in the United States, Marco managed his long days in Beverly Hills by imagining the fresh smell of pine wood and varnish and a better potential future. This Beverly Hills gig was not unique. In each job he held, "they exploit, they try to squeeze as much as possible [out of undocumented workers] for the same salary," he explained. Though Marco received TPS during the first years of the program in 1991 and eventually achieved permanent status (a green card) in 1997 through the Nicaraguan Adjustment and Central American Relief Act (NACARA), his experience as an undocumented immigrant stayed with him. "It's what saved me," he said, referring to the TPS-derived employment authorization that allowed him to return to custom woodwork. Although the work was still precarious and he had to work odd jobs to make ends meet, Marco's options had nonetheless widened.

A key part of undocumented worker degradation was racism and sexism. Undocumented workers felt that their lack of status made them particular targets of racial discrimination and sexual harassment. Suzette, an undocumented Haitian, worked a late-night shift manufacturing beauty products.[38] Her position had been shaved back just enough so that her employer was not required to give her a thirty-minute break. Her employer also regularly paid her late and pushed Suzette to work at a fast clip. Compared to her documented coworkers, Suzette felt uniquely surveilled. She could never risk being even a minute late and was under constant threat of firing if she was. She felt constantly harassed. As a Black undocumented woman, Suzette felt multiply vulnerable, declaring, "There are always difficulties when it comes to maneuvering through this world as a Black woman. And now to add that you also do not have papers, it is worse."

Suzette's undocumented status added a layer to the racism and sexism she endured, and her experience was not an outlier. Scholars have documented that in workplaces Black workers experience heightened surveillance, which contributes to a comparatively higher likelihood that they will be sanctioned or terminated.[39]

The Temporary Worker Experience

Workers with temporary protected status (TPS) are only one category of temporary workers, but their experience provides a useful lens showing the impact of precarious conditions on workers with temporary employment authorization documents (EADs). These workers are neither fully undocumented nor on the path to a more permanent status. TPS provides temporary relief from deportation and temporary authorization to work, without tying workers to a specific employer, as guest worker programs do. The TPS program is meant to provide temporary humanitarian relief to individuals from designated countries that have experienced environmental disaster or civil strife. Individual countries are given a specific expiration date—typically six, twelve, or eighteen months. Either Congress or the secretary of homeland security—often at the discretion of the president—can choose to extend the designation.[40] The renewal of TPS periods has been the subject of intense political and social movement advocacy. In 2017, at the height of our study, an estimated 325,000 migrants from 13 TPS-designated countries were residing in the United States.[41] Of the total TPS population, 16,200 were in New York State, most of them in the NYC metro area.[42] Haitians and Central Americans, the focus of our research, have been among the largest beneficiaries of TPS.[43]

Geoffrey Heeren estimates that tens of thousands of migrants in an "in-between state" of "non status"—including TPS, whose defining qualities include temporariness with no pathway to citizenship—have "few rights besides the right to work" and endure a legally "hazy" existence.[44] The full alphabet soup of "non statuses" is complex, with several thousand to hundreds of thousands in each category. Collectively, an estimated one million migrants live in the United States in some form of temporary legal limbo.[45] Although we agree with Heeren's characterization of these workers as having a "non-status," we refer to these workers as "temporary," or as having "temporary status," to provide a clear contrast to undocumented and permanently documented immigrants. It is the experiences of workers with temporary EADs that we detail here.

Though many immigration scholars see immigration status as a documented-undocumented binary, temporary status also presents many challenges for immigrant workers. On the one hand, temporary status can open doors, yet it also promotes new forms of precarity. Scholars have widely observed the "precarity of temporality" in the workplace[46] and the "legal violence" that people with temporary immigration status experience in their work, family, and school lives.[47] TPS workers—whom we also refer to as "temporary" workers—were often reminded by their undocumented pasts and undocumented coworkers that some things were indeed better with TPS. When describing their experiences at 395 low-wage jobs (see table 2.1), the temporary workers we interviewed often compared their current work experiences to the dirtier and more poorly paid jobs they had when they were not authorized to work. Yet working with an expiration date, and in a context where their employer was viewed as an immigration enforcer, bred a unique form of precarity. The instability of the immigration regime, the inefficient immigration bureaucracy, and the immigration enforcement baked into worksite hiring practices fed a unique form of worker precarity for temporary workers.

PROMOTING INSTABILITY VIA TEMPORARY STATUS

All temporary pathways have an end date, and that end date always looms and may come sooner than expected. Employers' roles can vary, depending on the provisions of temporary programs. Some temporary pathways to low-wage work, such as the H-2A (seasonal agricultural) and H-2B (seasonal non-agricultural) guest worker programs, require employer sponsorship and tie a worker to a particular employer. Because these workers cannot change employers, worker exploitation is widespread, as the experiences of countless temporary foreign worker regimes in the United States and beyond have confirmed.[48] TPS workers are distinct from guest workers and those with other statuses that do not involve EADs.[49] Yet, as we argue, TPS provides a window into understanding the workplace challenges that persist for temporary immigrants with EADs, even if they have the freedom to work for any employer. For temporary workers, the "liminal legality" of their temporary status generates an instability that makes it difficult to build a life without fear of deportation and the loss of employment authorization.[50]

Workers with TPS can experience real consequences from shifts in the political landscape, which have implications for how laws and executive decisions are enacted and how bureaucracies implement these policies. This was clearly the case when the Trump administration announced the end of TPS designations for immigrants from Central American countries and Haiti in 2019.[51] The US Department of Homeland Security (DHS) can grant TPS status to migrants from countries where extraordinary civil strife or environmental disaster has occurred, but this designation is short-lived and subject to political winds, and it must be renewed.

Although TPS does not tie a worker to a particular employer, workers with TPS have a temporary EAD. Because EADs have end dates, and because employers are required to verify that work authorization at the point of hire, the EAD is a major player in temporary immigrant worker precarity. Employers' ongoing role in re-verifying workers' status increases their power in an environment where workers' rights are already underregulated. Thus, while temporary workers are not undocumented and subject to immediate deportation, and even though they are not guest workers tied to one employer, the legal framework enforcing their status creates unique precarity multipliers. In other words, "TPS holders experience their own brand of state-induced precarity."[52]

SURVEILLING AND EMPOWERING EMPLOYERS VIA THE VERIFICATION REGIME

Temporary status wreaks havoc on an immigrant's ability to maintain stable employment in a system that requires employers to screen employees for valid work authorization. The practical problem is twofold. Workers seeking new employment cannot promise prospective employers that they will remain authorized to work past their EAD's expiration date. With no obligation to hire them, and the freedom to fire a worker at will, many employers simply either choose not to take the risk or threaten to let these workers go. Workers with TPS must reassure their employer at every renewal that they are still compliant and not putting it at risk of sanctions.

Indeed, communicating to employers that a country's TPS has been renewed by Congress or the executive branch can be a challenge. The immigration bureaucracy is often delayed in issuing documentation that signals an extension of work authorization. Such delays heighten job insecurity for temporary workers, who must already navigate an at-will regulatory environment. A risk-averse employer has little incentive to jump through the hoops required to hire and retain a worker with a temporary EAD. It also has little disincentive to simply hire another worker who does not require the same hassle of jumping through hoops. Employers can often legally choose to not hire or rehire a worker with TPS, given the weak employment discrimination protections for noncitizens. In response to civil rights concerns raised during the legislative process, Congress added specific provisions to IRCA to protect against some forms of discrimination on the basis of immigration status and national-origin discrimination.[53] TPS recipients, however, are generally not viewed as "protected individuals" who are intended to benefit from prohibitions against employer discrimination "on the basis of citizenship status in recruiting, hiring or referring for a fee."[54]

WORKERS IN LIMBO

Working While Undocumented Is Worse Compared to life as an undocumented worker, temporary immigration status and the work authorization that accompanies it bring some critical relief.[55] TPS allows immigrants to access more jobs and to move or be promoted into better jobs via regular employment channels in the formal economy.[56] This leeway undoubtedly generates a sense of improvement in one's circumstances. "TPS changed my life," said Hugo, a Haitian housekeeper who worked in a hotel, first in housekeeping and then in maintenance.[57] Once he received TPS, he kept working at the hotel, but he was also able to obtain a driver's license and certification to drive a school bus, work that brought in another $1,200 to $1,400 per month.

Workers like Hugo often talked about how TPS gave them a feeling of greater mobility. They felt that they could leave a job and find a new one if working conditions got bad. Lucrecia, a Salvadoran worker with TPS who had cleaned houses and then worked in retail, put it bluntly: "The first thing they ask me is to show them my papers, and they quickly say, 'Yes, I want [to hire] her.'"[58] She described how her life had changed since receiving TPS. "You have a huge advantage. Now, with TPS, you can get a job wherever, in clothing stores, supermarkets, and you don't have to go far to work." In contrast, when you are undocumented, you are stuck, she said; "without [status], you have to be like a slave." When you are undocumented, she added, you "work where you can, not where you want." With an authorized immigration status, Lucrecia said, "you can choose your job.... You can choose where you feel better, where you are more comfortable." Low-wage workers like Lucrecia viewed TPS as an improvement over undocumented work.

Workers who had TPS also expressed an overall sense of relief when they came out of the shadows of undocumented work. While TPS was not a cure-all, in very practical terms, they could now confidently use their own identity when filling out an application. They could apply for a wider range of jobs and be choosier about the conditions they were offered, and they were also less concerned about workplace surveillance by immigration authorities. Lucien, a Haitian immigrant who delivered newspapers prior to receiving TPS, went on to get a restaurant job.[59] He explained that, "when, for example, I apply for a job, they [ask] me for ID.... This makes me happy, this makes me confident, you understand? I am as comfortable as another citizen here, with the TPS, understand?" Though immigrants with TPS lack many of the benefits of a pathway to citizenship, TPS allows them to "pass" as any other authorized worker, and at least for their brief period of authorization, they feel relieved to be able to do so.

The benefits of "some" status compared to "no" status are apparent and palpable. For low-wage workers who previously faced enormous immigration precarity in one of the most expensive metropolitan areas in the country, particularly in a volatile political environment and with a recession looming, TPS was better than the undocumented alternative. Nonetheless, workers with TPS were also clear about the particular precarity imposed by their temporary immigration status.

Working with an Expiration Date Temporary status is a double-edged sword. As a "documented" status, TPS provides deportation relief and work authorization. However, temporary status also creates vulnerability. "It's like you live in a carton of milk . . . you have an expiration date," explained one labor union leader.[60] TPS does not guarantee a future in the United States, and recipients are required to register their information with immigration authorities—the same authorities many of them have spent years evading—every six to eighteen months. Thus, unlike most undocumented workers, TPS immigrants are explicitly known to the US government, which can find them and forcibly deport them if the political winds shift in a way that erases their temporary authorization. This possibility was an acute concern during the first Trump administration (2017–2021) for migrants from dozens of countries where war, violence, and economic strife persisted and for whom a return home was untenable.[61] While these concerns dissipated somewhat under the Biden administration (2021–2025), uncertainty over the exercise of executive power once again looms over migrants with precarious immigration status in the wake of Trump's victory in the November 2024 presidential election. This is true especially as other immigration policies have continued the status quo.

As Isaac, a Haitian computer assistant with temporary status, expressed this uncertainty in 2016, "You always have to keep your eyes open."[62] TPS holders commonly had a greater sense of confidence than their undocumented counterparts, but they paired that confidence with constant vigilance. Moreover, immigrants with TPS remained stuck in a limbo that made it difficult to settle into work and life more broadly.[63] This uncertainty made some immigrants think twice before applying for the status in the first place, despite the potential benefits. For example, Marco, the Salvadoran we mentioned earlier who eventually attained permanent status, recounted that he was very reluctant initially to apply for TPS and finally did so only after the strong urging of his wife. Understandably, he worried that having TPS would make him more vulnerable to government surveillance than living without documents, a life to which he had already adapted. He recalled thinking at the time, "If I register with immigration . . . they are going to know exactly where I live, and they can come and take me away at any time."

The precarity of TPS status stems not only from how it is administered but also from how it intersects with immigration enforcement in the workplace. TPS workers must show employers (or carry for inspection) up-to-date physical work authorization cards. Yet bureaucratic delays at the US Citizenship and Immigration Services (USCIS) can complicate their ability to meet this requirement. Workers like Manolo, a Salvadoran English-speaking college graduate, reported that employers wanted to see the physical EAD card to be assured of his work authorization.[64] These cards carry an expiration date, and the process of obtaining an updated card after successful renewal can drag on. This was the case for Manolo, even though other forms of proof (like a copy of the *Federal Register*'s confirmation of TPS extension) are legally acceptable.

Despite these burdens for workers, employers are required to verify work authorization under employer sanctions policies. This task often devolves to hiring managers and HR department employees, many of whom have very little knowledge of how the program works. Thus, when an expiration date is coming up or has passed, a context of risk aversion arises. If TPS workers cannot show physical proof of work authorization, employers—both nefarious and benevolent ones—leave themselves open to scrutiny. Advocates recounted spending a lot of their time clarifying for employers what to do when an employee's EAD card was expiring or had expired. These advocates often helped workers with temporary status to navigate work authorization questions with their employers. Some employers were simply nervous about running afoul of IRCA sanctions, while others were known for intimidating and coercing workers they felt were in their debt for the job opportunity.

This additional layer of employment insecurity—exacerbated by immigration policy—does not disappear once a TPS worker gets a job. Instead it persists throughout the renewal period, intensifying as the deadline approaches and the federal government must decide whether to extend or terminate TPS for migrants from a particular country. Besides remaining in good standing in order to be eligible for TPS renewal, immigrants must also gather funds to pay the costly fee required for each application round. At the time of our study, the fee to apply for employment authorization under TPS was a costly $410. Timing the application can be tricky—individuals must wait for the country's designation to be announced and then are given a sixty-day registration period.

Even when applications for renewal of TPS are approved, updated EADs do not always arrive on time. The process can cause anxiety for both the employer and the worker with temporary status.[65] A Haitian home health aide we talked to was "super stressed" whenever her temporary status was about to expire. Magdala feared losing her job, but she also wanted to avoid the bureaucratic burden and cost necessary to extend her TPS.[66] "Whenever I have to renew, I have to look for a lawyer, then find money to pay this lawyer. I am in a state of constant stress and distress."

Though grateful to not be undocumented, their lack of a pathway to permanent status was not lost on TPS holders. Even though they had built their life in the United States—some for over two decades—they knew it could be taken away. As Santiago, a Salvadoran with TPS who had worked in cleaning and factory work, put it, "I am not a resident, much less a citizen."[67] Santiago and others thought that permanent status would free them of the stress and costs of temporary status. Access to permanent status, they hoped, would solve many of their problems. Wistfully, Santiago remarked, people with permanent status "can move mountains . . . can do anything they want," without having to pay the costly application fees.

The precarity of working with TPS predated the first Trump administration but intensified when he came to power in 2017. One of his hallmark moves was to announce the intended cancellation of TPS designations for many countries. During the Trump administration, not only were undocumented workers targeted, but xenophobic rhetoric toward the entire immigrant community was deployed. Laura, a Haitian naturalized citizen, recalled that Trump's statements sent her family members with TPS "into a panic."[68] The TPS program became a political football, and advocates had to work hard to solidify its immediate future. Linda, the Haitian home health aide we met in chapter 3 who had become a naturalized citizen, knew several people with TPS and remarked that they were "very afraid," especially when "Trump came into power." She hoped that workers with TPS would get permanent status, and "for folks that don't have papers at all, my heart goes out to them," she said in solidarity.

These worker narratives confirm that immigration status does matter, but in diverse ways for different status groups. Workers with permanent immigration status confirmed that status mattered to them, but not singularly so. For them, reaching the apex of immigration status neither erased the underregulation of workers' rights they experienced nor served as a panacea for the persistent racism and xenophobia they continued to encounter in US workplaces.

The Permanent Worker Experience

Eighty-nine of the immigrants we interviewed had become either a lawful permanent resident or a naturalized citizen. Their accounts of their experiences at a total of 275 low-wage jobs (see table 2.1) revealed two things: First, that permanent status is more secure than undocumented or temporary status, can improve access to formal jobs, and enables workers to exit bad jobs, thereby reducing the entanglements of immigration enforcement at work and beyond; and second, that attaining permanent immigration status does not guarantee better work conditions or security for workers or their families. The long shadow of immigrant surveillance, criminalization, and deportation and the subordination of immigrant workers' rights can directly touch workers with permanent status as well as through the experiences of their families and friends. Xenophobia and racism persist despite immigration status improvements. And bad jobs remain ubiquitous given the ways in which the US government feeds precarity through its immigration regime and underregulation of workers' rights.

In 2022 the vast majority of immigrants in the United States have some form of "permanent" status—either as a lawful permanent resident (LPR) (24 percent) or as a naturalized (rather than US-born) citizen (49 percent).[69] Although these permanent statuses convey many of the same benefits—including the ability to legally work without needing an employer visa or an EAD—they do have some differences.[70] For instance, LPRs can be deported for an aggravated felony conviction, and only citizens can work in many public-sector jobs. Nonetheless, we consider the two statuses together here as they share permanent and easy-to-document work authorization, in contrast to undocumented or temporary status.

Unlike undocumented workers, who have no work authorization, and temporary workers, who have a temporary ability to work, workers with permanent status are less entangled with immigration law, are entitled to full workers' rights protections under labor and employment laws, are protected against immigration status discrimination under IRCA, and face fewer barriers to labor market participation. The perspectives of workers with permanent status can uncover the challenges that persist even after the perils of illegality are removed.[71] Their experiences caution us against overdetermining immigration status as the sole driver of precarious low-wage immigrant worker experience. As with their undocumented and temporary counterparts, the realities of low-wage work, racism, and xenophobia are also omnipresent for workers with permanent status. For those who remain in the low-wage workforce, permanent immigration status cannot magically render jobs more stable, dignified, and bias-free.

Permanent status does not insulate immigrant (or native-born) workers from workplace precarity. Two key mechanisms of the US immigration regime are at play for workers with permanent work authorization: the amplifying of racist anti-immigrant narratives, and the broad web of immigration enforcement that ensnares mixed-status families and communities, sometimes including even permanently documented immigrants. The relative permanence of immigrants who are lawful permanent residents or naturalized citizens does not free them from the inherent "enforcement bias" of the immigration bureaucracy, which affects all immigrants to different degrees.[72]

AMPLIFYING ANTI-IMMIGRANT SENTIMENT AND ILLEGALITY

Federal policies and practices subject immigrants of color to presumptions of illegality, both at work and elsewhere. For example, section 287(g) of the US Immigration and Nationality Act, passed in 1996, authorizes some state and local law enforcement entities to enforce federal immigration law, and the Secure Communities program allows federal US Immigration and Customs Enforcement (ICE) officials to enlist the assistance of state officials in detaining anyone suspected to be in violation of immigration law. Seline Szkupinski Quiroga and her colleagues find that, in the wake of these policies, "even legal permanent residents and other immigrants who are authorized to live and work in the United States had difficulty with employment based on the stereotype of the undocumented immigrant."[73] Similarly, Catalina Amuedo-Dorantes and Susan Pozo find that naturalized Mexicans in states with mandatory E-Verify policies experience more discrimination at work, with impacts on their upward mobility.[74]

The exclusionary immigration enforcement regime can fuel xenophobic and racist narratives that exacerbate everyday discriminatory experiences, even for immigrants with permanent status. The pervasive link between federal immigration enforcement and local policing puts workers of all immigration statuses at risk of being ensnared in surveillance and screening procedures. Regardless of their status, racialized immigrants are commonly stereotyped as immigration lawbreakers during traffic stops and everyday interactions.[75] Formally, lawful permanent residents are still deportable immigrants if found guilty of certain crimes, a policy that hardened following the 1996 "tough on crime" reforms.[76] Though naturalized citizens are largely safe from deportation, in recent years anti-immigrant policymakers have intensified arguments that instruments for "de-naturalization" are still very much on the books.[77]

Latino immigrants in particular have been racialized as "illegal" by public discourse and in political debate, though other immigrants also face the racialized nature of illegality.[78] While few studies have ascertained the impact of immigration policies on Black immigrants, we do know that they too face considerable occupational segregation and that some national-origin groups realize lower returns to human capital.[79] We also know that anti-Black racism intensifies both policing efforts and the immigration consequences of overpolicing in the criminal legal system, even for noncitizens with lawful permanent residency.[80] These experiences are not confined to the United States, and migrants bring with them their experiences of racism in their countries of origin, during their transit, and in other journeys. For example, much has been written about exclusionary tropes for Haitian immigrants in other major destinations, such as the Dominican Republican and Brazil.[81] Racist and anti-Haitian exclusion was a common complaint among the Haitians we spoke to, many of whom had also spent time in other parts of Latin America. This prior exclusion combined with their experience of racism in one of the most diverse regions in the country, where racism nevertheless flourishes.

RENDERING MIXED-STATUS FAMILIES AND COMMUNITIES VULNERABLE

Beyond how individuals experience anti-immigrant tropes and associated policies, punitive immigration policies can ripple across an entire immigrant family and community. Workers with permanent status are not immune from the intensified immigration enforcement system's "spillover effects," which have been widely documented.[82] "About 1.6 million unauthorized immigrants were married to US citizens and another 675,000 were married to lawful permanent residents (LPRs) in 2018. At the same time, 4.4 million US-citizen children had at least one unauthorized immigrant parent, as did 100,000 LPR or nonimmigrant children."[83] According to a Pew Research Center survey, over half (51 percent) of Latino immigrants reported that "they worry a lot or some that they or someone they know could be deported."[84]

Vulnerability at home can feed precarity at work. The possibility that their family and friends could be deported or fired can inform what workers are willing to tolerate at work. The threat of deportation also has enormous mental health consequences, especially for couples[85] and children.[86] Some permanently documented immigrants also have children and other family dependents back in their country of origin, many of whom have few if any legal pathways to join their loved one but rely on them as a source of support.[87] In other words, even migrants with permanent status must contend with the immigration regime's threats to the well-being of their family and their community.

While immigration policy alone cannot account for these inequities, it worsens already inequitable resource distribution, particularly in communities where access to social safety net resources is thin to nonexistent. As it is, the gap between Latinas and White men is one of the starkest: The former earn 54 cents on the dollar, with profound consequences for individual and family stability.[88] Despite conferring critical benefits, permanent immigration status does not erase these core precarities.

WORKER PRECARITY PERSISTS DESPITE PERMANENT STATUS

Working While Permanent Is Better Immigrant workers who had transitioned from undocumented or temporary status to permanent status repeatedly affirmed that their lives had improved. Lawful permanent residency and naturalized citizenship convey many benefits, including the ability to legally work without needing an employer-sponsored visa or a time-delimited employment authorization document. A permanent resident card (or "green card") has no end date and fulfills the requirement for DHS's Employment Eligibility Verification I-9 form. It establishes both identity and work authorization and does not require re-verification.[89] Permanent status provides permanent work authorization, thus improving the work experiences of immigrants by removing the hassle and anxiety of regular re-verification.

Workers with permanent status often reported being hired more easily than when they were undocumented or only had temporary status. They also felt more confident in leaving jobs to find new ones with higher wages and safer conditions. Since their employers were not required to re-verify the work authorization of lawful permanent residents or naturalized citizens, these workers felt that they now had an advantage in seeking better work. For example, Walder, a Guatemalan who became a naturalized citizen, left his job at a mall restaurant and doubled his wages by moving into mall maintenance work instead.[90] By the time we spoke with him, he was working in an office job.

Other workers who acquired permanent status—like Randy, the trucker who formerly had TPS and eventually became a citizen—were able to access new certifications and comparatively better jobs. Though these jobs were not always better paid or more stable, they allowed for more autonomy, giving workers more control over their schedules and mobility—a valuable job characteristic.[91] Some workers also reported better treatment. For example, Jocelyn, a Haitian registered nurse who became a naturalized citizen, was able to move from a low-paid home health aide (HHA) position to a position as a registered nurse (RN).[92] She described the difference between her former job and her new job as "night and day." She was paid three times more than she had earned as an HHA and got "more respect now."

Beyond gaining access to new certifications, workers also generally felt that having better papers would translate into better jobs—or at least hoped that would be the case. For example, Patricia, an undocumented Haitian immigrant cleaner, hoped to one day get permanent status so that she could leave her cleaning job, become certified in elder care, and "get a better job."[93] For these workers, the added benefits from better work lifted their whole family. Bertha, a Haitian worker who had worked in cleaning and later as a home health aide, was sure that the opportunities that came her way would not have been possible without her lawful permanent residency status.[94] "Before this I used to clean at [a fast-food restaurant]. I used to mop, wash equipment, etcetera. Now I work with old people. I make more money. I am more relaxed." Her hope was to get an even better job in the future, so that her kids would have a better life. "I would like my kids to learn to swim and learn piano," Bertha explained.

Beyond work, some immigrants with permanent immigration status also felt that their status opened doors for them to pursue higher education, travel to see family, and obtain driver's licenses. Martha, the Guatemalan migrant described earlier who arrived as a child without papers and later gained status through her husband, was now a naturalized citizen. She enthusiastically explained the utility of permanent status. She had worked jobs ranging from retail to high-ranking state government and felt that her life changed after receiving permanent immigration status. "Wow. It was a great feeling. It just opened so many doors." Martha was able to receive financial aid for college, job opportunities, and other tangible benefits. Attaining permanent status also relieved her of the fear "that one day ICE could knock on the ... door and take me and my parents." Her new permanent status motivated her "to get so many things done" from which she had been previously blocked. She was also able to petition for her parents' legal status.

Workers discussed the benefits of permanent status over both undocumented status and temporary status. Randy, whom we met earlier in this chapter, chose to finally marry his citizen wife and eventually naturalize, given the persistence of anti-immigrant policies in the United States. He, like others, felt that temporary status fostered instability and a sense of danger. "When you only have TPS," explained Maribel, a naturalized citizen from El Salvador who had worked a wide variety of low-wage service jobs, "you do not feel secure."[95]

Part of this sense of insecurity stems from the restricted mobility endured by both undocumented and temporary migrants. It is also harder to travel for those with TPS, who have to ask authorities for permission to travel and present an emergency justification for doing so. Anabel, a Salvadoran lawful permanent resident and paralegal, talked about "the privilege," "the great relief," and the "benefits of having citizenship."[96] When we spoke to her, she was awaiting her citizenship interview, which, she lamented, had been delayed by the COVID-19 pandemic. She recalled her failed attempt when she only had TPS to get permission to travel to El Salvador to visit her dying sister-in-law. Deeming her sister-in-law a mere distant relative, the US government declared Anabel ineligible for a humanitarian permit to travel. "These things are very difficult.... On one hand, things were okay [with TPS], but on the other hand... it's a golden cage."

Finally, permanent status leaves workers less reliant on agencies or other intermediaries to find work than workers without documentation. When directly employed by their employer, permanently documented workers are more able to negotiate formal work arrangements and payment options. And yet, such stability is not a universal experience. Permanent status does not relieve the deleterious pressures of the immigration regime on the families and communities of these workers. Permanent status alone cannot strengthen the weak workers' rights regime, nor can it eliminate the long shadow of racism and colonialism.

Precarities Persist Even for Permanent Immigrant Workers Ultimately, permanent status is a major asset for workers. Yet not all permanently documented workers felt that improved immigration status helped them very much. Indeed, research is mixed regarding the impacts of legalization or adjustment of status on formerly undocumented individuals.[97]

Permanent status does not automatically lead to a job. Workers like Rocio, described in chapter 3, told us that she still struggled to find work even though she had had permanent work authorization for the entire twelve years she has been in the United States: "A lot of times we have papers," she said, "and are still not able to work." After working for a temp agency, Rocio was let go and was still waiting to be called back. She believed that employers preferred Hispanics over Haitians, even when the Haitians had permanent immigration status and the Latino workers did not. "My family brought me here with all my papers, and someone else with no papers works 24/7?" Some employers' preference for the pliability and vulnerability of undocumented workers puts workers with a temporary or permanent status at a disadvantage. This preference for undocumented workers, which has long been documented in the literature, is a labor extraction strategy that employers deploy to craft a more compliant and divided workplace.[98]

Despite the benefits, permanently documented workers also described persistent unsafe work conditions, harassment, and discrimination. Working in a freezer "could have killed me," said Marcello, a Haitian lawful permanent resident.[99] But the company did nothing in response to his complaints about the dangerous temperatures (20 degrees below 0) he regularly endured. Even permanently documented workers like Marcello felt that they were treated like expendable, subhuman laborers at times. Irina, a warehouse worker we met in chapter 3 who had lawful permanent residency, longed for her life of being treated as a "princess" back in Haiti. In the United States, by contrast, she had "to work like a slave." For both Marcello and Irina, permanent status did not lessen their workplace precarity.

Permanent status also did not wipe away racism, language barriers, or sexual harassment. Diana, a Nicaraguan with lawful permanent residency described in chapter 2, had worked in jobs ranging from domestic work to restaurants. She recounted a time when an American coworker humiliated her, she felt, "for being Latina." As a domestic worker, she had experienced wage theft, back injuries, and dog attacks. The popular cleaning agency she worked for notoriously refused to provide breaks to her and other workers. Her accent—or rather, discrimination against her accent, she surmised—was part of the problem too. Indeed, many studies have pointed to English ability and other human capital as positive driving forces. Matthew Hall and Emily Greenman find, for example, that "the ability to speak English proficiently tends not only to reduce immigrants' exposure to risky work environments, but to partially attenuate differences between documented and undocumented workers."[100] Conversely, Pascale, a Haitian immigrant, found that her language limitations posed a continuous barrier, despite the permanent and secure immigration status she had attained through her green card.[101] To find a job while lacking English language skills, she said, you would need to have connections to other Haitians "at the place."

Beyond language, the first Trump administration intensified feelings of insecurity among all immigrants. Christelle, a Haitian naturalized citizen who worked as a home health aide, conceded that, "without my legal status, I wouldn't want to be in the US."[102] Others, like Marise, a Haitian with lawful permanent residency who had worked in fast food and home health care and was now employed as a medical assistant, cited the hateful political environment in the United States as a central concern, even though she lived in one of the most diverse regions in the country.[103] "With the way the country is going," she explained, "this President Trump, he is deporting people for anything. I had to naturalize." Workers expressed fear and unease about the constant threats emanating from the White House and were not convinced that they were shielded by their permanent status. Anabel, the lawful permanent resident from El Salvador, conceded that things had calmed down after 2021 with the new Biden administration, but she was dubious that President Biden had the power to enact meaningful change.

In sum, permanent status adds an extra shield, but it does not block the many forces that still drive immigrant worker precarity. Status matters, but it is not the only factor that matters in low-wage work in the United States.

Conclusion

The US immigration regime encourages a work environment of "bad jobs" with low wages, dangerous conditions, and degrading treatment. It imposes an additional layer of precarity on low-wage immigrant workers, who must already navigate an underregulated workplace. This chapter has affirmed that immigration status is consequential for workers in the low-wage economy. Each emblematic immigration status we looked at—undocumented, temporary, and permanent—generated distinct forms of precarity. Undocumented workers labor in the shadows, with few alternative pathways out. Employment verification requirements create very real threats to immigrant worker safety and limit their access to better wages and working conditions. The threat of deportability pervades a woefully underregulated workers' rights context, making job loss an extremely high-stakes prospect.

Temporary workers with an employment authorization document—like those with TPS—enjoy advantages unavailable to their undocumented counterparts, including temporary deportation relief and work authorization. Yet these benefits are temporary, must be fought for, and need to be reinstated every six to eighteen months. The renewal process creates stress and uncertainty for employers and workers alike. By amplifying the at-will employment insecurity inherent in the US legal system, temporary status disadvantages temporary workers with EADs in their job searches and disincentivizes employers from hiring or maintaining a worker who brings so much uncertainty and hassle.

Finally, permanently documented workers—lawful permanent residents and naturalized citizens—in some ways enjoy the holy grail of immigration status: citizenship, or a pathway to citizenship. With stable work authorization and a much lower chance of getting caught in the deportation dragnet, these workers have a palpable sense that they are protected in a way that their family and coworkers with undocumented or temporary status are not. That said, even permanently documented workers continue to experience precarious working conditions, the immigration state dragnet, racism, and the broader anti-immigrant sentiments pervading even the most immigrant-dense communities.

THE US IMMIGRATION REGIME AS BARRIER AND PATHWAY TO CHALLENGING PRECARITY 5

Beyond workplace conditions, the immigration regime shapes how workers consider attempts to improve their experiences at work. The structures and practices of immigration policy create formidable barriers over and above those imposed by pro-employer laws, a weakened labor movement, and regulatory reliance on workers themselves to bring forward claims.

These barriers function in at least three ways. First, the immigration regime deepens the precarity of at-will employment, amplifying workers' concerns about getting fired, detained, or deported if they rock the boat. Second, worksite immigration enforcement efforts confuse undocumented and temporary immigrants as to whether they have access to the same suite of labor protections as other employees. Third, immigration status differences can dissuade workers from mobilizing together by inhibiting their perceptions of shared identity and interests. Indeed, some employers may use retaliatory deportation threats or use immigration status differences to pit workers against each other.

Despite all these ways in which the immigration regime reinforces worker precarity, all three groups of low-wage immigrant workers sometimes demanded better pay, insisted on safer and more dignified work conditions, reported pernicious harassment to government entities, or found quieter ways to resist. Our interviews illuminated at least two main ways in which the immigration regime empowered workers even as it increased precarity. First, immigration status sometimes served as a basis for solidarity. Some workers, seeing the interests they shared with other workers of similar status, decided to

https://doi.org/10.7758/rioz4023.4272

mobilize with them. Others became empowered to push back against harsh conditions after their immigration status improved, either from undocumented to temporary or from temporary to permanent. Workers with temporary and permanent statuses signaled that they felt more freedom to demand better treatment because of their improved status.

Second, workers spoke about the importance of immigration advocacy groups and labor unions in supporting their resistance. Even though these organizations sometimes struggle to reach the most vulnerable workers, they can help workers advocate for their rights, and by fostering solidarity among immigrant workers, they can encourage them to bargain for more. Advocacy organizations, including but not limited to labor unions, become crucial instruments for breaking down the policy and organizing silos that too often separate labor, immigration, and racial justice issues.

Immigration Regime Barriers to Challenging Precarity

Immigrant responses to bad treatment at work must be considered within the broader framework of the US immigration regime. The criminalizing of immigrants, the centrality of the workplace as an immigration enforcement zone, and the unstable nature of immigration policy fortify the barriers to challenging precarity that all low-wage workers face.

THE IMMIGRATION REGIME PUTS AT-WILL EMPLOYMENT INSECURITY ON HYPERDRIVE

The vast majority of low-wage workers in the United States do not have job security through a collective bargaining contract. Simply put, most workers can be fired very easily and have no recourse. This pernicious, and completely legal, employment insecurity is a key feature of the employer-friendly legal regime and poses a major barrier to demanding improvements at work. Asking an employer to address a workplace issue might quickly lead to losing one's job and livelihood. The US immigration regime, and the hierarchy of statuses it fosters, exacerbates this insecurity, especially for undocumented workers. Indeed, many employers view the subordination and pliability of undocumented workers as a key asset.[1] Additionally, workers with temporary and even permanent immigration status feel squeezed, fearful of losing their job if they demand more from their employer. Some viewed their ability to endure poor treatment as a job requirement and felt that they had little power to complain if they wanted to keep their job.

Workers' fear of losing their job or of being detained or deported is a major barrier to coming forward, despite government agencies' proclamations of inclusive labor standards for all employees regardless of immigration status. Beyond the economic necessity of accepting poorly paid and hazardous work, undocumented workers often felt that their legal status put them at risk of deportation if they spoke up in any way. Workers have invested resources and risked a lot to come to the United States to work. Marco, the green card holder from El Salvador whom we met in the last chapter, captured a widely held sentiment among current and former undocumented workers when he said that, if you do not want to be deported, "you have to suck it up." Deportation would be a devastating and expensive consequence of speaking up. Like others, Marco left El Salvador at an early age: He was nineteen when he left the country in 1986, at the height of El Salvador's civil war. Marco felt that he would be killed if he stayed. In leaving behind his entire family, including his wife and baby, he was seeking both safety and economic security.

During Marco's harrowing journey from El Salvador to the United States, he was stuffed inside a trailer with more than thirty other immigrants and came close to death from suffocation and heat—a recurring scenario among immigrants that too often ends in mass tragedy.[2] When Marco reflected on his past experience as an undocumented worker, he emphasized that tolerating bad working conditions was the smartest choice he could have made for himself and his family. Living with a green card when we spoke with him, fifty-four-year-old Marco now felt better able to push for better working conditions.

Workers felt that they risked deportation if they spoke up. Like Marco, Samuel, an undocumented Haitian warehouse worker described in chapter 3, shared that undocumented status "puts you at risk" of employer retaliation and makes pushing for better working conditions more challenging. Glenda, referring back to when she was an undocumented Salvadoran supermarket worker, said that she was apprehensive about pushing back against degradation and harassment from a coworker. She feared that the employer "would call the police" if she did. She was also afraid that "she would go to prison and be deported" if she spoke up at work in any way. Instead of asking for better treatment, she would often "go to the bathroom and cry" until she could contain herself enough to continue working.

Workers with temporary status reflected on the fear that they too once felt when they were undocumented. Anis, a Haitian temporary worker, reflected on his undocumented work experiences, which he contrasted with the relative security of working with his current temporary status through the TPS program.[3] He explained that when you are undocumented, "you're scared to go to the police," and knowing that, your employer pays you less than the documented workers for the same work because you "can't protest." These workers' undocumented status gave their employer more power and put them at a disadvantage.

Unsurprisingly, given that demanding better wages and treatment is a risk for undocumented workers, we found that workers often stay quiet, even when enduring sex discrimination and harassment. Lilian, an undocumented Haitian warehouse worker, shared a story that was all too commonly told by the undocumented women workers we talked to.[4] At one warehouse packing job, she refused the sexual advances of a supervisor and was subsequently demoted. Though this was a clear case of retaliation, she felt that she could not go to her harasser's superiors for help, given her undocumented status and the likely possibility of additional retaliation. Lilian, as well as various other undocumented workers, were unwilling to take this risk.

These fears were not unfounded. Indeed, workers reported that some of their employers explicitly had threatened to have them deported. Others mocked their undocumented status as they threatened to fire them. For example, Jacinto, a Honduran construction worker who had TPS when we spoke to him, came forward to contest his employer's nonpayment of over $2,000 in unpaid wages when he was undocumented.[5] His employer responded with insults and threats of deportation. "He'd insult us, tell us we were illegals, that he was going to fire us," Jacinto explained. It became clear that "it wasn't going to be possible to do anything, so I just let it be." His employer would go on to file for bankruptcy, torpedoing any chance

Jacinto had of restitution. Indeed, the hassle and risk of coming forward had not been worth it.

Workers were understandably fearful of losing their job and not being able to find a new one. In addition to the general challenge of job transitions, undocumented and temporary workers felt that it was harder to find jobs because they either lacked work authorization or had it but the process was simply too complicated. Because immigrants of both statuses faced challenges in their job search, they were wary about coming forward to lodge demands and thus risk losing their job and having to start the search all over again. For undocumented workers, it was not easy to find an employer willing to hire them off the books or not look too closely at their identity documents. Search costs were even higher for workers who relied on temp agencies and had to pay the agency a fee. Julian, whom we met in chapter 3, was an undocumented Haitian worker who found his job through a temp agency. He lamented that "[you] don't have your full autonomy or independence to quit and find something else." He described workers in this position as "almost like a slave," because the employer "knows he can do anything to you." Julian and other undocumented workers in subcontracted arrangements had multiple levels of gatekeepers to get past.

Temporary workers also face heightened concerns about their job security, albeit via different mechanisms. These workers are more of an administrative headache for employers because their work authorization documents are consistently expiring and the replacements are often delayed. Temporary workers therefore felt it was more difficult for them to find employment comparable to what they would have found if undocumented. They were acutely aware that they were more of a hassle for employers, given the temporary nature of their status and the bureaucratic delays around work authorization documentation. Their temporary status made them more vulnerable to employer retaliation and raised the stakes for coming forward to demand more dignity and better working conditions.

Abel, a Haitian immigrant who used to work security and was driving for a rideshare company at the time of his interview, did not go to the Department of Labor to complain about wage and hour violations when he had TPS.[6] He recounted, "I was scared because, you know, I have TPS. If I went there, so my boss gonna stop me and say so, I'm going to stop you to work there. That's why I was scared." For Abel and other workers with temporary work authorization, going to the Department of Labor could lead to being fired. Even though labor and employment laws make it illegal for an employer to retaliate against an employee for making a complaint, they are difficult to enforce. For workers like Abel, the risks of demanding improvements at work mostly outweighed the rewards. His worker rights on the books seemed out of reach in practice.

THE IMMIGRATION REGIME CONFUSES IMMIGRANTS ABOUT THEIR ACCESS TO WORKERS' RIGHTS

Even workers who might have been willing to push past their fears of being detained, being deported, or losing their job were confused about their rights as employees under US labor and employment laws and knew little about how to access them. All low-wage workers struggle to know their rights, to know where to go to enforce their rights, and to gather the resources to see the struggle through. Yet the messages that immigrant workers received confounded this struggle even further.

Undocumented workers sometimes assumed that they had inferior rights under labor and employment laws in US workplaces. Indeed, undocumented immigrant workers talked about not having the right to complain about wage abuses, sexual harassment, safety concerns, and other indignities *because of* their immigration status. Lilian, the undocumented Haitian warehouse worker we described earlier, said that she was unable to report the repeated sexual harassment she faced at work because "I didn't have my papers." She explained that when you are undocumented, they take advantage of you because "they know you can't go to the government, you can't report them." Similarly, Samuel, the undocumented Haitian factory worker we mentioned in chapter 3, argued, "The treatment is different because I am not treated the way you should treat other humans with papers—because in their minds you can't really do much or complain." To undocumented workers such as Lilian and Samuel, lacking legal immigration status meant that they could not claim their rights as employees.

To be clear, immigration status generally should not alter an employee's ability to vindicate their labor and employment rights in formal or informal forums. Federal, state, and local agencies often make statements to this effect and assure employees that their immigration status is not relevant to their labor and employment law claim. The US Department of Labor's website in 2022, for example, forcefully stated that the DOL "enforces the law without regard to an employee's immigration status" and that "no employer should have an unfair advantage because it employs undocumented employees and doesn't pay them."[7] The National Labor Relations Board (NLRB) sent the message that undocumented workers have NLRA rights even though the *Hoffman* decision reduced some of the remedies available for legal violations. As former NLRB General Counsel Jennifer Abruzzo declared in May 2022, "All too often, immigrant workers are subject to unlawful intimidation tactics that seek to silence them, denigrate their right to act together to seek improved wages and working conditions, and thwart their willingness to report statutory violations. The NLRB will do everything we can to protect immigrant workers to exercise their rights under the NLRA."[8] These governmental assurances, however, neither reached nor assured some respondents who saw their immigration status as an insurmountable barrier to challenging their employers.

The frequent use of intermediaries (such as temp agencies and informal contract work) in low-wage immigrant workplaces inhibits access to justice too. Undocumented immigrants often turn to intermediary companies to get around their work authorization challenges. Subcontracted arrangements can buffer lead employers from the responsibility to verify workers' authorization under immigration law while also shielding them from labor and employment law liabilities.[9] These same entities also sometimes took advantage of workers' vulnerability and fear of speaking out. For example, during weeks when Lilian was able to obtain sufficient work in the packing warehouse, the driver offered to her by the temp agency demanded higher rates. As an undocumented low-wage worker at the time, Lilian lacked both legal access to a driver's license (which would not be available to this population in New Jersey until 2019) and the funds to pay for other transportation. She desperately needed rides from the temp agency's driver to get to work and other destinations. This driver was the only person she knew who could take her to cash her checks at the bank so that she could pay rent and utilities.

Speaking up to complain about the kickbacks to the temp agency driver seemed unwise. Reflecting on her undocumented experience, Lilian felt certain that she simply had to tolerate the extortion, "because you don't have your papers." Where individual workers failed to find a willing employer to hire them directly, temp agencies proved a reliable, though no less exploitative, alternative.

Indeed, immigration status, paired with nonstandard work arrangements, complicated some workers' ability to access their rights.[10] Besides getting workers through a temp agency, some employers simply classified undocumented workers as independent contractors, often illegitimately. The misclassification of undocumented workers is a well-documented practice, though workers seldom understood whether it was legal. In other cases, undocumented workers just worked off the books, often being paid in cash. As informal workers, they were spared the required deductions from their pay, but they also were not afforded the rights extended only to "employees." To prove they had a legal claim, workers had to fit the legal definition of an "employee" and be able to name the responsible employer to a labor standards enforcement agency or court. Cash payment and informal work were both exceedingly common practices for undocumented workers seeking to avoid formal employment verification mechanisms, but working this way made it harder to document a violation. Doing so often required time (which low-wage workers rarely had in excess) and access to an advocate who could help them navigate the claims bureaucracy.

Though undocumented workers described some of the most pervasive barriers to claims-making, they were not unique in facing challenges to coming forward and calling out abusive employers. Workers with temporary or permanent status also talked about ways in which the US immigration regime made them more hesitant to engage with government entities, even those that had nothing to do with immigration enforcement and were focused on enforcing labor and employment law. The anti-immigrant political rhetoric during the first Trump administration intensified this deterrent effect, creating more confusion among immigrants about the parts of the government with which they could safely interact. Even in places like New York and California, where state labor laws specifically prohibit immigration-based retaliation, the federal context had a chilling effect on immigrants who were even more reticent to engage with government officials and institutions with Trump in office.[11] Policies meant to create safe spaces for immigrants—such as schools, hospitals, and places of worship—were routinely disregarded during the Trump administration years, which encompassed much of this study.[12] This disregard, combined with widespread misunderstanding about the definition of "public charge"—a rule that penalized noncitizens who legally accessed social safety net resources—led many immigrants to avoid seeking health care, even during the COVID-19 pandemic.[13] Threats to take away citizenship from immigrants who had been granted US citizenship further stoked skepticism about the intentions of government entities, even the agencies charged with protecting employee rights.[14]

THE IMMIGRATION REGIME STYMIES COLLECTIVE ACTION BY ISOLATING AND DIVIDING THE WORKFORCE

Given the many barriers that workers face, groups of workers, rather than lone wolves, have a better chance of improving life at work. Yet collective action requires building relationships and trust with coworkers, or with others who may lend a hand. Racism and xenophobia can make it even more difficult for workers to come together around their shared interest in improving wages and working conditions. US immigration policies can also deter worker solidarity, further empowering employers in the low-wage workplace. Workers often reported that immigration policy concerns made them hesitate to reach out to others. Some were hesitant to trust coworkers, who they feared might turn against them. Indeed, workers reported preferring to stay quiet and isolated in order to protect themselves and their families from untrustworthy coworkers.

Undocumented workers and workers with temporary status reported feeling isolated, keeping their immigration status secret, and being harassed by coworkers. For Samuel, undocumented immigration status "is a situation that you don't need to publicize [to coworkers]. Because many times, if it is known, it puts you at risk." For others like him, sharing their undocumented status risked getting fired, arrested, deported, and harassed by coworkers, who often vied for limited resources and privileges. Dante, another undocumented Haitian warehouse worker, put an even finer point on it: "From what

I have learned, whenever a coworker learns of your status, you'll probably be immediately fired."[15]

Thus, immigration status was both a tool of control by supervisors and managers and something that strained coworker relations. Diana, a Nicaraguan with lawful permanent residency, as mentioned earlier, had worked the full gamut of low-wage jobs when she was undocumented, including stints in various forms of childcare and house cleaning and jobs as a dollar store cashier and a restaurant server. In these jobs, she said, her spiteful documented coworkers would say, "If you do something to me, I will call immigration to take you away." Though employers and coworkers alike lack the power to demand that someone be removed from the country, there is nothing to stop them from trying, or from sharing information about a fellow employee's undocumented status with the employer or with immigration authorities. The mere threat of doing so was enough to put undocumented workers on notice. For these workers, maintaining secrecy and privacy, rather than engaging in collective action with their coworkers to demand better treatment, was the most logical survival strategy.

Isolation and coworker harassment were also common narratives among workers with temporary status, even though they had both formal permission to be in the country and work authorization. For example, Abel, the Haitian security guard who did not feel safe going to the Department of Labor, said that temporary status made him fearful of reaching out to coworkers or others beyond the workplace, even for informal assistance. "I was scared because, you know, I have TPS. . . . I didn't talk to [coworkers], I never let anybody know I had TPS." Feeling that sharing information about his TPS status would make him vulnerable, Abel had decided that keeping his status to himself was the best way to keep his job secure. Similarly, Glenda explained, "Coworkers sometimes harassed me and told me to 'go back to your country.'" She felt isolated and vulnerable to harassment and did not see her coworkers as natural allies.

In sum, the immigration regime created barriers to speaking up and fostered worker isolation and division among workers. Nonetheless, some workers we talked to found ways to resist, and the immigration regime created some pathways for mobilizing workers.

The Immigration Regime and Pathways to Challenging Precarity

So far we have told a story about the immigration regime that is focused on the barriers it erects. But some people push through these barriers, and the immigration regime itself can carve out pathways to coming forward. For one thing, workers' shared immigration status can unify them. Further, an improvement in a worker's immigration status can embolden them to push for more. External organizations, such as community advocacy groups, labor unions, and worker centers, have been spurred by the emergence of exclusionary immigration policies to build organization capacity that enables them to help workers navigate the complicated interaction between their immigration concerns and their concerns about their rights as workers and to show them how to speak up.[16] Civil society can facilitate access to justice and cultivate collective actions across a diverse set of workers and a diverse set of concerns. Because these groups are often working at the intersection of labor and immigration, they are in a unique position to support workers in their efforts to improve their lives at work and beyond.

IMMIGRATION STATUS AS MOBILIZER

Whether by sharing experiences "in the shadows" or navigating the unpredictable and clunky temporary authorization regime together, both undocumented and temporary workers can encourage workers to act collectively to push for change. Here we do not offer a Pollyanna account of collective struggle. A sense of allied interests does not come automatically, nor is collective action inherently solidaristic as workers navigate any number of divisions, including ethnic tensions. But an effective strategy for change sometimes emerges from shared immigration struggles. For example, Randy, the Salvadoran truck driver introduced in chapter 4, recalled the Mexicans he worked with at a restaurant when he was undocumented. "We got along well. It didn't matter that we were different nationalities. The important thing was that we were all *illegal*." Randy's account of status solidarity features an important opening for worker mobilization. Indeed, a major push of the large-scale immigrant justice campaigns has been getting workers to think past their differences to find common purpose fighting for migrant worker justice.[17] Even at a micro level, we found evidence of some workers building connections with each other through shared experiences of exploitation.

In addition to their lateral collective organizing efforts, immigrants who achieved a better immigration status were also able to more confidently seek improvements for themselves and their families.[18] They did so either by using their worker voice to demand more from their current employer or by exercising their right to exit in search of a better job.[19] For example, Josefina, a Honduran TPS holder who had worked as a home cleaner and at a dry cleaner, reflected on now having temporary status and a work permit.[20] "If someone doesn't treat me right," she said, "I know I have the right to complain." Similarly, Marisol, a Salvadoran factory worker with TPS, commented that now that she had legal status and formal work authorization, her employer "paid attention" to her.[21] When she told her employer that she would call the Department of Labor if they did not pay her, it worked. Thereafter, her employer always paid her what she was owed. Marisol was willing to call out her employer repeatedly for wage violations because she had documents. Her immigration status motivated her to persistently nudge her employer to comply with baseline wage and hour laws. As long as her employer persisted in not complying, she kept holding them accountable by warning that she would complain to the government.

Some workers not only threatened to make complaints against employers but were more willing to seek out other resources and benefits. For example, Ricarda, a TPS holder from El Salvador, worked in a meat department and was fired for failing to lift heavy boxes.[22] She went to the union, but they were unable to help. On the suggestion of a friendly Puerto Rican supervisor, she went to the Department of Labor to file a claim for unemployment. She succeeded in getting unemployment insurance payments and felt that her work permit had given her permission to speak up—unlike undocumented workers, who had too much at risk.

Finally, perhaps the most powerful tool provided by improved immigration status was the ability to walk away from a "bad job" and seek better employment. For example, Marco, who had worked cleaning toilets and a range of construction gigs, remarked that receiving permanent status after twenty years without papers allowed him to now "look for a company . . . where the employment is better . . . the boss pays you better, respects you a little more . . . and if they do not respect you, [you] can say, 'I'm leaving.'"[23] Similarly, Maribel, the Salvadoran immigrant we met earlier who had held a wide array of low-wage jobs and was now a naturalized citizen, described her progression from undocumented to temporary to permanent status. The improvements in her immigration status empowered her exit from intolerable working conditions in search of greater workplace dignity. Maribel felt that her status improvements opened opportunities to leave her job and get a better one. She was more confident that her temporary status allowed her to find a job that would pay better than her assembly job at a factory. "I loved my job . . . but I left it because they didn't pay much, and since I had TPS, I could fly." She chose to leave the job she had when she was undocumented as a form of resistance, hopeful that something better would come along. For Maribel, immigration status improvements paved the way to empowerment at work and the freedom to change jobs rather than tolerate poor treatment at work.

IMMIGRANT ORGANIZATIONS, UNIONS, AND WORKER CENTERS AS VEHICLES OF EMPOWERMENT

Some immigrant workers empowered by their status changes were further emboldened by community advocates—members of organizations that can facilitate the overcoming of immigration barriers to worker mobilization. The labor movement has increasingly dedicated organizing resources to immigrant populations,[24] and indeed, the immigrant rights movement has functioned as "both a civil rights movement and a labor movement."[25] Collectives can tie these issues together while helping workers to access justice and build solidarity among coworkers and the broader community of low-wage immigrant workers.

Though few respondents were represented by a union, some unionized respondents identified labor unions as allies in their efforts to overcome exclusionary immigration policies and feelings of disempowerment at work. As labor unions resolve to address the needs of their diversifying membership, some are investing in organizers who speak workers' native languages and expanding their services to include immigration counsel alongside help with workplace issues.[26] Contractual provisions in collective bargaining agreements have the potential to provide immigrant workers with material benefits and more protections from deportation and harassment.[27] Though some respondents were deeply cynical about their unions, others talked about how unions made them aware of their rights in the workplace and their employer's responsibilities. Workers also lauded the benefits of being covered by a contract, despite the compromises that bargaining produced.

In practical terms, unions helped workers process grievances related to a range of issues. Germán, a Costa Rican migrant and former tech worker, became a lawful permanent resident when his daughter turned twenty-one and was able to petition for him.[28] He described his time working in food service as an undocumented immigrant as challenging. Now a union steward, he proudly described helping his coworkers by advancing their complaints in both English and Spanish. When his coworkers called him, he took them through the process. He informed them that employers "cannot be so abusive when the union is there to hold them accountable." Workers who successfully collaborated with their union leadership to put pressure on their employer or to enforce a contractual right saw the advantages of not going it alone.

Yet, in light of waning union coverage, community groups that advocate for worker justice (worker centers) played a key role in helping immigrant workers to surmount barriers.[29] The role included disseminating information about basic rights, such as informing workers in their native language about their rights and how to claim them.[30] These organizations also helped connect workers to government agencies, advocates, organizers, or lawyers, depending on the nature of the complaint. For example, it was a worker center that provided Glenda with the information and support to go to the Department of Labor (DOL) to register a complaint about withheld wages. The DOL "solved [her] problem, talked to the boss, and he paid [her] the hours that he owed." Some workers, like Mateo, simply felt better when an advocate, acting on their behalf, made demands on their employer. As an undocumented Guatemalan construction worker, Mateo felt that the contractor he worked for could no longer mess with him because the staff at the day laborer center would "send the lawyer to court" if that happened.[31]

Better immigration status alone cannot magically empower workers; they also need a strong advocacy base to help them mobilize the new confidence that comes with improved status. Beyond individual worker empowerment, fostering collective solidarity is also time- and resource-intensive, and not always successful. Nonetheless, organizational connections are another critical line of defense to help shift power from employers to workers and to advocate for meaningful change and justice at work.

Conclusion

Contemporary laws and practices disadvantage low-wage immigrant workers not only through the underregulation of workers' rights but also through the US immigration regime. The latter puts at-will employment insecurity on hyperdrive while confusing workers about their rights in the workplace and ways to access the system for gaining restitution. The immigration regime also fosters worker isolation and divisions among workers. The obstacles to mobilizing for change, both individually and collectively, are formidable. The story, however, is not entirely bleak. Improvements in immigration status can help workers overcome some of the barriers to stepping up to challenge precarious working conditions. Groups that serve immigrant worker communities can also help workers navigate both the thicket of labor and employment law and immigration policy, supporting them in their organizing and advocacy efforts.

When we asked workers to talk about problems, injustices, and barriers they felt at work, themes of discrimination, racialization, and demeaning treatment were prominent in responses across all three immigration statuses. Next we take a closer look at the dynamics of racism and xenophobia in the workplace.

PART 3
RACISMS AND COLONIAL LEGACIES AT WORK

In part 3, we document experiences of racism and xenophobia that persist in spite of "race-neutral" labor and immigration policies and examine exceedingly narrow antidiscrimination policies that fail to address these racist legacies. Workers doing many types of low-wage work and of all immigration statuses experience a broad spectrum of racism at work. We adopt a broad view of the government that captures its historical roots in racist systems and the realities of implementing the letter of the law. A consideration of global legacies of slavery, several waves of European colonialism, and contemporary US imperialism provides critical context for understanding contemporary forms of racialization at work[1] and the persistence of white supremacy.[2] We focus here especially on how workers themselves named and experienced racism and explicitly tied their experiences back to the past in their origin country and also to present realities. Chapter 6 ties these historical forms of racism and colonial legacies to workplace precarity today. Chapter 7 considers how these same forces shape workers' ability and willingness to resist disempowerment at work and demand a more dignified workplace.

Our interviews with Haitian and Central American immigrant workers revealed experiences of racism across all job types and all statuses for both sets of workers. Yet the form of these racialized experiences differed. As the work of Black feminists and postcolonial theorist Franz Fanon reminds us, there are "diverse oppressions" in the lived experiences of individuals.[3] Indeed, while Haitian immigrants recounted pernicious anti-Black and anti-Haitian treatment, Central American respondents described how employers, customers,

https://doi.org/10.7758/rioz4023.6500

and patients regularly engaged in degrading and homogenizing anti-Latino biases. Both sets of workers understood their workplace precarity in racialized terms and weighed the costs and opportunities of resisting the status quo. Memories of their arduous migrant journeys and the persistent realities of their countries of origin, where many maintained strong family ties and obligations, were front of mind.[4]

Ultimately, Haitian and Central American low-wage workers interface with three key facets of the government: As low-wage workers, they work in underregulated—some would even say unregulated—workplaces; as low-wage immigrants, they face a hierarchical immigration regime that separates them by status and sometimes criminalizes them or targets them at the workplace; and as low-wage immigrants of color, they encounter the ever-present legacies of racism in their countries of origin and now in the United States.

HOW RACISMS AND COLONIAL LEGACIES SHAPE WORKER PRECARITY

6

For low-wage immigrant workers of color, racism is yet another stark reality of low-wage work.[1] These experiences range from everyday microaggressions to severe disparate treatment. Throughout our interviews, workers pointed to racial subordination as a persistent factor shaping their precarious position at work. In sharing their stories, we contextualize the failings of the contemporary labor and employment law and immigration regimes within the longer history of government-sanctioned racial hierarchies.

Our interviews with Haitian and Central American workers exposed the various forms of racism at work, which begin with the process of racialization. Race scholar Carlos Hoyt outlines the five steps of racialization:

1. *Selecting* some human characteristics as meaningful signs of racial difference
2. *Sorting* people into races on the basis of variations in these characteristics
3. *Attributing* personality traits, behavior, and other characteristics to people classified as members of particular races
4. *Essentializing* purported racial differences as natural, immutable, and hereditary
5. *Acting* as if purported racial differences justify unequal treatment[2]

In this chapter, we focus on the final step of racialization: the unfair treatment of people based on supposed racial differences, which derive not just from phenotypical but also from linguistic

https://doi.org/10.7758/rioz4023.5580

differences. When employers, coworkers, customers, and patients treat workers differently based on their race, they are perpetuating racialization and harm to people of color, regardless of their individual intention and motivation.

Workers endured a broad spectrum of racialization and racism, including overtly racist remarks and multiple forms of everyday degradation. Workers talked often about experiences of humiliation that they felt were motivated by racial difference. Such experiences are difficult to operationalize in labor force surveys and seldom rise to the level of an actionable offense under current legal standards.[3] Workers described not only experiences with employers and supervisors but also what they perceived as racist treatment from coworkers, patients, customers, and the broader public with whom they interacted at work. These varied forms of racism (what we sometimes refer to as "racisms") remind us that job quality is not simply about wages, benefits, promotions, and safety. Workers also care about dignity and respect, which encompass far more than what is legally defined as "racial discrimination."

Workers chronicled a variety of racist tropes and other inequities at the workplace, but not all workers told the same story. Indeed, experiences of racialization differed among workers. For Haitian workers—including all three immigrant types (undocumented, temporary, and permanently documented)—both anti-Blackness and anti-Haitian bias were particularly pervasive at work. For Central American workers—again, across immigration statuses—anti-Latino bias was more salient than distinctions across national origins. Central American workers felt that their experiences of racial inferiority were reflected in their experiences of labor degradation, which was heightened by differences in language and accent.

Scholarship has chronicled the diversity of racisms. The long history of anti-Black policies and African American disadvantage, for example, has been shown to disproportionately impact Black migrants.[4] Further, Afro-Latinos have an experience "of *Latinidad* [different] from their lighter-skinned counterparts," and Indigenous Latinos sometimes face more severe discrimination than their mestizo coworkers.[5] While our sample of Central American immigrant workers did not include many self-identified Afro-Latinos or Indigenous Latinos, we acknowledge the extensive research that has documented the diversity of experience within the Latin American diaspora in the United States.[6] Those histories, along with state-sanctioned efforts to shape and reshape racial identities, are important for understanding how workers understand their experiences at the workplace.

We examine these contemporary accounts of Haitian and Central American workers alongside legal racialized labor hierarchies of the past. Though contemporary policies have largely been purged of explicit racial preferences—and as such are considered "race-neutral"—these once legal racisms continue to matter. Specifically, the devastating legacies of transatlantic slavery, lingering White European colonial privilege, and ongoing US dominance in Latin America (including the Caribbean) have cemented racial hierarchies that continue to reverberate for low-wage immigrant workers today. Beyond simply conjecture, these are connections that workers themselves make as they situate themselves within these histories. These ground-up views of race and inequality from "those who occupy the margins of American society" reflect what scores of race and inequality theorists have long documented.[7] In telling their stories, workers alluded to their national pasts and presents, as well as the conditions that shaped their migration journeys and subsequent work experiences. They invoked the enduring consequences of slavery and subjugated labor in the twenty-first-century workplace. The labor of immigrant workers of color "reproduces relations of servility" that "are reminiscent of forms of racialized labor demand during the colonial period," and their accounts of racialization and degradation at work recall "feelings of dominance rooted in white supremacy."[8]

The significance of these legalized racial labor hierarchies varies across different groups of low-wage immigrants from the Americas. Each country and region[9] has a unique history that generates particular stereotypes that travel with migrants and fuel their subjugation at work.[10] The transatlantic slave trade of Black workers feeds anti-Blackness at work, and the hostile global reaction to the Haitian Revolution feeds the unique nature of anti-Haitian sentiment at work. Though Central Americans experience distinct forms of racialization, dominant stereotypes about Latinos in the United States extend to a wide variety of Latinx peoples.[11] Central Americans' contemporary experiences at work must be understood within the longer history of degrading Latinos and framing them as a threat to society.[12] These tropes erroneously lump Latinos together into one monolithic group, casting aspersion across the pan-ethnic category in essentializing ways that also ignore Central American workers' unique national identities and home country experiences.[13]

The Haitian Immigrant Worker Experience

The Haitian migrants we interviewed described a variety of racist encounters, from outright racist comments to pay disparities stratified by race and disrespectful microaggressions. Workers across all immigration statuses (undocumented, temporary, permanently documented) cited a variety of racisms at work. These dynamics have both historical and contemporary foundations, rooted in racisms not only in the United States but across the globe. We focus on two of the most common themes: the prevalent accounts of anti-Black racism, and the particular dynamics of anti-Haitian sentiment. It is impossible to entirely disentangle anti-Black bias from anti-immigrant and anti-Haitian bias.[14] Nevertheless, we address each iteration of racial stratification in turn to unpack its particular historical foundations.

WHITE SUPREMACY AND ANTI-BLACKNESS AT WORK

Anti-Blackness, Moon-Kie Jung and João Costa Vargas contend, "stresses the uniqueness of Black positionality and experiences relative to those of non-Black social groups."[15] Anti-Blackness was pervasive for the Haitian workers we interviewed. They frequently recounted work conditions of unequal pay, scheduling, and promotions, alongside dehumanizing racist treatment. They were the target of both explicit statements degrading Black peoples and pretextual "colorblind" statements that singled them out for demeaning treatment.[16] To better understand the emergence of these inequalities and how workers experience them, we revisit the profound ways in which transatlantic slavery contoured labor relations and migration patterns.

Histories of Transatlantic Slavery, Anti-Black Laws, and Their Aftermath The injustices of the transatlantic slave trade, which sold and imprisoned

Black Africans as chattel for more than three centuries in the Caribbean and beyond, reverberate today for Haiti and the Haitian diaspora. The slave trade, which reached US shores in 1619, started more than a century prior on the island where Haiti now sits. Hispaniola, home of modern-day Haiti and the Dominican Republic, was one of the first sites of the western European slave trade in the Americas. Spanish colonialists built a settlement on the southeast coast of the island and dubbed it "Santo Domingo, after the revered founder of the Dominican order," from which they would go on to attempt the cultural, religious, and demographic extermination of Hispaniola's Indigenous population.[17] By the mid-sixteenth century, that population "of perhaps 500,000 to 750,000 people was almost completely eliminated through war, forced labor, and disease."[18] Spanish colonists subsequently began "importing" enslaved Africans as laborers in 1501. This history is central to understanding contemporary racial hierarchies in the Americas and across the globe, despite the fact that Haiti itself is often excluded from the imaginary of Latin America.

French colonizers displaced Spain from the western part of the island in the mid-1600s and renamed it Saint Domingue (modern-day Haiti).[19] In doing so, France expanded the slave economy on Hispaniola, relying on the labor of enslaved Africans to cultivate sugarcane and other cash crops. The French colony, often referred to as the "Pearl of the Caribbean," quickly became the most lucrative colony in the world. "By the late eighteenth century, it was the world's largest producer of sugar, exporting more of it than the colonies of Jamaica, Cuba, and Brazil combined," and it produced half of the world's coffee despite being roughly the size of Maryland.[20] France's profit came, however, at a devastating human cost: "Anywhere from 25,000 to 40,000 enslaved persons died each year due to punishments, work conditions, diseases, and suicide. Close to three million enslaved people were brought in total to grow and harvest Saint Domingue's many crops."[21] The contemporary economic realities facing the African continent and the African diaspora throughout these former colonies cannot be understood without first confronting these racialized histories.

Throughout the Americas, Portuguese, British, Dutch, and Danish colonizers joined the French and Spanish in enslaving millions of Africans. The Spanish and Portuguese also promulgated, through law, a racial caste system that privileged European "Whiteness" and subordinated peoples of Indigenous and African descent. Meanwhile, in what would become the US territory, slavery endured until the Thirteenth Amendment to the US Constitution formally abolished it in 1865. Formal abolition did not, however, put an end to legalized forms of racism and racialized labor hierarchies in the United States.[22]

Even post-emancipation, anti-Black laws, such as the "Black Codes" of the Jim Crow era, restricted African Americans' property rights, freedom of movement, and labor mobility in the United States. These legalized forms of racial segregation and degradation remained in effect in the United States until the 1965 Civil Rights Act, but the color-neutral era that followed failed to eradicate racial inequality, which persists today.[23] Contemporary iterations of anti-Blackness are encoded in and fueled by the continued criminalization and disproportionate imprisonment and policing of Black men in particular,[24] unequal health outcomes,[25] entrenched housing segregation and displacement,[26] political disenfranchisement,[27] and long-standing wealth gaps,[28] among many other forms of racism. These inequalities are relevant to the lives of native-born and migrant workers alike. Racial hierarchies and anti-Black biases operate in US workplaces and are key to understanding Haitian worker experiences in the United States. Our Haitian migrant interviewees recounted the challenges and barriers they experienced as Black workers, as well as the agency and adaptive strategies that they adopted in response (Hunter and Robinson 2016).[29]

Legacies of Transatlantic Slavery, Anti-Black Laws, and Their Aftermath
Though immigration status informs how workers relate to workplace precarity, achieving permanent status does not neutralize structural racism in the workplace. This insight has been confirmed by audit studies that reveal employer preferences when considering equally qualified applicants of different races.[30] Haitian workers of all immigration statuses recounted both overt and more subtle manifestations of anti-Black racism. The most blatant instances of racism came up in hiring. For example, Walter, a Haitian engineer with lawful permanent residency and an impressive résumé, surmised that he was frequently called in for an interview because his German-sounding

name made him look White on paper.[31] However, he was constantly denied job opportunities at the interview stage. Eventually, Walter landed a public-sector job.[32]

Racist hiring practices—which often intersect with gender identity—can block workers' attempts to climb the occupational ladder. Daphnée, a Haitian naturalized citizen, recounted being "passed [over for] many promotions."[33] She felt strongly that her difficulties climbing the occupational ladder stemmed from being both Black and a "strong-willed woman." Daphnée saw her intersectional identity as a double-edged sword sometimes: "I think that scares people away, and at the same time people respect me. I don't let my boss dictate my life." Her persistence was a key factor in her eventual success, but it also created conflict with her employers.

Haitian men were often criminalized, and employers often made enormous assumptions about Black workers' criminality. For example, when Georges was applying for a job as a driver, his prospective employer was "shocked" that he had never been arrested.[34] The employer ran a background check and, finding no record, hired him on the spot. Such assumptions about Black workers' supposed criminal associations create disproportionate labor market penalties for them over the long term.[35]

Beyond hiring and promotion, Haitian workers reported pay disparities between them and their non-Black coworkers. Laura, a Haitian immigrant introduced in chapter 4 who was now a naturalized citizen, had this experience working at a retail store where she and her White friend worked together. Even though they were the same age, had received the same education, and had the same minimal work experience, Laura's White friend received pay that "was considerably higher than" hers. Laura clarified that this was "not because she worked more hours than I did, but simply because her pay rate was higher than mine." Though our data cannot confirm employers' pay practices, these accounts of unequal pay were common among the workers with whom we spoke.

Along with discrimination in hiring and promotion as well as inequities in pay, Haitian workers reported scheduling disparities. Managers did not accommodate Laura as much as they did her White friend in setting the work schedule. Her friend, according to Laura, could just say that "she wasn't coming in today and it wouldn't be a big deal." Laura had to play by different rules. She "couldn't get a day off," and even though she often worked more hours to try to increase her income, she still could not bridge the pay gap with her friend. Similarly, Juan, an undocumented Haitian who worked in a grocery store, explained that he was penalized for taking time off, even as White workers freely took vacations with no repercussions.[36]

Labor force studies confirm these forms of White advantage—and especially Black disadvantage. For example, based on within-firm data, Adam Storer and his colleagues argue that the "persistence of racial bias in the workplace does not seem to be the effect merely of relational dynamics in a workplace, but a reflection of the racial hierarchy in the United States."[37] Undocumented Haitian workers like Juan offered a similarly clear-eyed analysis of their racialized position at work. Juan named anti-Black racism directly: "And this had everything to do with the color of my skin," he said.

In fact, Haitian workers reflected on anti-Blackness in the United States with an understanding of its historic and global foundations. As workers described degrading and deplorable treatment by their typically White bosses and customers, they would invoke histories of enslavement and the "slave-like" tasks they were now made to perform. Marise, a Haitian lawful permanent resident introduced in chapter 4 who now worked as a home health aide, recounted the humiliating nature of her work at a fast-food chain.[38] She regularly had to clean vomit and feces that were "all over the toilet." No other workers were willing to do it, and to put it simply, Marise could not risk losing her job if she refused. She generally enjoyed her job and wanted to keep it. But being targeted to do tasks like cleaning toilets felt demeaning and humiliating, and like the epitome of anti-Black racism. "I felt like a slave. I even cried. I love to work, and I depend on it to live. I felt really low."

Haitian workers across the board offered accounts of workplace racism, drawing parallels to histories of enslavement. For example, Rocio, the Haitian worker with lawful permanent residency we first met in chapter 3, talked frankly about her boss's failure to pay her for all the hours she worked, the dangerous nature of the work, and, most poignantly, the "mean-spirited" treatment she received. Though clearly bothered by these features of her workplace, she felt trapped and humiliated. "Sometimes I am crying," she told us, "because there are things to which I have to [be resigned]. It's worse than being enslaved." It is also true that undocumented workers faced an added layer of disempowerment. For Stefano, an undocumented Haitian warehouse worker and cleaner who was also introduced in chapter 3, the racialized legacy of slavery was an especially salient reference. He framed his experience bluntly: As a low-wage Black worker, "you are just a slave who is pushing some time ... without respect or anything and that's it." The lack of respect at his current warehouse job was evidence of pervasive racism. His supervisor, Stefano explained, "[spoke] to us as if we were slaves. The only thing he is missing is a whip. He has no respect for us." For Stefano this disrespect was compounded by an endless accumulation of other problems, such as low pay, bounced checks, impossible schedules, overwork, and his constrained options in the labor market.

The anti-Black racism that Haitian respondents described was also deeply gendered. Workers recounted being subject to daily gendered tropes about Black men, who were often portrayed as "bad," "lazy," or "criminals." These comments were common in service and customer-facing jobs during encounters with management, coworkers, and the general public. Marcello, a Haitian lawful permanent resident, was a recurring gig worker who also worked at fast-casual restaurants. He felt especially targeted for disrespectful treatment as a Black man. These worker observations are consistent with scholarship that has widely documented the ways that Black men, in particular, are subject to pervasive stereotypes of criminality.[39]

In addition to assembly-line speedups and the many tools of flexibilization,[40] humiliation is a dominant form of control over low-wage workers.[41] Though deeply salient to our respondents, humiliation alone is rarely a legally actionable offense, or even a focus for standard labor force research. Irina, a lawful permanent resident working in packing, found this kind of treatment so intolerable and reminiscent of deep-seated anti-Black racism that she wished she had just "stayed in Haiti" rather than coming "to the States [and] working like a slave." Indeed, Irina's remarks accord with Saidiya Hartman's analysis that the "'time of slavery' has yet to pass, that the present is still in its grip."[42]

PERVASIVE ANTI-HAITIANISM: GLOBAL MARGINALIZATION

The racial hierarchy that centers White supremacy and anti-Blackness was salient for our respondents. Haitians, however, often felt targeted not only for being Black but specifically for being from Haiti, an island with a deep history of enslavement, followed by revolution and emancipation and, more recently, political unrest, violence, and disaster.[43] These histories were part of the repertoire of meaning-making that respondents drew on to understand their social position. In the experience of workers like Roselaure, a Haitian naturalized citizen who worked at a fast-food hamburger chain, Haitians were given less leeway and were more frequently targeted for firing than other immigrant workers.[44] Repeatedly, Haitian respondents invoked their country of origin's position in the global order to help understand their own subjugation at work.

Foundations of Haiti's Global Marginalization, Past and Present For Haitians, contemporary anti-Black racism is directly tied to the ongoing price their country pays for revolt. The Haitian Revolution (1791–1804), when nearly half a million enslaved Africans led a successful slave rebellion, struck a significant blow against European colonialism. One of the most unprecedented events in modern history, the Haitian Revolution precipitated centuries of collective punishment.

On August 14, 1791, a gathering of the enslaved for a Vodou ceremony on a plantation in northern Saint Domingue (near present-day Cap-Haïtien) launched an uprising that turned into a "successful revolution that toppled both slavery and the French colonial order."[45] On January 1, 1804, nearly thirteen years from that slave revolt, Haiti emerged as the first Black republic in a world where "the power structure was overwhelmingly White—and Whites held a rigid, hierarchical view of the world that they refused to have challenged at the time."[46] In the wake of revolution, Haiti emerged as a "Black utopia"—a beacon of Black liberatory futures in a White supremacist world.[47]

Though on its face this era was simply a vestige of conflict in the "old world," the Haitian Revolution is a living memory in the ethos of Haitians that has had lasting, real-world effects on the island and in the diaspora.[48] Following the revolution, political isolation and constant threats of invasion and re-enslavement curtailed Haiti's early nation-building efforts. These challenges were not simply symbolic but reflected very real financial extraction and military threats. In 1825, France threatened Haiti with war if it refused to pay a hefty monetary indemnity in exchange for French recognition of its sovereignty. To pay this egregious debt to France—ten times Haiti's annual budget—the new republic, ironically, had to accept loans from French banks.[49] Haitian leaders also had to borrow from US financiers, who demanded power over political decision-making in exchange for funds. Nearly two centuries later, a tumultuous and interventionist relationship continues between the United States and Haiti.[50] The strain of these debts on the Haitian economy also explains much of the political and economic unrest in Haiti today. The "independence debt and the resulting drain on the Haitian treasury were directly responsible not only for the underfunding of education in 20th-century Haiti but also lack of health care and the country's inability to develop public infrastructure."[51] It was from this ravaged reality that many Haitian workers we spoke to had fled, leaving behind families who continued to suffer the ongoing effects of this debt, political unrest, and violence. These long-standing postcolonial traumas in Haiti drive migrant displacement today.[52]

The United States continues to play a central role in shaping Haiti's global marginalization. By the early 1900s, "the demands of the French were . . . surpassed by the pressures of a new and powerful force": the United States.[53] "In the early part of the [twentieth] century, the United States was engaged in a kind of imperial competition with Europe . . . determined to keep the Americas for itself."[54] With Haiti thus becoming of great interest to the United States, US military officials "considered Haiti strategically important, while entrepreneurs were eager to build new plantations in Haiti as they had elsewhere in the region. On July 28, 1915, US Marines landed in Haiti, ostensibly in order to reestablish political order after a bloody coup. They stayed for twenty years."[55] Years later, the United States would intervene in Haitian affairs through its support for the François "Papa Doc" Duvalier regime and the subsequent "Baby Doc" regime of his son, Jean-Claude. The Duvaliers ruled Haiti with brutality from the late 1950s to the mid-1980s.[56] The US occupation of Haiti and its aftermath would continue the cycle of debt, dependence, and political interference that began with the French indemnity a century and a half before.

The deep-seated relationship between Haiti and the United States has shaped migration aspirations and intentions, as well as the experiences of Haitian migrants once they arrive in the United States. These histories of colonialism, resource extraction, and ongoing military intervention are key to understanding Haiti's poverty, political instability, and mass emigration. Haiti's historical and contemporary marginalization is also reflected in the heavy toll of the AIDS crisis of the 1980s, recent environmental disasters, and ongoing violence and political upheavals. Despite its rich history of triumph and revolt, Haiti is often cast as a poorly understood regional pariah. This positionality has been cemented in the US psyche by some politicians, most recently Donald Trump, who, early in his first term as president, pointed to Haiti as one of the "shithole" nations overwhelming the United States with its migrants.[57] Trump again stoked this vitriol during a televised presidential debate on September 10, 2024, when he repeated groundless and vicious claims that Haitian immigrants in Springfield, Ohio, were eating people's pets. Trump's comments, used as a voter turnout strategy, contributed to the rise in discrimination and racist violence against Haitians in Springfield and elsewhere.[58] We found that a sometimes thinly veiled, but often blatant, anti-Haitian sentiment was a core theme among the Haitian workers we interviewed.

Aftershocks of Haiti's Global Marginalization Acutely aware of their position as Black workers in the United States, Haitians also felt targeted by their national origin. For example, Peterson, a Haitian lawful permanent resident who had worked in a variety of warehouses and factories, attributed some of the "horrible treatment" he experienced at work very directly to anti-Haitianism.[59] He felt that employers were more than simply anti-Black. They also made assumptions about Haitians, who were then shunted into the worst jobs. They "put them in a box," he explained. They "would say our country [Haiti] isn't good, it's a bad country." Bosses and coworkers would even invoke Haitian enslavement, the price Haiti had to pay for its slave revolt, and the modern realities of dictatorship, poverty, corruption, and violence, which were seen as evidence of Haiti's inferiority. Peterson believed that being Haitian carried an extra stigma, especially for those who did not speak English. The idealized image of New York City as a hyperdiverse global city that was a haven for old and new immigrants alike was far from Peterson's reality.

The particular marginalization of Haitian Kreyòl-speaking peoples is well documented. In Haiti, Kreyòl is denigrated as below French, and throughout Latin America the language distinguishes these Haitians from the rest of the Spanish-speaking region.[60] Even white-collar workers had experienced both anti-Black and anti-Haitian bias; for Laura, such bias had "played out" over her entire life and across several jobs as she attempted to ascend the occupational ladder, from her early work as a cashier to her current job as a compliance consultant. Her Haitian origin, she shared, was stigmatized for being associated with a history of dysfunction. Indeed, upon learning that she "[comes] from the poorest country in the Western Hemisphere, people tend to pile on that and try to make you feel like you're less than," Laura explained. Once people realized she was from Haiti, Laura often felt them changing their view of her talents and potential. She described the typical trajectory: "I could start at a job and do everything well. But the minute they find out I was born in Haiti, all of a sudden I don't have what it takes to become a VP [vice president]. Even though I was being groomed, almost promised the position." The dual biases against Blackness and Haitian origin reflect the long historical arc of resource extraction and impoverishment but also the contemporary political abandonment and rejection of Haiti by world powers, including the United States, where leaders have passed their disdain along to the US public.

In the ongoing global marginalization of Haiti, it is commonly asserted that Haiti is the "poorest" country in the Western Hemisphere. Instead, argues Haitian American anthropologist Gina Ulysse, we need a new narrative about the intentional, dehumanizing, and ahistorical underdevelopment of the country.[61] Haiti's complex colonial histories (and ensuing tensions) shed light on how Haitian immigrants like Laura navigate power at work, especially in relation to other migrant groups in New York City, including fellow Latin Americans who speak Spanish. These often strained relationships must be understood not simply as inherent animosity or just a vestige of US race relations, but also as echoes of colonial pasts on Hispaniola.

PERVASIVE ANTI-HAITIANISM: COLONIAL TENSIONS AND RACE RELATIONS ON HISPANIOLA

Persistent Colonial Tensions The most fundamental aspect of Haiti's history is the colonial duel between Spain and France on the island of Hispaniola. When Spain started conquering massive territories in mainland Latin America, Santo Domingo began to wane in importance. French colonialists soon took advantage of Spain's preoccupation with South America and began occupying the western half of the island. Through the Treaty of Ryswick of 1697, the Spanish officially ceded the western half of the island to the French as what would become Kreyòl-speaking Haiti, and the Spanish kept the eastern half, which is now the Spanish-speaking Dominican Republic. Linguistic differences were the most obvious lasting effect of this splitting of the island.[62] It also pacified the colonial playground and shaped the current conditions for both Haitians who remain on the island and those who leave to work in the United States.

The reality on the island is complex. An artificial cleavage, created by colonial forces, produced a tumultuous border inhabited by an ethnic and linguistic mixture of peoples. The hypernationalism of these colonial legacies has created massive tensions and resentments that have been well documented by Latin American and Caribbean scholars.[63] As recently as 2015, the Dominican Republic attempted to denationalize hundreds of thousands of Haitians (including those born in the territory). And over time, the United States itself has used the Dominican Republic as an outpost for its "empire of borders" to keep Haitians from leaving the island.[64] This reality is reflected in the anti-Haitian bias of Spanish-speaking supervisors and coworkers. It also broadly framed how the migrants we interviewed thought about their own contemporary subjugation.

The Reverberations of Race Relations on Hispaniola The dominant colonial tension on Hispaniola between Dominican and Haitian peoples was carried throughout the migrant diasporas of both countries. To be sure, these two emigrant populations find themselves in community and competition in New York City, a dynamic covered well by many Caribbean scholars and by race and migration scholars.[65] Yet our findings reveal that tensions on Hispaniola and the entrenched anti-Black realities throughout Latin America inform Haitians' relations with all Spanish-speaking workers. This complicates the typical White-Black binary and the dominant focus on White supremacy and the subjugation of Black and Brown communities.

These racialized pasts and presents cast a pall over Haitian exchanges with all Latinos (or "Hispanics," or "Spanish-speaking," as they were often referred to by our interviewees). The not uncommon feeling among Haitian respondents that Spanish-speaking workers received more job opportunities and were treated better revealed that colonial pasts and contemporary tensions on Hispaniola informed their understanding of the inequities they faced in the United States. These disparities pose challenges for building solidarity across racial/ ethnic migrant groups (as discussed in the next chapter).

The historical racial and linguistic tensions on Hispaniola are important for understanding Haitian immigrants' understanding of their racialized treatment at work in the United States vis-à-vis their Spanish-speaking counterparts. For example, Benjamin, whom we met in chapter 2, was a Haitian with lawful permanent residency who had worked in factories. Frustrated about not being able to get a job even though he had immigration "papers," he expressed a belief that employers preferred Latinos. Employers might hire "one Haitian but [will] mostly recruit Hispanics," he said. The subjugated experience of Latinos, even at the hands of the coethnics who help build social capital for recruiting and hiring, is well documented, but inequality at work is multifaceted.[66] Thus, relative to Latinos, Haitians saw themselves as racially disadvantaged, owing to the anti-Haitian bias of both employers and coworkers. For them, the racial tensions in New York City coexist with the racial tensions on Hispaniola and the anti-Blackness entrenched throughout Latin America (vividly experienced by some Haitian migrants in transit).

Many Haitian workers felt that they were treated unfairly relative to their Spanish-speaking coworkers not only in hiring but in task assignments. Conceding that her work at a factory was vastly different from her current work in health care, Ana, a Haitian lawful permanent resident described in chapter 3, nevertheless maintained that the racial dynamic remained the same. Relative to "lighter-skinned Spanish people," she was "assigned tougher work" under "worse conditions." Ana was not alone in being frustrated by this reality, which muted the aspirations for occupational mobility and advancement of many Haitian workers.

The structural disparities that disadvantage both Latino and Haitian workers also sow discord between groups. Employers' preference for undocumented Latinos in particular was not lost on Haitian workers. Stefano, an undocumented Haitian who worked in manufacturing and was mentioned earlier, was indignant that, by his estimate, 80 percent of the people he worked with were Spanish speakers "without papers." Despite their status, he felt that they were treated better than undocumented Haitians: "[If] something goes down on the floor, the first person they will fire is you, because of your color." Such prejudice reflects racialized management hierarchies and well-documented forms of "social closure" around out-groups.[67] While immigrant Latinos are often the target of these exclusions, employers also strategically incorporate them into the firm in order to exclude others.[68] This frustrated workers like Stefano, who felt targeted by "Spanish" managers who let other "Spanish" workers "slide" when a problem arose. This latent solidarity, he believed, was entirely due to their shared racial identity and found expression in the exclusion and targeting of Haitians like himself.

These tensions between Haitian respondents and their Latino supervisors multiplied the forms of degradation they felt and created a sense of perpetual persecution. For example, Irina described her sense of the power and authority that "Hispanics" in her manufacturing workplace enjoyed that Haitian workers simply did not have access to. "If the Hispanic does something and goes to complain," she explained, managers never failed to find that "the Hispanic is always right." Meanwhile, her Latino managers responded harshly to Haitians when they faltered even in small ways, such as taking more than their allotted fifteen-minute break. "The Hispanics take longer breaks than us, and they don't say anything to them." To keep her job and avoid getting her pay docked, Irina, fully aware of this disparity, was careful to return to work before the fifteen minutes were up. As a result, she had to cut her breaks short and "always rush to eat or stuff the food in [her] bag," in order to avoid conflict. Irina had little room for error—or even full humanity—compared to her Hispanic coworkers.

Though these perspectives clearly elide the complex dynamics of racial capitalism that subjugate Latino workers as well, the narratives of Haitian workers featured racialized divisions that left them feeling marginalized. These experiences of anti-Blackness at work compound the sequelae of the colonial violence on Hispaniola and the enslavement of Black Africans in the Americas. We turn next to the parallel, though distinct, racialized experiences of Central Americans.

The Central American Immigrant Worker Experience

While undocumented and temporary immigration status fueled worker precarity, permanent legal status did not erase racism at work for either the Haitians or Central Americans we interviewed. Their experiences highlight the wide-ranging racialization to which migrant workers are subjected while also confirming that racism is multifaceted and manifests in distinct ways. Central American respondents reported a range of aggressions, from overtly hostile statements about "Latinos" or "Hispanics" to everyday degradations like coworkers snickering about their accents.

Racism is a system, not simply an individual prejudice. It is contextual and far from uniform, and multiple forms of racism can coexist. While Haitian workers reported experiences infused with anti-Black and anti-Haitian sentiment, Central American workers recounted experiences of being homogenized as Latinos and having their national-origin identities erased. Central American workers often expressed, for instance, that White Americans did not see them as a Salvadoran or Honduran or Nicaraguan, but simply as one of many expendable Latino laborers. As before, these narratives implore us to grapple with US intervention in Latin America, the long history of US labor extraction from Mexico and Central America, and contemporary anti-Latino politics in the United States. We turn now to these histories and presents.

THE ROOTS: SPANISH COLONIAL RULE AND ITS AFTERMATH IN CENTRAL AMERICA

After centuries of Spanish colonial rule in Central America were followed by independence from Spain, the colonial rulers who took power engaged in a forced homogenization of the population, while subjugating Indigenous and Black laborers. Reliance on cash crops from the region required an expansion of farmland acquisition and the further dispossession of Indigenous people from their communal land. These actions led to ongoing revolts and civil unrest throughout the region. Colonized lands were highly dependent on single export products—indigo in El Salvador and Guatemala, tobacco and silver/ore in Honduras and Nicaragua. By the end of the 1800s, coffee, sugarcane, and bananas had replaced indigo in most of the isthmus, increasing the Central American region's reliance on the unstable global market for cash crop commodities. Predictably, the labor hierarchy in these industries was highly racialized. Agricultural laborers were mostly Indigenous Mayan descendants—who had been forced to become agricultural laborers—and the descendants of African enslaved persons, known at that time as "*mulatos, negros, morenos*, and *pardos*."[69]

Ultimately, the ruling White Spanish elites engaged in "indigenous extermination" as well as the expulsion of Afro-descendants from specific Central American territories, like El Salvador and Guatemala. This ethnic polarization is best exemplified by "La Matanza" in El Salvador, the genocide of forty thousand Mayan peasants in 1932. Carried out less than a century ago, *La Matanza* was one part of a broader terror campaign instigated by the military regime of President Maximiliano Hernández Martínez to quell dissent and force the Indigenous population into compliant labor. The genocide, which violently forbade the "public displays of indigenous dress and language," impacted the psyches of Salvadorans for generations to come.[70] It also fostered a hostility and shaming of the native population not just in El Salvador but throughout the region.[71] In the decades that followed, El Salvador and Guatemala also enacted a series of race laws that expelled Afro-descendants from specific territories and halted any further migration of African and Asian immigrants.[72] While histories of racialization and violence vary across Central American countries, the result was a racialization of the working class via a terror campaign that negated Indigenous and Afro-descendant populations from the public imagination throughout the region.[73] Honduras would become the military base of operations for deadly US imperialistic actions that replaced Spanish coloniality.[74]

Central Americanist Jorge Cuéllar stresses the importance of interrogating past "colonial terror" as such: "Violent events have a direct effect on the social and psychic life of aggrieved communities: they affect the processes of memorialization, change the stories people tell themselves about their own history, generate resentment toward those culpable for the events, and shape the political imagination of future generations."[75] The Central American respondents we interviewed felt the weight of these pasts.

THE ROOTS: US IMPERIALISM IN LATIN AMERICA AND DOMESTIC POLICIES TARGETING LATINOS

Anti-Latino biases abound within the United States and rest largely on the view that Latinos are inferior to Whites in the workplace.[76] A staple of US race relations, these tropes are also rooted in the long history of US imperialism throughout Latin America. As Latin American countries gained independence from their colonial rulers in the early nineteenth century, the United States expanded its economic and political domination over the region. It also made territorial expansions, most notably after defeating Mexico in the Mexican-American War (1846–1848) and the acquisition of 50 percent of Mexico's territory. This era cemented the role of the United States throughout Latin America.

The United States would go on to make inroads into the political leadership and economic agendas of Central and South American countries. It did so through US-backed coups and wars that fed instability and underdevelopment in the region, displaced communities, and prompted migrations north. Many different countries besides the United States have pillaged Latin American environments and resources, but resource extraction and economic destruction by US capital have left an indelible mark on communities and economies throughout the continent.[77] The impact of the expansion of the US "sphere of influence" remains palpable today. Despite the postcolonial linguistic, racial/ethnic, religious, and cultural diversity of Latin America, it became expected that "everything south of the continental United States must . . . be homogenized—as 'Latin' or 'Latino.'"[78]

Despite this attempt at homogenization, Central American immigrants have had distinct experiences in the United States, owing in large part to the particular US foreign policy interests in their home region. In 2023, Central American migrants were the second-largest group of foreign nationals arriving from the Americas.[79] Largely excluded from asylum protections following the first postwar mass exodus in the 1980s wars, today Salvadorans, Hondurans, and Nicaraguans who ultimately qualified for temporary protected status find themselves in a position of permanent temporality that has lasted over twenty-five years. Meanwhile, the initial denial of political asylum foreclosed many economic opportunities for Central Americans and limited their access to social protections such as affordable housing and health care. These exclusions have influenced the nature of Central American immigrant civic engagement and political demands in the United States.[80]

The shop-floor experiences of migrant workers must be understood within this historical context and in the light of subsequent US foreign relations and immigration policies. Interventionist and extractive US policies helped fuel racist domestic policies. Even as administrations change, policies are overhauled, and justice movements demand change, these pasts have lasting impacts on contemporary inequality, as the example of South African apartheid has shown.[81]

In the migration context, origin-country governments curate their labor export in many ways. One key strategy in the Americas has been to construct the Whiteness of migrants as an asset connected to their emigrant labor value.[82] These migrants then arrive at destinations where racist laws have permitted discriminatory businesses, segregated housing and education, English-only policies, and impunity for perpetrators of anti-Latino discrimination and violence.[83] Together, these histories continue to feed the collective degradation of Latinos as unequal to Whites.

The anti-Latino histories in the United States have become part and parcel of the racist border policies of recent decades, which have garnered significant political and public support. These exclusionary and criminalizing US-Mexico border policies have affected all migrants from not only Latin America but around the world.[84] Such enforcement policies criminalize immigrants[85] and feed the "Latino threat" narrative, thereby fueling a rash of state and local policies aimed at policing the interior, sometimes even through literal and legal racial profiling.[86]

The first Trump administration was explicit in its racist stereotyping of Latinos, in particular Mexicans and Central Americans. However, such stereotypes have deep roots as a popular homogenizing narrative that characterizes all Latinos as an "invading force."[87] This narrative "erase[s] within-group differences among Latinas/os" (for example, US-born immigrant Mexican, Central American, etcetera) that acknowledge the sociopolitical and cultural complexities that exist in shaping the diversity of Latina/o experiences.[88]

These wide-ranging forms of anti-Latino racism play out alongside a specific political narrative that criminalizes and vilifies Central Americans—for example, through a focus on the threat of the MS-13 gang in both national and local politics.[89] Region-specific vitriol accompanies efforts to erase complexities within the region and "homogenize[s] the Latina/o population to fit a monolithically subordinate category of people."[90] Though Latino homogenization can be place-specific, it often excludes immigrants from Central American countries, who have unique identities and home country experiences that consequently become subordinated to the generalized anti-Latino visage.[91]

US foreign and domestic policies have fueled the demonization of Latinos, which in turn fuels Latino immigrant precarity at work. These histories help contextualize the degraded laborer narrative that was so common and salient in our interviews with Central Americans. That employers and the public at large subjected Central American workers to degrading work should be understood as an outgrowth of immigration policy toward Latin American migrants. At the same time that contract labor laws continued to subjugate formerly enslaved persons in the US South, the United States was also advancing racist migrant labor policies. The racist "guest worker" schemes that emerged focused on temporary contracts for Asian and Mexican migrants who met specific economic criteria for advancing the interests of US capital.[92] The cultural and economic position of all Latino laborers in the United States today must be viewed within this broader context.

Latino immigrant labor is seen as both a threat and an "essential" ingredient for economic stability in the United States. Recurrent periods of "inclusion through illegalization" promoted segregated work based on racial hierarchies.[93] Maintaining these hierarchies, in turn, became critical to labor control.[94] In particular, the two-decades-long Bracero Program with Mexico (1942–1964) skirted the national-origin quotas of the day to create and then meet a demand for pliant migrant labor. Long after the program ended, labor recruitment practices and migratory routes from Latin America (especially, but not only, from Mexico) persisted, even as former *braceros* fell out of status and would later be targeted for "repatriation."[95] The active recruitment of Mexican migrants during this era also persisted alongside an ebb and flow of border surveillance at both Mexico's northern and southern borders.[96] The Bracero Program served as an anchor to labor export policy in Latin America, and it reverberates in the forms of labor recruitment and exploitation that persist to this day.

Workers widely felt that they were viewed at work as simply "Latino," even though they very much identified with their nation of origin. In the following section, we detail the core themes in Central American respondents' descriptions of their experiences of labor precarity as Latino workers: pervasive feelings of homogenization and erasure, and persistent forms of inequality and degradation tied to their Latino status.

THE SHADOW: A HOMOGENIZING ANTI-LATINO NARRATIVE

Haitian and Central Americans experienced many things in common, and both felt the aftershocks of centuries of racialized labor hierarchies in their many forms. However, rather than experiencing poor treatment based on their particular national origin, the Central American migrants we interviewed often described encountering a generalized anti-Latino sentiment and an aggressive erasure of their national identities in everyday interactions.[97] The broad category of "Hispanic" (and later "Latino") was created by state actors in response to demands from both civil rights groups and media markets, both of which stood to benefit from the creation of the category. The absence of such a category had helped elide deep-seated inequalities experienced by this population, and its creation opened up an untapped source of consumers.[98] Yet today this broad category has tended to erase the broad diversity of the population included in it. US imperialism in Latin America and anti-Latino domestic policies, old and new, have curated this universalizing anti-Latino narrative that elides the complexity of the region and diasporas.

Though the focus of much political analysis, the sensationalizing focus on "drug dealers, criminals and rapists" from Mexico[99] is less a story of specific Mexican exclusion than an entry point to a generalized anti-Latino narrative.[100] The conflation of Central America with Mexico is a geopolitical fiction (Mexico is in North America) that lumps together everyone south of the US border. Generalized anti-Latino narratives ignore realities such as the racialized and violent treatment of Central American transit migrants in Mexico, where state institutions and local populations read these migrants as decidedly foreign.[101]

While most of the Central Americans we talked to did not offer an Afro-Latino or Indigenous identity, they felt racialized primarily as Latino in the United States. Respondents repeatedly reported being homogenized by management, coworkers, customers, and the broader public as Latina/o/x—Hispanic—or as Spanish. Two key unifying features that respondents identified as their racial markers were language and accent, which marked them as foreigners and outsiders who should return to "their country."

Invisibilized as Central Americans and homogenized as Hispanics/Latinos in the workplace, respondents reported unceasing discrimination, harassment, and humiliation, which they saw as tied to this panethnic racialization. For example, Glenda, a Salvadoran TPS worker we first met in chapter 3, recounted her many racist experiences as a low-wage worker in the United States. Her racial/ethnic identify came to be conflated with her workplace precarity. She argued that "when someone sees you as Hispanic, there is always discrimination" at work.

Respondents like Glenda felt that their precarious work experiences stemmed from their subjugation as Latinos. For example, Alejandro, a Salvadoran medical supply store clerk with TPS who was also introduced in chapter 3, cited his "Hispanic" heritage as the source of many of his bad encounters at work. Declaring that "many Americans are racists who hate Hispanic people," he went on to describe a litany of racist encounters. Similarly, Wilmer, a Salvadoran with TPS described in chapter 3, explained that in his work in residential contracting these animosities translated into complicated interactions and double standards whereby "White Americans know that Hispanics have to work more [than them]." Thus, Wilmer was often asked to work longer and harder than what he had agreed to, while his White coworkers were able to relax and simply do the job they were contracted to do. "There are a lot of people," he said, "who try to . . . make us work too much for crap [wages]." Through these experiences of labor exploitation, Wilmer developed an identity as a Latino migrant worker marked for cheap, demeaning labor.

In an English-only context—even in the hyperdiverse and multilingual setting of New York City—the inability to speak "unaccented" English was the largest marker of Latinidad that widened the chasm between Central American respondents and White Americans. Language provided a platform for abuse and harassment.[102] For example, Alessandra, a Honduran lawful permanent resident described in chapter 3, admitted that her manager used her inability to speak English fluidly to ridicule her in front of others and declare that "she's stupid." She was humiliated, since she knew enough English to understand what this expression meant.

Even though Spanish is the second most common language spoken in the United States, the English-only imperative that has developed has become a major racializing force.[103] Workers recounted being ignored and dismissed for not speaking English, even when there was no occupational requirement to do so. Lucrecia, a temporary status bakery worker from El Salvador described in chapter 4, asserted that when a worker does not speak English, "people do not take you seriously. It is like you do not exist."

Other workers recounted similar feelings of invisibilization and dehumanization stemming from their accent and imperfect English. For example, Dario, an undocumented Honduran who sought day labor outside of a home improvement store, described being regularly demeaned by clients: "Sometimes they don't understand you, and they get mad and start to insult you."[104] Workers in public-facing low-wage positions regularly told similar stories of being insulted and ridiculed. Such experiences of exclusion were compounded by Central Americans' simultaneous quest to fit into a linguistic landscape where their Spanish revealed a minority vocabulary, accent, and intonation.[105]

Central Americans were also reminded—sometimes explicitly—that, as Latino outsiders, they did not belong and were perpetual foreigners. Workers recounted being told to "go home," a trope reminiscent of high-profile efforts to cast all Brown humanity south of the border as undesirable. Workers were often reminded—by management, coworkers, patients, customers, and clients—that they did not belong. For example, Glenda vividly recounted being belligerently confronted by a customer who declared, "This is not your country. Go back to your country, wherever you're from." The customer then uttered a string of insults for all to hear. This public humiliation was both *exact* (you do not belong) and *vague* (I don't know where you are from). Glenda surmised that she was simply another "Hispanic" worker to this bigoted client. Similarly, Guillermino, a Honduran bus driver with TPS, who was described in chapter 2, regularly contended with passengers who harassed him while he drove. They would yell, "Go back to your country," and "Why are you here taking our jobs?" Like other Central Americans we interviewed, Guillermino felt that he was simply another Latino being targeted.

The homogenization of Central American migrants in the United States, in essentializing differences among the workers with whom we spoke, mirrored a colonial legacy of ethnic and cultural erasure through Hispanicization.[106] Taken together, homogenizing anti-Latino bias simultaneously marked Central American migrants as similar to other Hispanics (who abound in the United States and New York City) and reiterated the trope that they were foreign invaders who did not belong.

THE SHADOW: THE NARRATIVE OF THE UBIQUITOUS BUT DEGRADED LABORER

Even as their national-origin differences were ignored in the workplace, Central Americans were unified in their subjugation as Latino *workers.* As Latinos, Central Americans, across all immigration statuses, perform a disproportionate share of low-wage, hazardous, and poorly paid work in the United States. In an indication of their precarity in the global economic and racial order, their labor is ubiquitous and expendable. As also noted by our Haitian respondents, some Central American workers felt that they were even preferred over their "American" counterparts for the dirtier, more grueling, more degrading work assignments.

Most of the immigrants we spoke to for this project, by design, were workers doing low-wage jobs, which are concentrated largely in underregulated industries. Central American respondents described extensive labor denigration in their workplaces alongside a generalized anti-Latino racism. For example, Diana from chapter 2, the Nicaraguan home care worker with a green card, reported that her supervisor often made derogatory comments about her intellect in general and about her abilities at work. When asked why her superior was treating her this way, Diana responded that she felt she was being "humiliated for being Latina." Her supervisor, whom Diana described as a poor White woman, would say to her repeatedly, "You are nobody." For Diana, this form of denigration was intended not simply to assert class power and authority but also to invoke White privilege to subjugate her.

Racialization takes place in relation to those in power above you and those beside you. Oscar, the undocumented Salvadoran day laborer working in construction, felt like Hispanic workers were treated differently than "American workers." He explained that "sometimes they look at you like something that is worthless ... like something ... something that has no value." Oscar considered his location as a laborer at the bottom of a construction site crew inherently racialized. Racialization can isolate workers from each other, even in contexts where working-class experiences could be an otherwise unifying force.

When compared to the anti-Blackness and anti-Haitian sentiment we uncovered in the accounts of Haitian respondents, the experiences of both Central Americans and Haitians illustrate the varying hierarchies in the lives of immigrant low-wage workers. At the top of every hierarchy sits White supremacy. Indeed, Central American workers seemed acutely aware of the privilege afforded to White Americans over Latino workers. According to Oscar, "White Americans give us the more difficult jobs that they do not want to do." Rather than champion this popular advocacy slogan, which assumes a uniquely heroic capacity for enduring worse conditions that should be celebrated, the decades of policies that legitimate poorer treatment and working conditions for workers of color help illuminate these employer strategies to sort workers.

Not only were Central American workers expected to do more degrading work than their White peers, but they also felt that they were given a heavier volume of work. Arturo, an undocumented Guatemalan worker with a long work history in the United States, recalled that in all the jobs he had held—at a car wash, in a laundry, on a construction site, with a landscaping company, and as a cleaner—it was "always" the same story.[107] He put it simply: "They give the White Americans the easier work and the Hispanic workers get the tough work." This ethnic antagonism has been long documented by dual labor market theorists, who see the divide-and-conquer strategy as a way to deter labor solidarity.[108] Such antagonism intensifies the structural forces that have created secondary labor markets for Latino immigrants and other immigrants of color.

Indeed, workers saw themselves as stuck in the doldrums of their low-wage jobs, while employers doled out the limited benefits to their White counterparts. For example, Alessandro, an undocumented Salvadoran construction and manufacturing worker, noted that his boss gave White coworkers "more opportunities" and "more breaks."[109] Central American respondents like Alejandro felt that they were run more ragged on the shop floor and pressured to work faster, just as they were blocked from opportunities for mobility to more desirable jobs, which were reserved for workers with Whiter bodies.

These data confirm neither the racial landscape of the workplace nor the full range of respondents' racial attitudes. Yet we know that White supremacy works not simply as a system of contestation over power but also as a way of framing how workers understand and perform their own racial identity. Eduardo Bonilla-Silva has written extensively about the "honorary" Whiteness of some racial categories and the aspirational Whiteness that becomes embedded in some immigrant communities.[110]

To be sure, workers' accounts sometimes signaled very flagrant violations of labor and employment law. For example, one Salvadoran construction worker with temporary status shared that his boss commonly asked the Latino construction crew to do dangerous work that did not comply with occupational safety and health standards.[111] He contrasted this treatment with the high safety and health standards he knew were upheld for the mostly all-White unionized construction work. Structural inequalities like these were clearly and severely marked by racial difference, even if they did not constitute "racism" under narrow civil rights laws. Yet they were a central aspect of our interviewees' racialized identity as Latino laborers.

For Central Americans, the erasure of their national identity, subsumed under "Latinos" writ large, positions them as beneath White America. Meanwhile, the long sequelae of the legalized racisms of previous eras continue to shape immigrant labor precarity today for Haitian immigrants. All these forms of belittlement reinforce a strategy of racialized labor extraction meant to deter solidarity and to benefit capital (Gleeson 2015).[112]

Conclusion

This chapter has identified a variety of ways in which workers of color are racialized, despite race-neutral contemporary laws and formal protections prohibiting discrimination and harassment. For both of the populations we detailed here, Haitian and Central American migrant workers, the US civil rights framework is insufficient for defining and addressing racism at work. Federal civil rights laws in the 1960s made some headway by outlawing the most egregious workplace practices, but lawmakers did not design them to address the root causes of structural racism and xenophobia. Indeed, the spectrum of what counts as actionable "employment discrimination" under civil rights laws is quite narrow. The law, as Samuel Lucas explains, tends to focus on "identifiable acts, committed by specific, identifiable individuals (or corporate persons)."[113] This highly individualistic approach leaves much of exploitative and degrading relations to be "condoned." Put simply, current civil rights protections do not adequately define the mechanisms of racial discrimination, nor do they capture discrimination's impacts on workers of color. Many racist encounters are intangible, historically rooted, and entirely legal. Ultimately, racism is "a fundamentally damaged social relation that takes place in a wider environment rarely captured by these legal frameworks."[114]

Acknowledging that employers, coworkers, and the public engage in a broad spectrum of racist behavior (intentionally or not) pushes scholars and advocates to think beyond the typical markers of job quality and overt acts of racism. Indeed, canonical studies of immigrant work tend to home in on key outcomes, such as employment trends, wage parity, and exposure to hazards, as described in part 1.[115] Beyond material inequalities (in pay, hours, scheduling), we should not underestimate the significance of "degraded work."[116] Workers experience racism in a variety of mundane—though no less significant—ways on the job. Our worker interviewees recounted racial inequalities not only in hiring, firing, and pay but also as reflected in disrespectful and dehumanizing statements and treatment by management, coworkers, customers, clients, patients, and the general public. Beyond driving job satisfaction, these relational aspects of work expand the gamut of racialized worker precarity that ethnographers have documented in detail through long-term observations at workplaces.[117] Taken together, a variety of racisms—old and new, explicit and implicit, international and domestic—mark the experiences of low-wage workers across immigration status. Racism functions differently according to national (or regional) origin, color, and even language.

We also call for looking at low-wage work through a broader lens of historical and structural racism. Histories of White supremacy are key to understanding the forces driving low-wage immigrant work and the racist experiences that workers endure. While this book has not attempted to capture the full histories of our respondents' national or regional origins, a rich tradition of ethnic and area studies has brought such work to labor scholarship. We also acknowledge that this book provides necessarily incomplete histories of immigrant racialization and the long durée of racial capitalism.[118] At the same time, however, we have elevated the work of other Central American and Haitian studies scholars who have documented these histories.[119]

By centering worker voices and historicizing their experiences, we can better "account for both institutional and grounded day-to-day practices of racialization."[120] We can also connect these experiences to long legacies of slavery, colonization, and legalized racisms.[121] In the next chapter, we revisit the potential of worker mobilization at the individual and collective levels, despite the obstacles that disempower workers. We argue that race and national origin compound existing barriers to claims-making that all low-wage immigrant workers face but also provide opportunities for building solidarity across difference.

RACISMS AND COLONIAL LEGACIES AS BARRIERS AND PATHWAYS TO CHALLENGING PRECARITY

7

Along with the contemporary labor and immigration regimes, persistent racisms and colonial legacies narrow the available pathways to worker empowerment. Achieving work authorization and permanent immigration status is a critical support for migrant workers, but doing so, on its own, does not address all the factors driving worker precarity. Immigrant workers also report racist supervisors, coworkers, and publics who commonly deploy damaging stereotypes, ethnic slurs, and blatant preferential treatment. Beyond individual prejudices, persistent racisms—which can be traced back to historical racisms and colonial legacies and often masquerade as benign race-neutral policies or cultural preferences—also matter. They can deter workers from demanding on-time payment, reporting harassment, or requesting safety equipment. Racial (and ethnic and national-origin) tensions also can divide workers in racially stratified workplaces.

Workers grappled not only with how to respond as individuals but also with whether and how to band together with coworkers in the same boat. Both the Haitians and Central Americans we interviewed often struggled to find solidarity with other workers. As chapters 3 and 5 revealed, a myriad of barriers block worker voice and divide the workforce. Low-wage workers, vying to keep their precarious positions in an at-will environment, can be divided across immigration statuses and, as we also find, across racial/ethnic identities. Some employers stoke these divisions, aiming to stymie any collective solidarity on the shop floor that could reduce company profits.[1] In considering their options in contesting their work conditions, migrant workers draw not only on their position within the US racial hierarchy

https://doi.org/10.7758/rioz4023.5660

to understand alliances and fractures but also on their racialized experiences in their country of origin. Further, transnational obligations to those they have painfully left behind can raise the stakes of losing their job and inform their decisions about what they are willing to tolerate in order to keep that job.

Still, workers have agency, and sometimes they find ways to navigate these barriers. Origin-country conditions and trauma from the migration journey weigh heavily on workers but also can inspire them to come forward. This chapter demonstrates how race and national origin can help propel workers to challenge precarity at work. Resistance can take many forms—sometimes enacted through government channels, sometimes through informal channels, and sometimes more subtly, as quiet resistance (see also chapter 3). Some workers opt for bold and explicit forms of resistance, such as filing a lawsuit. Others engage in persistent nudging or "dragging foot" (sometimes referred to as "quiet quitting").[2] Some individuals go it alone, while others team up with a group. Inspiration comes from many sources, and revolutionary histories and symbols can serve as touchstones. Aside from scholarly analysis, we find that workers themselves make connections between the shadow of US foreign policy in their origin country and the inequalities they now face in the United States as migrants.

Race and Colonial Legacies as Barriers to Challenging Worker Precarity

Contemporary laws and historical inequalities shape both working conditions and opportunities for worker mobilization. That is, even as new protections emerge and old forms of discrimination are repudiated, structural inequalities persist. Workers are constantly considering whether and how to demand more for what is often back-breaking, grueling, and undignified work. Some worker demands are protected by the law, while others are broader appeals for greater respect and recognition from their employers, even if not legally required. The US labor standards enforcement system, which relies almost entirely on these worker claims to function, has declined in regulatory capacity over the last fifty years. The system is compromised. Workers have a lot to lose if they come forward to complain, organize a union, or make collective demands.

We know that immigrant workers of color may lack the resources and networks available to their White counterparts, such as access to legal counsel or even basic information and leverage to buttress their claims.[3] We have demonstrated that workers in the new "fissured workplace" are often independent contractors, who lack the same rights as employees.[4] This form of employment is especially prominent in certain migrant-dense industries, such as landscaping, construction, and other gig work.[5] On the whole, the greater likelihood that workers of color will gain work through less stable intermediaries (franchises, subcontractors, temp agencies) makes it more difficult to hold employers responsible for meeting pay and health standards.[6] For some underrepresented immigrant workers, linguistic barriers and cultural misunderstandings further complicate the bureaucratic process of claims-making.[7] Each of these barriers, aside from being tied to the labor and immigration regimes, has created deeply racialized inequalities in the low-wage workforce by making immigrant workers of color more vulnerable to workplace precarity and placing significant burdens on their ability to defend their rights.

We propose three ways in which racism and colonial legacies make worker resistance harder and demonstrate how racial/ethnic inequality throws up barriers for worker mobilization efforts: (1) racist supervisors abound and represent a primary barrier to worker voice; (2) worker solidarity is far from abundant or easy, given that workers must often navigate long-standing competition and racial/ethnic tensions with their coworkers; and (3) immigrant workers often have a "dual frame of reference" anchored to origin-country conditions and transnational obligations, which feed worker calculations and concerns about what could be lost if their efforts fail.

RACIST SUPERVISORS BLOCKING WORKER RESISTANCE FROM WITHIN

One route for speaking up is to request help from a community organization in filing a complaint with a government agency.[8] This form of co-enforcement, as we have shown, is critical, but also challenging to access and navigate. Workers may instead opt to first push for incremental and low-profile changes within their workplace. In this case, they often need to carefully engage with a supervisor or other management actor. Some workers have had success with persistent nudging in the hope that their employer will stop evading liability.[9] Workers opting for this form of resistance must choose when to push forward and when to back off in order to keep their jobs. Resistance for some workers looks like softly refusing an unjust order or negotiating with willing, even sympathetic supervisors or human resources representatives with the power to make some changes. More often, management actors are less responsive, finding ways to placate workers without addressing their complaints in their entirety. Workers asking for help in addressing basic legal obligations, such as payment in full and on-time, sometimes find themselves facing a brick wall.

In truth, employers generally have few incentives to acquiesce to worker demands and have a variety of strategies to deflect them. Workplace inequality is deeply racialized, as are employer strategies to subjugate workers and deflect their complaints. Our aim here is not to rank racist employer practices on a scale of severity. Instead, we argue that individual racial prejudice and structural racism come in many forms. Together they shape not only the conditions to which workers are subject but also their ability to push back, both individually and collectively.

In chapter 6, we outlined the role of anti-Blackness and anti-Haitianism at work, along with the homogenizing and degrading anti-Latino narratives to which Central Americans are subject. Here too we show that the experiences of both Haitians and Central Americans reveal the variety of racisms in the workplace and the many actors with whom workers must contend. White supervisors with prejudicial attitudes are certainly a common fixture in the stories told by workers. However, many other racial groups are capable of engaging in discriminatory behavior, and certainly do, especially in the hyperdiverse metropolis of New York City, where race relations are complex and ever evolving. Our data are not designed to directly compare the interactions between Haitian and Central American workers. Yet, as we have already established, the experiences of the two migrant worker groups provide insights into the various manifestations of White supremacy, anti-Blackness, and tropes about certain immigrant origins that hinder attempts to create worker solidarity.

Some Haitians identified their Latino supervisors (whom they also labeled "Spanish") as a major source of tension and conflict. One Haitian undocumented worker, Jorge, recounted being verbally abused by his Latino supervisor at a fast-casual restaurant.[10] He told his supervisor not to call him *"negro"* (the Spanish word for "Black") and pointed out that his Latino coworkers were doing less work than he was doing. Jorge's supervisor responded by telling him that he was "lazy" and should get back to work. The supervisor then threatened to call the main boss if Jorge persisted in his complaints. Since he really did not want to lose his job, Jorge dropped the issue. Weighing the costs, he concluded that pushing it was ultimately a waste of his time, and that there was no "need to complain" because "they won't even listen to you." Similarly, Rocio, the Haitian factory worker with permanent status mentioned earlier, reported experiencing racial tension with her Latino supervisor. She concluded that it was no use to "even bother to report anything"—being given heavier workloads and not enough breaks, preferential schedules that excluded her—because "the Spanish people stick together," even when one of them was "at fault." Even highly educated workers like Walter, the Haitian green card holder who worked in a state job and had an advanced degree in civil engineering, felt that his position in the US labor market was forever marked by his accent and foreign credentials. His focus was on keeping his head down and staying employed.

Central Americans also felt that racist supervisors were a major barrier to pushing for change in the workplace. Their racialized experiences, however, were different from Haitians'. For instance, Glenda, the Salvadoran with TPS discussed in the last chapter, said that her English-speaking supervisor at the supermarket where she worked regularly discriminated against "Hispanic" and favored White and Black Americans. She tried to speak up, but her complaints went nowhere. Like Jorge, Glenda concluded that it was pointless to complain because Hispanics were not taken seriously at her job. Similarly, Oscar, the undocumented Central American construction worker introduced in chapter 3, felt that his African American manager hated Hispanic workers, gave them too much work, and mistreated them. On one occasion Oscar failed to complete the tasks he was given, and the supervisor told him he was fired and told him to leave. Oscar protested, explaining that he had been given more work than was possible in the time allotted, and he refused to leave. The supervisor eventually called the police, who arrived and affirmed that Oscar needed to leave the property since he had been fired. He eventually complied and was left feeling ashamed, defeated, and afraid to discuss the incident with anyone. When asked if he ever spoke to his coworkers about the problems he was having, he responded plainly, "No, I never talk about it with anybody, not even my kids. . . . I don't like to do it, because it dispirits the other person. . . . It certainly does for me, and I don't want to put that on them."

The racisms that immigrant workers confront are complex and also reflect ethnic and regional divisions that cross borders. Colonial histories carved national borders, which in turn fomented competition between immigrant communities in the United States, hardening existing racial hierarchies. Even within ethnic groups, animosities may emerge between cohorts of migrants, which can also split along ethnic and linguistic lines.[11] Leslie, an undocumented worker from Guatemala described in chapter 3, felt that Mexican supervisors mistreated her because she was Central American. She and her coworkers felt that "the Americans" were a lot nicer and more understanding. "Hispanics," she explained, "only have demands, and don't care how you are doing, they only want your labor and that's all." Consequently, she did not even bother approaching her supervisor to request changes.

Taken together, these tensions reflect differential forms of privilege and disadvantage that become deeply racialized as some immigrants and workers of color move into positions of power at work and others do not. These racialized divisions then become institutionalized and create cleavages even within racial groups.

LIMITS ON COLLECTIVE RESISTANCE FROM RACIAL TENSIONS AMONG WORKERS

Beyond employers fostering racial division, tensions among coworkers also threaten efforts to fight for better work conditions. Inadequate labor and employment law protections and the US immigration regime combine to disempower and divide workers. Racism, in its many forms, can also make collective action and solidarity among workers even more difficult. Workers' ability to join with each other across racial lines can create alliances against employers, but such efforts are often fraught.

In part, racial tension and division is baked into the low-wage labor force. Many workers described their work environments as segregated by race or national origin. In his workplace, said Julian, an undocumented Haitian warehouse worker we met in chapter 3, "Spanish workers received the most preferential treatment, followed by Africans, and finally Haitians at the bottom." In the diverse low-wage workplaces of metropolitan New York, tensions within the Black diaspora can make joint actions to push for change difficult. Merlet, a Haitian worker with lawful permanent residency, described her experience as a certified nursing assistant: "Black Americans hang out with other Black Americans" and "Jamaicans are with Jamaicans."[12] Given their different national origins, she shared, both groups "don't communicate with Haitians." It could be difficult to break through national-origin divisions, she explained. She felt the animosity to be pervasive, as coworkers would rebuff her even when she asked for help with minor things.

Julian also pointed to the racially stratified workplace as a barrier to collective resistance. He described his fellow delivery service workers as "divided into clans . . . Africans have their clan; Latinos have their clans." Language differences also prevented him from communicating or collaborating with other workers, who left him to finish tasks alone. As a result, he also often fell behind and was pressured by management to keep up. This treatment made Julian feel resentful and isolated: "While the Spanish is comfortably sitting [down], he is getting paid the hours. . . . I was [still] loading the container." Nevertheless, Julian felt that he would be "crazy" to report problems about the uneven workload and the unreasonable pace he was expected to keep up with. There was too much division among workers, even those from the same region of the world. "It is all about clan—it is divided into clans," he explained. With no "community of Haitians" with whom he could band together—there were only a handful of Haitians in his workplace—he felt alone.[13]

Despite having their unique regional and national-origin cultures and identities so often ignored by those who homogenized Central Americans, tensions within the Central American community also festered. These tensions also created significant barriers to speaking with a collective voice at work. For example, Miguel, a Salvadoran with temporary status who had worked as both a cleaner and in restaurants, talked about the competition between his fellow Central Americans, who vied for both hours and prime positions.[14] He recounted a tense situation between a Honduran and a Nicaraguan that ended in punches and eventual dismissal. "They were fighting for hours. . . . Their [supervisor] gave more to [one], and [the other] got mad, and they ended up in a fistfight." Much has been written about national-origin differences—and even regional distinctions—between Latinos that can be traced to tangible differences in the relationship of each Central American country to global power and US foreign policy. Despite the similar colonial and linguistic roots shared by Central American countries, political tensions often pervade social relations among the different countries and their diasporas.[15] Even though they are lumped together as a "Latino" monolith by their employers, customers, and patients, rivalries among Central Americans further fueled competition among workers fighting for their employer's favor.

Management's racist behavior and racial and ethnic tensions among coworkers in their US workplaces played out alongside current events in their origin communities. Workers were frequently burdened not only by their responsibilities in the United States but also by their transnational obligation to their community of origin. Workers considered all these factors as they weighed the necessity and costs of engaging in workplace resistance.

ORIGIN-COUNTRY REALITIES AS BARRIERS TO RESISTANCE

Current conditions and past realities shape how immigrant workers resist disempowerment at work and how they judge their work conditions in the United States using what Michael Piore calls their "dual frame of reference."[16] This peripheral vision, as Patricia Zavella also terms it, compounds the barriers to speaking up produced by a weak workers' rights regime (part 1) and immigration status challenges (part 2).[17] Conditions in their country of origin were often so severe that the workers with whom we spoke were primarily responsible for supporting their family members who had remained behind and depended on their monetary support for survival.[18]

Aside from their practical assessments of the relative severity of workplace precarity and consideration for the many people relying on their income, migrant workers also internalize a narrative that values them primarily as economic contributors to both the community they left behind and US society.[19] In a context where immigrants are valorized as "essential," narratives about ability to work hard and endure are compelling pathways to inclusion in an increasingly hostile political environment.[20] By contrast, complaining about workplace conditions and demanding higher wages, better protections, and parity with other workers negate this image of exceptionality. Workers often referenced the many people they left behind, whose well-being depended on their ability to keep their job and stay under the radar of government surveillance to avoid deportation. These deep feelings of obligation often neutralized workers' voices and raised their level of risk aversion.

Practically speaking, workers commonly compared their work experiences to alternatives in their countries of origin and almost always saw their conditions in the United States as preferable, even if challenging. In their eyes, they had to put up with bad treatment at work because they had suffered and invested a lot to get to the United States. Their investment was simply too great. For example, Gessica, a Honduran woman with temporary immigration status, explained that the poverty she fled gave her strength to confront the challenges she faced in New York.[21] For her, those challenges and the exhaustion of work were burdens she carried in the name of the family who now relied on her. After enduring domestic violence, losing her mother to cancer, and finally being able to bring her children to the United States, she had concluded that she just needed to "take care of" what she had. Pushing for more at her manufacturing job when she felt fortunate to have a job at all felt irrational.

Similarly, Maribel, described in chapter 2, left El Salvador in the throes of the civil war and eventually transitioned from temporary to permanent immigration status. She had come so far, she reasoned, while also frankly admitting her distrust of US government officials, even when they were trying to help her. It was hard to "shake" those feelings, she said. The experience of war in El Salvador, combined with living without permanent status in the United States for so long, "marks a person." Indeed, research has highlighted the lasting impact of precarious immigration status over time, even after immigrants achieve permanent and even citizen status.[22]

We observed these narratives across genders, though for the men we interviewed, notions of masculinity and caring for their family were also a powerful narrative.[23] Gustavo, a temporary Salvadoran migrant with only a ninth-grade education, worked in warehouse packing, at a supermarket, and in construction.[24] His focus was on producing the best work possible, and he took on the challenges at work with the family he left behind constantly in mind. His wife, kids, and grandchildren all remained in El Salvador. His daughters' successes, only possible because of his migration, were a major point of pride—one had become a professor, and two others were engineers. Because he was working in the United States, Gustavo said, "they have been able to do, let's say, what I could not have done [for them] there [in El Salvador]." Gustavo now had temporary immigration status and believed in the dignity of hard work, a central point of pride for him. He described Salvadorans as "workers," and said that "[we] should hold our heads up high, work hard, and move our people forward." Similarly, when asked whether he pushed back against rampant bad treatment at work, Dario, whom we met earlier, was focused instead on keeping his job. As an undocumented construction worker from Honduras, he explained, "we just keep working, you know, we need the job, we need to work." For these workers, and others we spoke with, the best way to fight back was to work as hard as possible under the conditions provided.

Aside from losing their job and putting the well-being of their families both here and abroad at risk, workers were also often genuinely afraid of being deported, given the rampant violence and economic devastation that would await them back in their country of origin. For Haitian workers, instability in Haiti, perilous journeys to get to the United States, and the ongoing impacts of a devastating earthquake in 2010 were barriers to taking on the risks of challenging their working conditions. Jessica, an undocumented worker who juggled various precarious gig jobs, shared that if she had to go back to Haiti, she was "going to have problems" because of the "gangs and thieves, riots, and protests" and "all of that."[25] For Jessica, staying in the United States was a matter of life and death. If she was deported, she feared that she and her child "might die" back in Haiti. Jessica did sometimes speak up at work but was cautious and judicious in how she did so. Similarly, Michaelle, a home care worker with temporary immigration status, felt that Haiti was too difficult after the earthquake to risk return.[26] Mexico, to which she first fled, was also plagued by crime, she lamented. Her top priority was to stay in the United States and keep her job, however difficult it was.

Returning to their country of origin was a daunting and potentially lethal prospect, despite the longing they all had for those they had left behind. These excruciating dilemmas stem from deep histories of racial inequality on top of workplace inequality in the United States and Haiti's global subordination today. Haitian American leaders echoed these sentiments as important narratives in their communities. One advocate and elected official emphasized that the historical isolation and abandonment Haiti experienced even before the earthquake and hurricanes remains a barrier to social change today.[27]

Further, the isolation and rejection Haitians endure within the Caribbean immigrant community in the United States deepens these inequities. A relatively weak civic infrastructure for Haitian immigrants compounds feelings of Haitian exclusion. Haitians have fewer powerful advocacy groups representing them than do other communities.[28] They are also newer migrants in New York: Their first arrivals date back to the Duvalier dictatorship era (1957–1986), and thus they must rely on churches and hometown associations as well as established groups like powerful unions.[29] Yet, within mainstream groups, organizing and education approaches often exclude, even if unintentionally, Haitian sensibilities and histories. One Haitian American labor leader offered a poignant example from immigrant outreach efforts: "Having a flyer with ... 'TPS' [temporary protected status] is not the best way [to reach out]." Instead, direct appeals to participate in the TPS program would garner negative attention for residents who were acutely aware of immigration surveillance in their communities. Seeking anonymity instead, many Haitian immigrants distanced themselves from such efforts, and public-facing outreach posters would be ripped down. Many Haitian community members instead sought online forums or web links for quieter forms of engagement.[30]

For Central Americans too, political instability, economic inequality, and the grueling migration journeys they had endured shaped their evaluations of their conditions at work in the United States and their willingness to fight publicly for improvements. Historical context matters. Central American civil wars and revolutions of the 1970s and 1980s marked a time when marginalized peoples fought for representation in government and redistribution of wealth from an oligarchic system that had concentrated wealth in the hands of a few. The United States, fearful of regional instability and the rise of communism, supported right-wing responses to these events and contributed to militarization, violence, and instability that still has reverberations today. These histories remained palpable for some respondents and marked not only their decision to leave their origin community but also the risks they were willing to assume in the United States. The United States occupies a contradictory space for Central American immigrants: It is a haven from the inequality and violence in Central America that has driven "ordinary people to leave their homes and put their lives at risk crossing deserts with smugglers" but in addition, "the US has long played a defining role" in "Central America's history of inequality and violence."[31] Thus, it is not particularly surprising that origin-country experiences and familial obligations inhibited some workers from challenging disempowerment at work.

The reverberations of origin-country realities and her difficult journey north were ever present for Belén, a childcare provider with temporary status.[32] Belén left war-torn El Salvador in the 1980s. The town had been bombarded, and her house was set on fire. She left her four small children behind with her mother and other family members, hoping that she could provide for them by sending them money from the United States. She did not want to subject her children and her mother to a dangerous clandestine journey north. Losing her job would have had wide ripple effects for Belén's family members in El Salvador. Her support helped her children attend universities in El Salvador that led all of them to promising careers as an architect, a business administrator, a lawyer, and an engineer. Even though she was now disabled from a car accident and a bout of cancer, she felt conflicted about returning to El Salvador, given the state of the country. She insisted, however, that if forced to go, she would choose dignity and return voluntarily, unwilling to risk detention. "I would not risk having police one day show up at my house to take me to jail.

... I have [trauma] from the war and will never return to that type of situation."

Such risk aversion took many forms and was a powerful force for many migrant workers. It was rooted deeply in the national histories that migrants from each Central American country recounted with surprising clarity. However, it is important to also mention the protest and organizing that marked these histories of resistance. Indeed, throughout the periods of repression in both Haiti and Central America, collective engagement always played an important role, though it is important not to romanticize these struggles as universally empowering for all who lived through them. For some of the migrant workers with whom we spoke, a sordid experience with labor advocacy in their origin country had affected their willingness to join a union in the United States. For example, college-educated Julian, when asked about union presence at his manufacturing job, was adamant that he did not know and did not *want* to know if one existed. "In Haiti, I actually got fired at one of my jobs because I was part of a union," he said. The idea of unions in the United States "frightens me" as a result, he said. The giant power imbalance between employers and low-wage workers was not lost on him. He knew that workers were "a tool for [employers'] gain" and that employers treated a worker as "an object" rather than a human being. But for Julian, trying to resist poor working conditions through collective action was a fool's errand, and he would not risk losing his job, especially given his undocumented status.

All of these barriers to improving work conditions and wages, however forbidding, are not absolute. As we have seen throughout the book, this is not just a story of powerful employers and powerless workers. Sometimes workers defy the odds, take the risks, and demand more respect and better wages and working conditions, as we discuss next.

Race and Colonial Legacies as Pathways to Challenging Worker Precarity

Although most workers we talked to felt that they had no chance to change things, some workers of all statuses creatively pushed back, either through individual action or with the support of their coworkers or advocates. Some sought common ground, which they found in many forms. Some workers joined with others through racial, cultural, or linguistic ties to find common ground in the workplace that propelled them to push for change, as many scholars have documented.[33] Some workers drew inspiration from their background in their origin country to push for better conditions for themselves or others. Race and national origins bred divisions for some but were critical sources of solidarity too.

ORIGIN-COUNTRY REALITIES AS PATHWAYS TO RESISTANCE

While many workers thought of their families first and foremost when they decided to lay low and not challenge the status quo at work, others had those same obligations to their loved ones in mind when they decided to resist the status quo. Despite the myriad challenges we have described that can dissuade workers from resisting business as usual, some low-wage immigrant workers found strategies and narratives for taking action in their own premigration experiences. Our data do not allow us to pinpoint a precise formula for determining when workers will draw on these histories to step up or step back. Instead, we draw from our interviews to acknowledge the importance of these past experiences that sometimes help migrant workers fight for justice.

The duality of motivations for taking action is a foundational reality in much of social movement scholarship. Social movements often rely on particular frames and narratives to mobilize their base and their allies.[34] Individuals also rely on psychological heuristics, drawing on broader cultures of action to become socialized into claims-making.[35] Past origin-country experiences can be symbolic touchstones and catalysts for change that give migrants the strength to step forward to demand change. For some who endured difficult pasts and harrowing journeys, there is too much to lose. Others find the strength and motivation to push for better in the United States because everything has already been lost.

Indeed, a number of workers we spoke to had fled political persecution, such as Nelda, an undocumented woman who fled El Salvador and settled in Long Island.[36] She had worked for a political party in

El Salvador, and many of her coworkers had been murdered. She did not wait around to be next. As the country descended into "political and economic chaos," her cousin helped connect her to a coyote. In 2004, she spent $8,000 and a harrowing twenty-seven days to make the trip. She went on to clean houses under brutal conditions for $7 per hour, then shifted to home health care. When asked what she thought of work conditions in the United States, she noted immediately the irony that an advanced country was replete with exploitation and impunity. "A lot of us had the thought that they respected the law . . . but we see that even US citizens are affected. . . . One of the things that really affected us . . . there's a lot of abuse." Recognizing the injustice, and despite the difficult conditions she had fled, Nelda was clear-eyed about the need to change and refused to romanticize work in the United States.

Workers also harbored a sense of survival and dignity from their origin-country experiences.[37] For example, Candelario, a Salvadoran worker with temporary immigration status, drew on his challenging experiences in El Salvador as inspiration for demanding his employers' respect in the United States.[38] Candelario had spent time in a Salvadoran prison, where standing up for himself had become a mode of survival. In his low-wage jobs in the United States, he called upon the strength he had gained living "under the law of the jungle" in prison. He went on to stand up to employers who were not paying what they had promised at his various construction jobs pouring cement and installing roofs and siding. Many other migrants, like Candelario, arrived in the United States with a sense of empowerment borne of the persecution they had faced in Central America for their organizing activity.[39] Having fled war and lethal military impunity that targeted activists, some felt that they had far less to lose in the United States.

Others drew inspiration from their country's revolutionary past. The Haitian Revolution (1791–1804) quite explicitly played a prominent role for many active Haitian migrants.[40] Jeff, an undocumented Haitian working in manufacturing and packing, drew inspiration from Jean-Jacques Dessalines, a key leader in the Haitian Revolution and the first leader of independent Haiti in 1805.[41] For Jeff, Haiti's revolutionary past was a source of inspiration to speak up and organize his coworkers, who often looked to him for leadership when things went wrong. Taking such action, he felt, was his calling. Jeff saw his fate as intimately tied to his coworkers' fate: "You hurt one of us, [you] hurt all of us." Invoking his origin country's past, he exclaimed, "I know I must revolt against injustice. We have Dessalines's blood running through our veins. We have the power of all our presidents within us. We won't be defeated without a fight." Jeff's account is consistent with other contemporary accounts about the role Haiti itself has played in inspiring "other enslaved peoples to envision and fight for Black utopias."[42] The history of their origin country still reverberates for Haitian migrant workers in metropolitan New York and helps them link the aims of achieving racial and economic justice.

SHOP-FLOOR SOLIDARITIES: RACIAL IDENTITIES AND SHARED LANGUAGE

The project of building racial solidarity is fraught. Organizers and advocates described the challenges of fomenting solidarity between Dominicans and Central American workers in a context where warehouse managers tended to be Dominican and leaned more heavily on Central Americans to "move faster."[43] Similarly, solidarity between Black migrants and African Americans was not at all a given, as labor ethnographies also show.[44] Haitian respondents felt that Black US-born workers perceived them and other immigrant workers as a threat, as willing to work for less pay.[45] Pan-ethnic cultural ties and even language are insufficient bonds. Employers can use racism to divide workers of color, even within the same racial, regional origin, or linguistic groups. And coworkers themselves bring their own "racial baggage" to these relationships.[46]

However, this was not always the case among the immigrant workers we interviewed. Some workers found solidarities along racial, coethnic, or linguistic lines, and sometimes country rivalries were overcome. For example, Stefano, the undocumented Haitian immigrant working in the manufacturing industry, told us that he developed solidarity with his (non-Haitian) Black African immigrant coworkers, who helped open doors for him. Social capital bonds were formed through job referrals and by lending a hand on the shop floor. And despite long-standing tensions on the island as well as in the United States, sometimes Haitian and Spanish-speaking workers were able to join forces. In an era when many Haitian immigrants are taking the dangerous passage through Latin American countries, some of those shared experiences became a basis for cooperation. Though most Haitians spoke Kreyòl as their dominant language, their transit journeys sometimes resulted in long stays throughout Latin America, and some had been able to learn Spanish. Some Haitians had even begun learning Spanish on the border with the Dominican Republic.[47] Similarly Central Americans sometimes built connections with other Latinos (with whom they were often grouped racially). Despite the erasure of their core national identities by outsiders, these connections also became a basis for exchange, including the sharing of information about workers' rights and how to enforce them. Though far from the norm, these cross-pollinations sometimes became a first step toward deeper solidaristic actions.

Shared national origin, however, was not a magic bullet for achieving solidarity, as countless labor ethnographies have confirmed.[48] Coethnic exploitation was rampant, and jealousies and competition abounded even among compatriots. Yet Haitians sometimes came together as Haitians. As previously mentioned, Roselaure, a naturalized Haitian fast-food worker, teamed up with her Haitian coworkers to jointly approach the restaurant owner to denounce a blatantly discriminatory manager. They demanded that management address the issue of Haitians more frequently being fired. "After two weeks, the owner of the restaurant had a big meeting and fired the accused assistant manager." Roselaure suspected that solidarity among the workers, as well as the threat of community solidarity, had strengthened the impact of their efforts. "There are a lot of Haitians in the community in which I work," Roselaure said. She believed that, "if word got out that they were mistreating Haitians," the community would have seen it as a problem and responded. Strength in numbers at work, and in the neighborhood, mattered for business.

Conclusion

The inadequacy of workers' rights protections under contemporary labor and employment laws and the US immigration regime are critical components of workplace injustice, but only part of the story.

Migrant workers discern the possibilities to come forward, alone or collectively, in a context of racial and ethnic tensions with deep roots in racist and postcolonial histories and presents. As seen in the accounts of the Haitian and Central American migrant workers we interviewed, the critical context for understanding these dynamics reaches far beyond the New York City metropolitan region. Histories of transatlantic slavery, colonialist interventions, and subsequent revolutions, not to mention ongoing US interventions in Latin America and the Caribbean, all remain salient factors for worker mobilization. White privilege has been baked into labor and immigration regimes in ways that still reverberate for low-wage immigrant workers of color today.

Racist supervisors and coworkers can make it even more difficult for workers to come forward. Far beyond individual experiences of prejudice, however, race must be read into the deep-seated systems of inequality in origin and destination countries. Poverty, strife, and underdevelopment in their countries of origin mark workers' perceptions of what they are willing to endure and risk. For those who have left loved ones behind, their role as an economic lifeline weighs heavily on them and makes them incredibly cautious. Yet these histories cut both ways. Race and national origin can also sometimes fuel worker resistance. Migrants' experiences in their country of origin can provide inspiration and the skills to seek restitution in their US workplace. Defying the structural odds, some Haitian and Central American workers did come forward to demand better treatment in the low-wage workplace, sometimes through formal complaints and other times through quieter forms of resistance. While racial tensions can isolate workers from each other, solidarity sometimes does break through.

Part 3 has laid bare the importance of looking beyond labor and immigration policy to understand the experiences of low-wage immigrant workers of color. Individual forms of racism and xenophobia matter—in the actions, for example, of prejudiced bosses and coworkers—but so do long-standing racisms and global geopolitical inequalities. These forces shape workers' perspectives on what is tolerable, what is possible, and what resources are at hand to use in fighting for better.

CONCLUSION 8

The voices of Haitian and Central American workers and their advocates have communicated that forces beyond their control keep their wages low, lock them into substandard working conditions, and minimize their opportunities to push for change. These forces are endemic to contemporary US labor and employment law, the immigration regime, and enduring racial inequalities. Centuries-long periods of the legalized slavery of Black people, colonial expansion to the Americas, and US imperialism in Latin America and the Caribbean have left long legacies of racism and xenophobia. These histories are key to understanding the experiences of low-wage immigrant workers today. There were (and still are) winners and losers in the global competition over land and resources. This book has aimed to reinsert these histories of the past (alongside accounts from the present) as a core aspect of understanding the realities of labor for low-wage immigrants of color. It has disentangled three vectors of the government's role: underregulating workers' rights (part 1); promoting an immigration regime that disempowers workers (part 2); and perpetuating legacies of racism and xenophobia (part 3).

Contemporary labor and employment laws in the United States privilege employers' interests over workers' interests. They place few restrictions on employer power given the default at-will employment system that makes it easy to lose a job in the low-wage economy. Basic protections do require employers to pay a minimum wage, to keep a safe workplace, to allow for collective efforts, and to avoid some forms of discrimination. Yet these protections are under-enforced and often lack "teeth." They do not meaningfully repair the harm to employees, nor do they deter employers from continuing to violate the law. Workplace violations become the normal way of doing business in many low-wage industries. Because unlawful retaliation against workers who do stand up for their rights individually or collectively is hard to prove, employers enjoy unfettered liberty in the low-wage workplace. Workers themselves, rather than government agencies, drive workers' rights enforcement efforts, even in the face of abundant barriers to coming forward.

The enactment and implementation of current US immigration policies further disempower low-wage immigrant workers. Exclusionary immigration policies push at-will employment insecurity into hyperdrive and make workers even more concerned about speaking out against mistreatment. These policies empower employers to act as private immigration law screeners at the hiring stage and add immigration consequences to the list of worries for workers considering coming forward to demand better. Exclusionary immigration policies also confuse workers about whether their immigration status curtails their rights as workers and sow worker isolation and divisions among workers.

The indignities workers experience at work reflect a racial hierarchy that places workers of color at the bottom. The racism and xenophobia generated from four hundred years of the transatlantic slave trade of Africans to the Americas, more than three hundred years of European colonial rule of Latin America and the Caribbean, and decades upon decades of policies that advantage White workers require significant intervention to eradicate and remedy. Even though discrimination on the basis of national origin or race is now formally prohibited under a variety of laws in the United States, these protections are insufficient and hard to access. The government's inadequate investment in ensuring employer compliance and worker redress perpetuates legacies of racism and xenophobia. Workers of color widely report anti-Black, anti-Latino, and anti-immigrant treatment, not only from supervisors but also from the customers, passengers, patients, and coworkers with whom they regularly interact in their low-wage jobs. Even low-wage workers who ascend the immigration status hierarchy and achieve permanent immigration status through naturalization or lawful permanent residency face racism and xenophobia at work. These narratives illuminate how racist supervisors can block worker resistance from within, racial tensions among workers can limit collective action, and origin-country realities can discourage workers from pushing for improvements at work.

The workers we interviewed also reminded us that they were not just disempowered victims of a powerful structure that advantaged profit-seeking employers. Despite the odds, immigrant workers of color do sometimes resist. Their resistance is sometimes subtle, sometimes confrontational. Workers are not always successful in achieving the goals of their resistance efforts, but their willingness to resist must be recognized all the same.

Workers were creative and sometimes found ways to push back without risking their jobs. Engaging in "persistent nudging" (chapter 2), for example, allowed some workers to push for change without rocking the at-will boat too much. Some workers were able to topple barriers to bringing formal legal claims to courts or government agencies by working with a community group, worker center, or labor union. Some came together, despite their linguistic, racial, or national-origin differences, around their shared experiences of unpaid wages. Immigration status was a unifier in some contexts where workers saw their shared reality of undocumented status or temporary protected status as a rallying call. And such efforts were not always segregated: Haitians and Central Americans sometimes came together around their shared interests to come forward and challenge employer power. These rare successes in the face of major disadvantages are worth highlighting because they highlight the potential for worker agency and show that workers are not passive victims. Nevertheless, that does not change the reality that they lack power in the low-wage workplace and face widespread disrespect and substandard treatment.

Our study suggests fruitful avenues for future research and has a number of practical implications for the government leaders, workers, worker organizations, and advocacy groups that aim to level the playing field for low-wage workers. The study has implications for employers too. "High Road" employers can work to find ways to improve wages and working conditions while still meeting their profit-making goals.[1] They can use human resource practices that are responsive to employee voice to improve the culture of their workplaces for the benefit of all. They can cultivate managerial approaches that are more consultative and that foster dignity and respect in the workplace. We saw elements of this approach in chapter 2's worker stories about supervisors who listened to workers' concerns and resolved problems that were bubbling up rather than giving them the runaround. The difficulty in scaling up reliance on voluntary employer behavior, however, only makes realizing worker rights all the more elusive.

Crafting a Research Agenda

Choosing to center worker narratives in service of a bottom-up epistemology has allowed us to better understand how low-wage immigrant workers navigate the power structures that shape their experiences. Future research could build on this foundation to address some of the limitations of our qualitative approach. This research focuses on two migrant groups (Haitians and Central Americans) chosen initially as two of the largest groups receiving temporary protected status. Because of the relatively large size of these regional origin groups, we were able to meaningfully compare them by other immigration status categories (undocumented and permanent) in order to gain insight into how immigration policy had shaped their experiences. There are also other TPS beneficiaries, such as immigrants from Nepal, Sudan, and Syria, whose benefits have lapsed and TPS beneficiaries whose immigrant experience is too nascent to fit the period of our study—for example, Venezuelan and Ukrainian immigrants. These groups have particular racial dynamics, colonial histories, and geopolitical relations that merit separate analyses, even as their experiences take place within the broader context of the global dynamics of White supremacy, capitalism and xenophobia. In undertaking the ongoing comparative work across places and groups that is needed, scholars must take into account the specific histories of origin communities and destination contexts in each case. Extant studies such as ours can become a foundation for theorizing new empirical endeavors.

In focusing on the New York City region, our study complements other studies of Central Americans living in California (San Francisco, Los Angeles) and Washington, DC, and the rich history of Haitian immigrants in destinations such as Florida. Each of these communities reveals specific settlement patterns and local dynamics. In the

New York City metropolitan region, we have been able to sample migrants across neighborhood type (Long Island, New York City boroughs, New Jersey commuter ring). Given the relatively higher rates of union density and a rich collection of immigrant and other advocacy groups and legal services, not to mention relatively labor- and immigrant-friendly state and local policies, our focus on this region produced a "best-case scenario" for this study. The hyperdiversity of New York also provided an ideal context in which to understand how workers of color experience racism in a traditional immigrant destination. Additional research should consider the specific challenges for immigrant workers in other civic and political contexts, in particular industries, and within different demographic makeups.[2]

This book makes an important contribution to the long-standing focus on the documented-undocumented binary. By highlighting immigrant workers with temporary status, we have shown that possession of temporary "documented" status does not entirely ease precarity at work and in fact disempowers workers in unique ways. In some circumstances, undocumented workers who were not registered with the government felt more secure than temporary workers, who were under government surveillance and more easily deportable as a result of their status. We are not the first scholars to move beyond the documented-undocumented binary. Ming Hsu Chen's work on the "citizenship spectrum" offers a number of other categories (employment-based visas, international students, refugees) that also deserve attention.[3] Arguably, examining other TPS-like categories of liminal status are likely to generate similar results.[4] These categories include individuals who receive temporary work authorization while their asylum applications are either pending or flowing from one of the many forms of prosecutorial discretion that Shoba Wadhia outlines.[5] Long-standing work on the labor precarity built into temporary foreign worker programs, especially in Canada and the United Arab Emirates, could also inform efforts to expand US programs.[6] And the many studies on the Deferred Action for Childhood Arrivals (DACA) program provide important areas for continued research on the challenges of liminal status.[7] Our analysis reveals immigration status as a central—but not sole—source of worker precarity and disempowerment.

This book has focused primarily on labor, immigration, ethno-racial categories, and colonial histories. Yet these are neither workers' only identities nor the only power structures in which they are enmeshed. Notably, gender and sexuality often shape the kinds of degradation migrants experience at work and the barriers to contesting them. Although our study has illuminated these dynamics throughout, a study focused primarily through a gendered lens is warranted. Similarly, other forms of difference are likely to be salient for certain migrant groups, such as religion and caste. Research on Afro-Latinidad and Indigeneity within Central American migrant groups offers an additional window into the intersectional experiences of migrants, such as Garifuna Hondurans or Maya-speaking Guatemalans.[8]

Finally, our interview approach has provided critical insight often missed by census, administrative, and even survey data. However, interviews are not labor ethnographies that provide critical observational insights about a particular workplace. Our work is deeply informed by rich migrant worker ethnographies such as those produced by Ruth Gomberg-Muñoz, Vanesa Ribas, and Rocío Rosales.[9] More in-depth workplace ethnographies are key to gaining insight into coworker relations and employer strategies. Continued work with employers, even at the expense of not being able to speak with workers at the same firm, will continue to be important as well.

Qualitative work is essential to unpacking, as we have done here, how power, race, and the law operate in the low-wage immigrant workplace. Nonetheless, more studies like the ambitious three-city survey of unregulated work undertaken by Annette Bernhardt and her colleagues are important to situate the relative importance of key factors in shaping worker precarity and attempts at labor power.[10] Such work requires innovative sampling techniques and an on-the-ground data collection effort that cannot be replicated by the canonical telephone survey approach used by major labor force surveys. Similarly, innovative estimation techniques using broad-scale national data that include liminal categories like TPS, such as the American Community Survey, are crucial to conducting targeted comparisons across national-origin groups and gender, and across a range of work outcomes.[11] Qualitative work will help unpack the mechanisms driving these key findings, including the highly correlated effects of race and immigration status and industry.[12] It will also unpack the differential impacts of TPS on the labor force outcomes of women versus men. Only then can we enact the incremental and transformational measures needed to offset employers' outsized power in the low-wage workplace and redress the many injustices and indignities that it generates.

Policy Implications

LABOR AND EMPLOYMENT LAW REFORM

Entrenched government mechanisms disempower workers in the low-wage workplace. Our study suggests that bold actions will be needed to offset the deep inequality of bargaining power between employers and workers in low-wage jobs. In what follows, we describe the implications of our study for legal reform and advocacy movements. While a full reconceptualization of state power is beyond the scope of this book, we highlight key implications that flow from our analysis.

Expand Who Has Workers' Rights A key way to empower workers would be to expand the number of low-wage workers protected by workers' rights laws and the number of companies subject to collective bargaining and workers' rights requirements. There are some experiments afoot, mostly at the state level, to reduce exclusions from workers' rights laws and extend workers' rights requirements to more companies. Many of these efforts are connected to union and worker center organizing efforts. For example, a major goal of the National Domestic Workers Alliance has been making domestic workers eligible for workers' compensation. Legal reforms could end New Deal–era exclusions of agricultural laborers and domestic workers.

As we have seen in this book, some low-wage workers lack workers' rights (or think they do) because they do not meet the definition of covered "employees" under a particular labor and employment law statute at the federal, state, or local level. They may work informally, are classified (or misclassified) as "independent contractors," or fall into some exception. In 2019, California's Assembly Bill 5, legislation popularly known as the "gig worker" bill, narrowed the definition of independent contractor status and expanded the number of workers eligible for employee rights under California law.

Another common feature of the low-wage economy is the use of intermediary third-party companies, such as temporary staffing agencies or franchisees. Low-wage immigrant workers in warehousing, care work, and other jobs often go through a temporary staffing agency or other third-party intermediary to access a job. Their direct employer is the intermediary, not the entity where they perform their work. Being directly hired through another kind of third-party intermediary rather than the lead company, such as a subcontractor or franchisee, also leads to confusion over joint employers. These intermediary companies operate as "buffers" that shield well-resourced lead companies from having bargaining obligations and liability under labor and employment laws. Buffering can foster wage and hour violations as underresourced intermediary companies cut corners on legal compliance to remain competitive.[13]

To increase corporate accountability, it will be necessary to expand joint employer law. The proposed Protecting the Right to Organize Act of 2021 would do just that. Some state joint employer law reforms are afoot. New York and a few other states, for example, are proposing bills that would hold franchisors jointly liable along with their franchisees. New York's proposed bill would make food restaurant franchisors responsible "for ensuring that its franchisee complies with" various employment and worker safety laws.[14] These efforts aim to remove the franchisee as a compliance buffer, thereby acknowledging that powerful companies "have a superior ability to offset rising wage inequality and to improve working conditions in the fast-food industry."[15] This can matter when workers are trying to recover lost wages from a poorly resourced intermediary company,[16] or when workers or their organization are trying to pressure the entity that holds the purse strings and ultimate power over wages and working conditions.[17]

Increase the Volume of Workers' Rights Despite efforts to offset the inequalities in bargaining power, New Deal–era labor law has failed to address power inequalities between employers and their low-wage employees. Indeed, the National Labor Relations Act (NLRA) of 1935 has been roundly critiqued as "an elegant tombstone"[18] and a "doomed dinosaur"[19] that cannot keep pace with the power of multinational corporations and post-industrial realities in the low-wage US economy. Not only does New Deal–era labor law limit the ability of labor unions to organize large sectors of the low-wage workforce, but one of the fundamental reasons for weak workers' rights protections is the US at-will employment system. Fear of job loss means low-wage workers remain relatively compliant no matter how degradingly or unlawfully they are treated. Even if an employer is not firing anyone, our interviews revealed that workers' concern about losing their job can motivate them to accept dehumanizing and substandard conditions.

Proposed reincarnations of the NLRA could facilitate collective worker power and offset the government-supported employer power we reference throughout the book. One proposal, for example, advocates flipping the default status quo to make all workplaces unionized.[20] A project of the Labor and Worklife Program at Harvard Law School engaged more than seventy individuals to produce a broad roadmap for radical labor law reform. One of its main tenets promotes NLRA reforms that would facilitate bargaining between unions and industries.[21] Bargaining at the sectoral level rather than organizing firm by firm could offset employer power, especially in low-wage industries where unionization is most difficult.[22] This proposal could allow labor unions to organize companies en masse and improve conditions for whole industries at a time of massive corporate power. Some proposals advocate reforms that would promote a more cooperative, less adversarial model. These kinds of reforms could allow for "a broader range of participation and representation processes, including workplace committees, establishment-level councils, and worker representation on corporate boards of directors."[23]

State and local legal instruments could facilitate new forms of worker representation at the industry level. Congress could amend the NLRA to considerably reduce the NLRA's sweeping preemptive effect. Currently, the NLRA preempts all state and local laws that "arguably" touch on something the NLRA protects or prohibits.[24] Creatively working within these constraints, some states are experimenting with different kinds of industry-wide models. New York's proposed Nail Salon Minimum Standards Act, for example, would create a worker council with nail salon workers, government, and business represented. The council would have the power to recommend statewide pricing frameworks that could offset "the race to the bottom that's pushing salon owners to cut corners and wages."[25] The nail salon initiative emerged from an organizing effort involving advocates for labor, racial, and immigrant justice in this low-wage industry.

There are many ideas for major reform of the NLRA that would radically transform it or even throw it out altogether. But some scholars caution against scrapping all of the NLRA, noting that the problem lies not in how it is written but rather the extreme hostility with which courts and agencies have interpreted it.[26] Others, such as the general counsel of the AFL-CIO, redirected the focus away from legal reformers by advocating instead "that the task of constructing a new labor law falls to the labor movement itself."[27]

On the whole, legal measures that strengthen labor unions, including their ability to secure organizational funding, could offset employer freedom to fire workers at will. Collective bargaining agreements between employers and unions are a powerful antidote to employers' at-will power. These contracts typically contain a "just cause" clause that protects employees from unjustified discipline or terminations. Unlike the at-will environment, which allows employers to fire or discipline workers for no reason at all, these contracts require employers to have a just and fair reason to discipline or fire an employee. In practice, these contractual provisions are often interpreted to require that the employer have reasonable rules and adequately warn employees of the consequences of rule infractions. The rules must have some connection to the work at hand, and violations must be properly investigated before disciplinary measures are taken. Any discipline that does result from an investigation must be proportional to the level of seriousness of the offense and the past record.

Collective bargaining agreements, however, can only go so far, as they cover a tiny portion of the private-sector workforce. In 2022, only 6.8 percent of private-sector salaried workers were represented by a union, and that share was far lower in low-wage businesses, such as clothing stores (1.3 percent), and low-wage industries such as restaurant and food service (1.8 percent).[28] Legislation aimed at making it harder for employers to fire or discipline employees would help offset employer power and the injustices that flow from it. Scholars and advocates have long called for new legislation that would offset employers' at-will termination power for all employees, even those not subject to a collective bargaining agreement, but new federal legislation is unlikely in this area.[29] Wrongful discharge protections are often considered to be in the states' police powers purview, although New York City's limitations on terminations of fast-food workers are currently being litigated on preemption grounds. If the law survives judicial review, New York City fast-food workers will be terminated only for misconduct, following an unsatisfactory job performance, or for a "bona fide economic reason."[30] Currently, three subfederal jurisdictions have wrongful discharge statutes that require just cause for firing an employee—Montana, Puerto Rico, and the Virgin Islands. Some require the payment of severance pay as a disincentive for at-whim terminations. The expansion of wrongful termination statutes "would bring US employment termination law in line with that of all other nations with developed legal systems."[31]

Enforce Workers' Rights More Effectively Expanding the number of workers who receive protections and the number of companies held responsible, while also creating new protections, amounts to just words on paper in the absence of compliance or a lack of enforcement when compliance falters. Underregulation is both a matter of not having sufficient protections on the books and not making those "rights real" through adequate follow-through enforcement of those protections.[32] A reform agenda to better enforce protections would need to be comprehensive and well resourced. One challenge to better enforcement of protections is the system's complete reliance on worker claims-making, a private mechanism of enforcement that is often untenable for low-wage workers. Instead, a greater focus on public enforcement—and especially collaborative, tripartite co-enforcement approaches—is needed.[33] Our analysis suggests a few areas of consideration, many of which scholars and some government agencies have proposed.

More resources are needed. Government agencies' "light enforcement," which we described in chapter 2, is in large part a matter of insufficient resources. For example, as of April 2023, the US Department of Labor's Wage and Hour Division had fewer than 800 employees charged with regulating 9.8 million workplaces across the United States.[34] There are similar resource limitations at the federal Occupational Safety and Health Administration and the Equal Employment Opportunity Commission.[35] These agencies are also often the only line of defense in jurisdictions where state and local oversight is practically absent. Moreover, the organizational design of these agencies, their relation to each other, and their state counterparts deserve strategic thinking about how to move away from their currently fragmented and labyrinthian nature.[36] The workers in our study had difficulty navigating the thicket of agencies. How could they be restructured to make the organizational design more intuitive and accessible to workers on the ground?

The underfunded and fragmented nature of labor and employment agency design makes strategic enforcement efforts, meant to target big actors and widespread lawbreaking, even more important. Even underfunded government entities can go after employers in a targeted way if they choose to, as many advocates and scholars have long championed.[37] Agencies, along with district attorneys and state attorneys, can use their discretion to take strategic, higher-impact actions.[38] In February 2023, for example, the Manhattan district attorney announced the creation of the Worker Protection Unit, which will bring legal actions in response to companies that are "taking advantage of our most vulnerable populations, including low-income and undocumented New Yorkers, and abusing power imbalances to line their pockets."[39] To address the fragmentation that hampers enforcement, multiple agencies can work together. For instance, licensing agencies, local prosecutors, and the DOL can effectively work together to tackle issues like independent contractor misclassification.[40]

Reducing barriers to workers' complaints and collective activity is key to advancing proactive compliance and enforcement of the law. A first-order reform is to make changes in a way that enables workers to know what their rights are as employees. Workers' rights information should be made easily available to workers. Agency outreach efforts and public information campaigns can be helpful on this front. A rule proposed in 2011 by the National Labor Relations Board—and invalidated by two federal courts of appeal soon after—would have required employers to place a poster about employees' right to take collective activity in a "conspicuous" place.[41] This kind of information requirement for employers is a step in the right direction, as is requiring employers to give workers information about where and how to file a claim.[42]

Governmental information campaigns can help, but so can intermediaries, or "brokers"—entities that can help bridge the gap between an aggrieved worker and the bureaucratic enforcement process.[43] Unions are key, but outside the unionized workforce, other advocates, such as lawyers, matter too.[44] Besides lawyers, worker centers have also played this role.[45] Any reforms that can bolster these intermediaries' ability to connect workers to rights enforcement would help to break down these barriers. Changing the rules around the Legal Services Corporation (LSC) program so that undocumented workers as well as low-income workers with labor and employment law grievances can receive free legal representation would be a prudent reform to better uphold the rights of all workers.

Another way to enforce workers' rights more effectively is to increase grants and funding for chronically underresourced worker centers that assist in government co-enforcement efforts.[46] Scholars have chronicled the many successes of this model.[47] Worker centers have helped workers find their way to government enforcement agencies and shown them how to stay engaged and empowered throughout the often lengthy and confusing agency enforcement process. Worker centers are based on many different organizational models, but on the whole they are a key way to connect government enforcement initiatives to low-wage workers, who are often the ones experiencing the most egregious abuses of their rights as workers.

A move toward agency-driven measures can mitigate the reliance on worker claims. Although worker claims can still be the spark, when agencies leverage a small number of complaints to identify problems endemic to an industry, and then take the lead in holding employers in that industry responsible, unscrupulous actors "take notice."[48] The Bureau of Field Enforcement of the California Department of Labor Standards Enforcement, for example, has been critical in carrying out strategic investigations—in partnerships with worker organizations—that aid in creating a "culture of labor law compliance."[49] Simultaneously, the time it takes to process a traditional worker-driven claim must be reduced by orders of magnitude.

Finally, the "cost of doing business" must reflect a system that is serious about upholding worker rights. For example, Benjamin Sachs proposes that "immediate injunctive relief, and robust damages" would deepen incentives for employers to comply with the law.[50] The more employers comply with legal requirements as a regular way of doing business, the less need there is for workers to come forward to enforce their rights in the workplace. The multilayered oversight of federal, state, and local agencies can strengthen this culture and scaffold the burden on vulnerable workers, including immigrants.[51]

IMMIGRATION LAW REFORM

Labor and employment laws do not exist in isolation. In addition to fixes within labor and employment law, immigration law needs an overhaul to offset its deep-seated injustices and the employer-employee power imbalances that flow from it. Comprehensive immigration reform, which could eliminate immigration status hierarchies, would be a bold intervention in this regard. Although comprehensive immigration reform is a formidable goal in the existing political climate, it is nevertheless a key way to offset the power imbalances that have downstream impacts on the low-wage workplace.[52] Immigration reform would also send a powerful message to states and localities that, by doubling down on anti-immigrant measures, have emboldened the exploitation of immigrant workers. Florida is the latest in a long line of states that have not only re-entrenched the role of employers in immigration enforcement by mandating the use of E-Verify but also added criminal penalties for unauthorized workers.[53] Besides an overhaul of immigration law that would mitigate the political agenda of restrictionist lawmakers, other shifts are also needed.

Beyond strengthening existing protections, new immigrant worker protections are needed, and employer sanctions must be rescinded. In general, employers can legally opt to not hire noncitizen workers who lack permanent work authorization. Concerns over being audited or sanctioned if they fall out of compliance may lead employers to avoid the risk of hiring workers with expired employer authorization documents.[54] Given this inherent dilemma, temporary workers should have the same discrimination protections as permanent workers.

While the devolution of enforcement roles to private actors may seem desirable as a cost-saving measure or as a way to curb the availability of unauthorized work, it comes at a cost.[55] It also empowers lawbreaking employers to use immigration enforcement, or the threat thereof, as a way to silence their employees and bolster a compliant workforce. For law-abiding employers, enforcing immigration law can create confusion and delays that disadvantage workers with temporary status, who rely on continual reauthorizations of EADs. The expectation that employers will play this role can also confuse workers who face egregious violations of their wage, health and safety, and other rights about whether they make claims to the government to expose workplace rights abuses. Removing employers from immigration enforcement would take a key arrow out of their quiver of power.[56] At the very least, Congress could reform the process around EADs to make it automated and immediately available to employees and employers when an immigrant's EADs have been reauthorized.

The decriminalization of immigration infractions would also recalibrate the power relationship between employers and their undocumented workforce. Local law enforcement involvement in immigration regulation and penalties that can land a worker in prison are powerful disincentives to come forward about workplace degradation or violations of labor and employment laws. Some states have amplified federal criminalization of immigrants by creating new identity theft laws that increase criminal penalties for workers. We must foster reforms that conceive of undocumented workers as "laborers," not "criminals."[57] Law and society scholars have pointed to the criminalizing nature of immigrant law[58] and the "legal violence" it inflicts on immigrant communities.[59] While such laws are acutely damaging for undocumented workers, they also have an impact on other "more documented" low-wage immigrant workers, who are disproportionately subjected to surveillance and feel that their temporary status is unreliable and time delimited. The stress on undocumented individuals also has wide-ranging mental health impacts on their friends, relatives, and coworkers who worry about them and adjust their own behaviors to keep them safe.[60]

Finally, while comprehensive immigration reform, a major amendment to IRCA, and decriminalization initiatives are uphill battles, legislative interventions could find smaller-scale ways to better protect undocumented workers and workers with temporary status. As one example, federal and subfederal governments could legislate a "*Hoffman* fix" that would reinstate monetary remedies for undocumented employees who experience labor and employment law violations. Although courts have widely concluded that undocumented workers have "employee" rights, some workers and employers continue to see undocumented status as a rights-altering condition when it comes to rights in the workplace. In response to *Hoffman*, some states, such as California and New York, have added explicit protections to their labor statutes directed at undocumented employees' rights in the workplace.

REDRESSING RACISM AND REFORMING CIVIL RIGHTS LAWS

Workers' narratives underscore what many scholars and advocates have long argued: The civil rights framework does not go far enough to address racism and xenophobia in the workplace. While strides toward progress have been made and US law no longer explicitly differentiates by race, there is much more to be done. Cultural representations, institutional mechanisms (including labor and employment laws and immigration laws), public policies, and other norms continue to reinforce a system that ensures the continued exploitation of immigrant workers of color.[61] Tracing the lasting impacts of historical racisms and colonial legacies is imperative, even if traditional theories and tools of social stratification research struggle to measure—and thus to center—their role in contemporary forms of inequality. Doing so requires moving away from a purely individualized conception of discrimination and thinking more historically.[62] For example, work by Raj Chetty and his colleagues has documented the real costs of these long-standing racial inequalities across the life course and generation.[63]

While radical transformation is necessary to root out the legacies of racialized labor hierarchies, improvements to the Civil Rights Act of 1964 could meaningfully address some of the problems raised by the workers interviewed for this book. Title VII of the Civil Rights Act and several acts that followed prohibit discrimination based on "protected categories" such as race, color, sex, national origin, age (over forty), disability, and genetic information. These laws put important legal restrictions on employers. Given that racism and xenophobia persist in the low-wage workplace, however, a radical rethinking of the civil rights framework is called for. Our analysis points to a few themes that are worth considering.

First, discrimination law does little to recognize or remedy the realities facing workers of color in the era of "race-neutral" and dog-whistle racism.[64] Reforming discrimination law, however, is a tall order. Some have advocated for adding more "protected categories," such as weight or caste. Others have called for rewriting the legislation in a way that acknowledges that discrimination and harassment are not encountered only by individuals of certain race, sex, or national-origin categories or some other protected category. Jamillah Bowman Williams, for instance, uses the unique discrimination against Black women as an example of the need for civil rights law to move beyond isolating protected statuses into discrete categories.[65] Williams proposes a "more flexible approach . . . that will force lawyers, law students, and judges to see the whole person rather than picking apart a person's identity in such a way that minimizes experiences of discrimination."[66]

Second, reformers should find ways to make it easier to prove that prohibited employment discrimination has occurred. Dated requirements to prove the smoking gun of a racist manager or coworker reflect willful ignorance of how racism works today.[67] Reformers must balance making it easier to prove discrimination with not opening the door so wide as to let in potentially spurious claims. Proposals to reduce the proof burden in part stem from acknowledgment that a large swath of workplace discrimination is implicit rather than explicit.[68] Scholars have debated the extent to which legal inventions can curb implicit discrimination.[69] Meanwhile, a number of proposals have emerged that aim to aid employee plaintiffs in these cases. One reform urges that victim perspectives rather than the "objectively reasonable" perspective should have more sway in determining whether discrimination has occurred.[70] Another proposes altering the burden of proof that each party must carry.[71] A reduced burden for plaintiffs would steepen the incentives for employers to take measures to avoid discrimination and bias claims.

Some organizers and reformers call for state and local expansions of civil rights frameworks in the absence of federal action.[72] For example, California advocates have recently won protections against caste discrimination,[73] and New York City prohibits employers from engaging in hairstyle discrimination.[74] Some have called for additional protections to better protect workers' dignity concerns, many of which are tied to forms of individual prejudice and difference. Unions have worked to integrate these innovative standards into their collective bargaining agreements. David Yamada has led calls for a private cause of action against workplace bullying as a way of furthering dignified treatment at work.[75] Such protections would not require workers to prove that the intent was based on membership in a protected class, such as race, sex, or religion. Some states have proposed model bills, but none have been ratified to date. Anti-bullying protections would go beyond existing anti-harassment protections because they would apply even when there is no identifiable connection between the bullying and a worker's "protected status."

These proposals view pressure from unions, worker centers, and communities as key levers to pushing for less bias and more dignity at work.[76] César Rosado Marzán, for example, concludes that "the worker center, its resources, and the perceived protections of work law, which the worker center let the workers know about, contributed to successful dignity restorations where workers rose from subordination."[77] As Rosado Marzán argues, some efforts to push back may not fully restore a worker's wages, but there can be critical dignity wins as workers push back against employer "dehumanization or infantilization." These claims in turn can become, Rosado Marzán contends, effective ways to frame coalitional worker campaigns across a range of statutory protections.[78]

The Agenda for Organizing to Advance Reform

Laws do not enact or implement themselves. Radical legal reform is necessary but insufficient, and it is also unlikely unless the government has the political will to enact and enforce that agenda. Current political conditions and the power that corporations hold make legal reforms in favor of workers difficult to imagine. To get there, a robust social movement that includes labor, immigration, and racial justice advocates will be needed. Too often, racial justice and immigrant rights are seen as tangential to the core issues facing working people today when in fact they are central issues.[79] Labor unions, an important institutional actor in progressive politics, could play a leading role in bringing such a coalition together to enact meaningful policy change on behalf of immigrants and workers of color, but it would take a "racial reckoning" and deep commitment to immigrant and civil rights goals.[80]

The labor movement has made a long transition toward "total person unionism"—that is, treating a range of policy issues as core to the working-class struggle.[81] A sordid history of racist and nativist practices in the labor movement has kept—and continues to keep—immigrants and workers of color out of membership and leadership positions.[82] AFL founder Samuel Gompers, for example, famously rallied for immigration restrictions, in particular Chinese (and Japanese) exclusion and what would become the 1921 and 1924 national-origin quotas. And while his solidarity with Black workers has become a core issue for the AFL-CIO, the labor federation's stands on issues of racial equity and justice have been marked by significant compromise.[83] The history of racial politics in the labor movement warns that progress does not always march forward with time: the anti-communist hysteria of the Cold War, the racism and xenophobia that emerged during recessionary periods, the calls within the farmworker movement to deport undocumented workers, and the complicity of the nation's largest labor federation (AFL-CIO) in the creation of IRCA's employer sanctions in 1986 are all part of labor unions' past, with legacies that still linger.[84]

There is evidence of movement toward viewing racial and immigrant justice as a core worker issue. The AFL-CIO has placed these issues on its national agenda, though the building trades federation has remained relatively silent.[85] Both the AFL-CIO and other major non-affiliate unions have spoken out—even if sometimes ambivalently—on issues of police brutality and the Black Lives Matter movement, and Black labor leaders have long centered race in the labor federation's agenda.[86] Meanwhile, the influence of police unions and immigration enforcement officers continues to foster major debate.

Responding to pressure from organizers of color, in 2017 the AFL-CIO appointed the AFL-CIO Labor Commission on Racial and Economic Justice, partially in response to the 2014 shooting in Ferguson, Missouri, of Mike Brown, a young Black man whose lifeless body was left to lie in the street for four hours. This powerful and devastating reminder of the ever-present stamp of racial inequality in the United States became a call to action for many in the labor movement and beyond. That call has been reinforced repeatedly by subsequent killings, including George Floyd's murder at the hands of a White police officer in Minneapolis and the endless reports of migrant deaths in detention and along the southern US border.

Many union locals on the ground have hired organizers to do the work of incorporating race and immigration issues into labor rights campaigns. Indeed, unions have been a key factor in disrupting White identity politics within the labor movement and in the broader communities where labor organizations operate.[87] These efforts, however, are not a panacea. Though it has become increasingly clear that class solidarity alone does not bind the working class, maintaining racial inequality remains an effective tool for building employer power and attempting to limit worker power. Efforts to address the legacies of racism within and beyond the labor movement and beyond unions and worker centers have had to not only invest in training this rapidly diversifying and increasingly immigrant workforce but also shift to new forms of organizing that can reach the vast swaths of the low-wage workforce among whom unionization is unlikely to ever take hold in significant ways.[88]

These are not simply reflections on the state of labor and immigrant politics in the United States. Our respondents often talked at length about the fractured solidarity on the shop floor and the competition and division between racial and national-origin groups. For the labor movement, one aspect of building worker solidarity across racial, cultural, and ethnic differences will continue to be labor education, for both union members and working families more generally. Providing such education is a way to build solidarity by enabling union members to learn about historical realities for workers of color, which may lead them to question the stereotypes propagated by media tropes around the inherent criminality of some racialized communities. In doing so, these organizational spaces challenge divisive narratives about the exceptionality of certain immigrants historically compared to today[89] and the "culture of poverty" plaguing Black communities.[90] Both narratives pathologize immigrant and other communities of color while ignoring the structural factors that have allowed social inequality to widen. While worker centers have traditionally been expert at organizing workers around racial-ethnic identity and solidarity, they alone cannot shoulder this burden. Their distinct organizational missions, memberships, and legal frameworks limit their reach and necessitate the ongoing support of unions to enact these sweeping reforms.

Organizers we spoke to over the last decade noted the importance of embracing these histories, even if unflattering. However, on-the-ground training of labor leaders, who in turn translate these new labor values to their locals, takes time and resources. Groups and convenings like the National Labor Leadership Institute, the Union Labor Institute, the UCLA Labor Summer, and the Labor Notes Conference have long pushed workers to confront the blunt realities of workplace inequality and recognize the particular burdens that immigrant workers of color shoulder. These efforts not only build community but help neutralize the divide-and-conquer strategies used by pro-business and right-of-center political forces that oppose any efforts to confront our country's racist and xenophobic past. Immigrant rights leaders have worked to turn this narrative around, realizing that all these battles need to be fought, and "that it should be us [the labor movement] that's organizing."[91] The political strategy needed to achieve these political reforms is the subject of other important volumes.[92] However, the parting lesson of this book, informed by the everyday lives of immigrant workers of color, is that these reforms will need to happen across the variety of domains that continue to shape the low-wage workplace.

METHODOLOGICAL APPENDIX

The Goals of the Study

While labor, race, and immigration scholars are often writing in separate silos, our multidisciplinary team of authors has woven these three fields together. This trifecta approach is critical to reveal the ways in which power operates through the labor, immigration, and race dynamics that intersect in the experiences of low-wage workers. It also allows us to connect the realities facing low-wage immigrant workers of color in the United States today to the varied legacies of transatlantic slavery and colonialist interventions in Latin America and the Caribbean. Our goal is to bring the sociology of immigration and race perspectives to labor scholarship, while also bringing a labor studies perspective to studies of immigration and race.

This study focused on the experiences of two of the largest groups of temporary protected status (TPS) recipients, Haitian and Central American immigrants, to better understand how three systems of power operate in low-wage work. After laying the groundwork by showing how labor and employment law fosters worker precarity, we outlined the impact of immigration status on worker experiences, looking beyond the literature's predominant binary of undocumented and documented. As we observed, vestiges of racism and colonialism persist in the experiences of immigrants even after they achieve permanent immigration status. Scholars working in a rich tradition of Haitian studies and Central American studies have long explored how the historical legacies of global White supremacy and coloniality mark the lives of these migrant groups. Once here, these migrants are incorporated into the US racial hierarchy, and the work of US race scholars provides important theoretical models for understanding

https://doi.org/10.7758/rioz4023.6065

the anti-Blackness and anti-Latino biases with which they must contend.

Gleaning observations from over three hundred interviews, and building on the work of critical race theorists, we came up with an integrated approach to understanding how immigrants experience workplace precarity and the challenges to mobilizing for change at work. Using this approach, we examined: (1) labor and employment laws that relate to workers' rights, (2) immigration policies, and (3) histories and present-day realities of racialization and coloniality.

To unpack how these systems of power operate, we applied an interdisciplinary sociolegal lens to understanding how the state both empowers and *disempowers* workers. To do so, it was critical to map the "black letter law" for both workplace rules and immigration regulations and outline how they are implemented. In particular, we spent time examining the statutes and administrative guidance on issues such as workers' rights and employer obligations to verify immigration documents. By interviewing workers across various immigration categories, in addition to their advocates, we were better able to understand how policies created unique barriers, or exacerbated common ones, encountered by other immigrants.

We have taken a critical approach to understanding the ways in which certain groups continue to benefit from the consequences of legalized racism and colonialism, even as others suffer. The many exclusionary government-sanctioned policies throughout history that were unabashedly racist and xenophobic are well documented. The formal repudiation of these policies did not bring about racial equality overnight, nor did it repair the structural inequalities baked into US labor and employment law and immigration policies. As such, we refer to racist pasts and *presents*, and we take a critical view of claims that the United States has a race-neutral legal system.

Bottom-Up Epistemologies: Worker Narratives

Our research began with a series of legal analyses to try to understand the parameters of labor and immigration policies in the workplace. To do so, we had to triangulate the US government's formal policies and the experiences of workers of three different immigration statuses on the ground. Interviews with over fifty key informants engaged in the immigrant worker advocacy space became critical. These key advocates—lawyers, labor leaders, and immigrant rights leaders—helped us piece together a detailed picture of how workers in the New York City metropolitan area experience immigration restrictions and the barriers to implementing the labor and employment protections enshrined in federal, New York State, and local laws.

Immigrant narratives about their experiences in the workplace are the central component of our data. Our interview team conducted nearly all of the interviews with Haitian respondents in Kreyòl. Similarly, the majority of interviews with Central American respondents were in Spanish. The research team coded each interview with a deductive set of conceptual codes drawn from the literature and added additional inductive insights. Through iterative coding and memos, we cross-checked key emergent themes to identify common narratives.

Workers reported common workplace violations such as nonpayment for hours worked, missed breaks and rest periods, supervisor refusal to provide basic safety equipment, sexual harassment, and egregious forms of employer retaliation following worker attempts to demand better conditions. We also recorded workers' narratives about moments of disrespect and feelings of degradation, regardless of whether formal laws provided protections in that area. We mapped their experiences onto existing laws and the secondary literature about legal violations and justice in low-wage work. Semistructured interviews reflect workers' own perspectives. As such, we avoid attributing intention and causality to employer and coworker actions.

Research Site and Comparative Design

The research design for this book is inherently comparative and an important part of the study of migration[1] and racialized individuals.[2] While many studies have focused on specific ethnic groups or immigration categories, we vary our sample in order to understand the unique and crosscutting ways in which workers experience labor policy, different types of immigration status, and racialization.

We focused first on the varying experiences of work authorization. To be sure, the alphabet soup of US immigration categories is vast. It was never our goal to take account of these distinctions (all of which have implications for work) and many other rights, including access to social protection and political voice.[3] But we wanted to move beyond the typical binary of documented-undocumented migrant. We ultimately focused on three general categories of work authorization: undocumented (unauthorized); temporary, as embodied by the work authorization provided to migrants with temporary protected status; and permanent, as is the case for lawful permanent residents and naturalized citizens, whose new status provides them with work authorization indefinitely.

Because we seek to understand migrants' distinct racialized experiences, we focus on two migrant groups that are well represented across each of these three types of immigration status. The largest two categories include Haitians and Central Americans—in particular immigrants from El Salvador, Honduras, and Nicaragua. Although a good deal of work has begun to examine the specific experiences of temporary status, a lot necessarily focuses on the experiences of guest workers (also known as temporary foreign workers).[4] Temporary protected status and similar temporary work authorization programs are an apparent improvement over guest worker programs because they do not require an employer sponsor.

Focusing on Haitian and Central American migrants in the New York City–New Jersey metro area permitted us to compare both an immigrant population racialized as Black and one racialized as Latino, with differing language sets (primarily Kreyòl and Spanish). This focus is certainly not intended to discount the ethno-racial diversity in each region, including the dynamics of race and color in Haiti[5] and the experiences of Indigeneity and Afro-Latinidad in Central America.[6] But by focusing on these two communities, we could examine how distinct systems of racialization shaped the challenges posed by a weak workers' rights framework in the United States as well as their impact on both the mundane and enforcement arms of the US immigration bureaucracy.

New York City's five boroughs and their neighboring communities in New Jersey and Long Island are by no means monolithic. Spreading out across this metro area, however, allowed us to capture various ethnic enclaves (for example, Haitians in Brooklyn, Central Americans on Long Island) and industrial variation. Where we went also reflected the community networks we had cultivated and the residential patterns of their clients and members.

Sampling and Recruitment Considerations

The goal of the project was to interview low-wage workers in both the Haitian and Central American communities across three legal status categories. Fifty-nine of our respondents were from Long Island, 149 were from New Jersey, and 90 were from the New York City boroughs (see table 1.1). On twelve occasions, the birth country of workers who responded to our recruitment efforts was outside our two main regions (Colombia, Ecuador, Guinea, Jamaica, Mexico, and Peru). Understanding the significance of their effort, we proceeded with an interview and provided them with a cash incentive. Their perspectives also informed our analysis.

We began with seed funding from the Cornell Institute for the Social Sciences and a small grant from the Russell Sage Foundation to recruit migrants who had temporary protected status. We identified several community-based organizations in our region of study (mostly legal services providers) that regularly processed renewals for TPS beneficiaries. In our initial round of recruitment, we collaborated with five organizations to do a series of mass mailings to their TPS clients. In the New York–New Jersey region, legal aid for TPS renewals in Haitian and Central American communities is relatively bountiful. We also relied on referrals facilitated by community contacts. Organizations distributed flyers in both Kreyòl and Spanish, providing information about the project and contact information for our research team and describing the $50 cash incentive (an important feature for this low-wage population). Research team members often would attend community meetings to explain the purpose of the study and to recruit volunteers. Additionally, to gain the trust of the leaders of the TPS community, members of our research team would spend time at community events or church gatherings to foster trust and familiarity with local communities. Our human subjects approval expressly prohibited us from contacting migrants directly, a safety feature meant to ensure participants' voluntary consent.

While our TPS interviewees referred workers with undocumented and permanent status to us, our sample for those two statuses was insufficient for meaningful analysis. Thus, the subsequent rounds of recruitment (for both undocumented and permanent status immigrants) necessarily took a different approach. We worked through legal services providers to reach TPS migrants, as they often needed legal help to tackle their regular renewals. Undocumented migrants' connections relied more on mutual aid organizations, community groups, and worker centers. Our recruitment efforts often required multiple attempts, as workers were typically difficult to reach and often had to cancel interviews, frequently with no notice. Flexibility was key.

We utilized a more diffuse recruitment strategy to connect with workers with permanent status, who now mostly had legal paperwork into perpetuity. We continued to post flyers across a broader range of organizations, and the leaders engaged in each of these communities with whom we spoke recommended former clients who had become lawful permanent residents or naturalized citizens through their services. We also relied on the social networks of our research team members, who were rooted in these immigrant communities. Given the complexity of workers' schedules, our research team had to adapt to the times and places where the workers gathered and had to be on call to respond to their availability. This often happened at the last minute, on weekends and after hours.

Project Timing: The Bumpy Road of Research

Data collection for this project spanned several years—across three presidential administrations and a global pandemic. The collection of data began in mid-2016 and wrapped up in 2022. The inauguration of Donald Trump in 2016 sent a shock wave of panic through the immigrant community, including the New York City metropolitan area. Local officials there had long espoused seemingly pro-immigrant policies and positions, but here too a pro-Trump base flourished and was now emboldened.[7] Specifically, in Long Island, New York gang violence became a talking point for President Trump's border wall agenda.[8] These local events animated our conversations with all groups of immigrants. Meanwhile, the murder of George Floyd in 2020 made conversations around racial injustice all the more poignant. All of these current events served as an important backdrop to conversations about racial discrimination as well as for questions about civic engagement and worker empowerment. Workers often commented on the injustice of police impunity and noted the theme of anti-Blackness, anti-Latino bias, and xenophobia in American life.

Initially, all interviews took place in person, at a place that was conveniently located for the respondent—interviewees' homes, library community rooms, fast-food establishments, park benches, the offices of community organizations, churches, and other public spots that were easily accessible by train and foot. When the COVID-19 pandemic hit in March 2020, in-person interviews ceased immediately. However, we were able to shift to interviewing virtually. While the loss of in-person interviewing was unfortunate, moving online was a shift that the entire world was making, and a necessary one that helped ensure researcher and respondent safety. The COVID pandemic introduced pressures across the project. Both respondents and our research team members had to contend with personal and family illness. The slow crawl back to collecting data after the initial shock of shutdown had to be done very carefully. In our analysis, we engaged workers about how COVID was impacting their lives at work, with a careful eye to the ways in which the pandemic was either creating new challenges or exacerbating long-standing ones.

Interdisciplinarity and Research Positionality

In her iconic article "Learning from the Outsider Within," Patricia Hill Collins outlines the importance of bringing an insider perspective to sociological research.[9] Rejecting the typical scientific norm of "objectivity," Collins and other Black feminists have argued for the utility of "subjectivity" in order to reveal the "interlocking nature of oppression" and the importance of cultural context. As such, it was important to us to coauthor with scholars (and receive feedback from scholars) who brought expertise from the fields of Haitian and Central American studies. Research team members who were coethnic and spoke the language were critical to building trust and gaining access with respondents through the series of challenging questions (on workplace abuse, immigration enforcement, and family dynamics, for example). Our colleagues could help us understand the trauma of displacement and the racialization of immigrant experience. As insiders to these ethnic communities, they were able to bring this contextual lens to the interviews as they were happening and during the phase of data analysis.

    Ultimately, this research study is the product of multiple disciplinary traditions, as well as practitioner and scholarly perspectives.

Kati Griffith is a labor and employment law scholar, Shannon Gleeson is a mixed-methods sociologist, Darlène Dubuisson is an anthropologist and transnational ethnographer, and Patricia Campos-Medina is an interdisciplinary social scientist with deep roots in the labor and immigrant rights movements. Interdisciplinary approaches are a mainstay of critical race theory and social justice–oriented work.[10] Yet they do not come without challenges and in fact have been scrutinized severely by some critical disciplinarians.[11] For this project, disciplinary collaboration was essential both theoretically and empirically.

Each of the authors brought specific scholarly and community expertise, including Griffith's Fulbright research in El Salvador and legal expertise, Gleeson's work on immigrant civil society and worker claims-making, Dubuisson's long-standing work in Haiti and Haitian communities at the southern border, and Campos-Medina's scholarship focused on Central American workers engaged in various labor struggles and the TPS solidarity movement. Dubuisson and Campos-Medina conducted the bulk of the interviews in the Haitian and Central American communities, respectively. However, we also hired several community-based interviewers, each of whom brought particular access to and knowledge about the community to the project. This approach helped us build a rich team of researchers.

In sum, our research represents a collaborative effort and a research team that includes scholars at various stages of their career, dozens of students, and many community partners whose participation was invaluable to data collection and analysis.

NOTES

Chapter 1: Introduction

1. Bernhardt et al. 2008b; Bernhardt, Spiller, and Polson 2013; Kalleberg 2011; Munger 2002.
2. Gelatt et al. 2022.
3. Shrider 2023.
4. Doussard 2013.
5. See, for example, Boris and Klein 2015; Newman 2009; Sherman 2007.
6. Berrey et al. 2017.
7. Gleeson 2016.
8. Bureau of Labor Statistics 2024a.
9. Calavita 2016; Lipsky 2010.
10. Lieberwitz 2022.
11. Robinson 2019.
12. Andersen and Collins 2004; Collins 2003; Crenshaw 1991; Lee and Tapia 2021; Zavella 2011.
13. MacKinnon 1987.
14. Piven 2008.
15. Rhomberg and Lopez 2021.
16. Brookes 2018; Dahl 1957.
17. Wright 2000.
18. See Scott 1985.
19. Gates 2002.
20. Scott 1985.
21. Acharya et al. 2018.
22. Leroy and Jenkins 2021. Here we reference White settler colonialism in the Americas (Dunbar-Ortiz 2021), while also recognizing the many different varieties of colonial and neocolonial relations and the varying forms of resource extraction and violence that empires generate (Mayblin and Turner 2020).
23. Grosfoguel 2003.
24. Ngai 2004; Perea 2011.
25. Saucedo and Rodriguez 2022.
26. Bonilla-Silva 2021; Carbado and Harris 2008; Ray 2019.

27. Lee and Tapia 2021.
28. Lee et al. 2022.
29. Gomberg-Muñoz 2010.
30. Scholars use various terms to describe workers who are not legally authorized to be present in the United States as defined by immigration law. Here we use both "unauthorized" and "undocumented" when we talk about immigrant workers who lack legal presence or work authorization. Even though the US government uses the phrase "illegal alien" to refer to this population, we reject this language, as it is not necessary to the analysis and advances pejorative characterizations (Guskin 2013).
31. To be sure, the Haitian diaspora has not been uniform. From a country that is currently home to 13.4 million people (Population Reference Bureau 2023), the United States is the largest destination for Haitian migrants—705,000 as of 2020 (Yates 2021). Of those, an estimated 163,000 migrants live in the New York–New Jersey metro area, behind only the Miami–Fort Lauderdale–West Palm Beach metro area (Olsen-Medina and Batalova 2020).
32. Central America typically is described as encompassing seven countries: Belize (0.4 million), Costa Rica (5.2 million), El Salvador (6.3 million), Guatemala (17.8 million), Honduras (9.6 million), Nicaragua (6.7 million), and Panama (4.4 million) (Population Reference Bureau 2023). An estimated 376,000 Central Americans live in the New York–New Jersey metro area, a population second in size only to the Los Angeles–Long Beach–Anaheim metro area (Ward and Batalova 2023). The "Northern Triangle" of Central America (on which much of US immigration policy is focused) encompasses El Salvador, Guatemala, and Honduras.
33. Abrego and Villalpando 2021. Given the complicated political histories of US interventionism and foreign relations in Central America, and the solidarity movements of the 1980s and 1990s, temporary protected status has been extended only to El Salvador, Honduras, and Nicaragua. Ongoing calls to extend protections to Guatemala as well have never been heeded (see, for example, the calls for such an extension from the group TPS for Central America, https://tpsforcentralamerica.org). As such, despite key differences, we include Guatemalans in our comparative sample, given their shared regional origin and colonial histories, their presence in the low-wage industries in the region, and their similar participation in the civic spaces from which we sampled (Abrego and Villalpando 2021; Menjívar 2021; Rodriguez and Menjívar 2015).
34. We maintain that the distinctions between lawful permanent resident "green card" holders and naturalized citizens are less relevant for our analysis, particularly in the low-wage private sector. We did, however aim to capture both categories of immigration status. Among the twenty-seven permanently documented Central Americans we interviewed, sixteen (59 percent) were naturalized, reflecting the longer tenure of this community in the United States. By contrast, of the sixty permanently documented Haitians we interviewed, only eighteen (30 percent) indicated that they had naturalized.
35. For example, among Haitians, 44 percent of respondents were permanently documented, compared to only 17 percent of Central Americans. This difference partly

represents the greater challenge we faced in recruiting Haitian immigrants with precarious legal status, in particular the undocumented Haitian community. A slightly smaller proportion of the Haitians we interviewed were undocumented, compared to Central Americans (20 percent versus 32 percent). This also reflects a more recently arrived Haitian population that is not as well connected to community resources, many of which we relied on to build trust and recruit respondents. By comparison, across each immigration category, Central American respondents had been in the United States for far longer. The average undocumented Haitian had been in the country for only 4.0 years at the time of the interview, compared to 11.1 years for undocumented Central Americans (see table 1.2).

36. The 301 respondents discussed at least 888 jobs in their interviews. To make sense of this variation, we constructed loose work histories for each respondent, identifying the number of discrete jobs they mentioned and the industries in which they worked. The North American Industry Classification System (NAICS) recognizes twenty industry sectors that encompass thousands of classifications. We instead devised a classification system that captures a far more straightforward rendition of the variety of jobs in which a low-wage immigrant worker in the New York City metro was likely to be employed. On the whole, 8 percent of workers were in administrative positions, 18 percent were in manufacturing/warehouse/packing, 15 percent in care work, 9 percent in retail, 18 percent in restaurants, 11 percent in landscaping or cleaning, 10 percent in construction, and 12 percent in other types of jobs. There were some clear trends by gender, origin, and immigration status. For example, documented Haitian workers were more likely to work in the formal arenas of care work (for example, as home health aides) compared to their Central American counterparts, even when adjusting for sample distribution across origin. Construction jobs were overwhelmingly held by men, while women dominated (though to a lesser degree) in the care sector (see table 2.1).
37. Milkman and Luce 2021; Milkman and Ott 2014.
38. Hirsch et al. 2024.
39. Racabi 2022; Tomassetti 2022.
40. Bernhardt et al. 2008b.
41. Estlund 1995.
42. Bernhardt et al. 2008b.
43. Rhomberg 2012.
44. Harper et al. 2021.
45. Carré 2015; Doussard 2013; Weil 2014.
46. Griffith 2019a.
47. Garcia 2011.
48. Abrego et al. 2017.
49. Armenta 2017.
50. Griffith and Gleeson 2017.
51. Unstable immigration policy has impacted the Haitian community in a number of ways. For example, the Biden administration's 2023 humanitarian parole program—Processes for Cubans, Haitians, Nicaraguans, and Venezuelans (CHNV)—created a two-year,

nonrenewable status for certain migrants from those countries (American Immigration Council 2023).
52. Gleeson 2016, 7.
53. Stainback and Tomaskovic-Devey 2012.
54. Kahn 2018.
55. Migration Policy Institute, n.d.
56. Campos-Medina et al. 2023.
57. Vogt 2018.
58. Lacarte 2022.
59. To be sure, the Afro-Latino experience, and specifically the Afro-Central American experience, could provide a unique and important perspective on the operation of anti-Blackness in the workplace (Bush et al. 2019; Jiménez Román and Flores 2010; López Oro 2021). In our sample, however, the vast majority of Central American workers neither identified as Black nor reported anti-Black bias at work.
60. Gleeson and Griffith 2021.

Part 1: Underregulated Rights at Work

1. Glenn 1992; Hill 1985; Kessler-Harris 2007; Perea 2011.
2. Garcia 2012.

Chapter 2: Worker Precarity in the Low-Wage Workplace

1. Ceron 2022.
2. Bureau of Labor Statistics 2021a.
3. Mishel and Bivens 2021.
4. Carré and Tilly 2017.
5. Hirsch et al. 2024.
6. Rosenfeld 2014.
7. Bartley 2018; Dreiling and Darves 2011.
8. Gates 2009; Levine 1988.
9. Prechel 2003, 315; see also Prechel 1990, 2000.
10. Bartley 2018.
11. Akard 1992.
12. Bernhardt et al. 2008b; Estlund 1995.
13. US Department of Labor, n.d.-a.
14. Best et al. 2011.
15. Estlund 2002; Sachs 2007.
16. Lucas 2008.
17. Bernhardt et al. 2008b.
18. Rainey 2022.
19. Duncan 2003.
20. US Department of Labor, n.d.-c.
21. Occupational Safety and Health Administration, n.d.-a.

22. Piore and Schrank 2018.
23. Gleeson 2016.
24. Gleeson 2012.
25. Ritchie et al. 2023.
26. Rosenfeld 2014, 30.
27. Rosenfeld 2014; Troy 2000.
28. Sachs 2007.
29. Fisk and Malin 2019.
30. Gross 1995.
31. Rosenfeld 2014, 4–5.
32. Rosenfeld 2014.
33. Fine and Gordon 2010.
34. Galvin 2016.
35. Fritz-Mauer 2020, 735; Oswalt and Rosado Marzán 2018.
36. Lee and Smith 2019.
37. Epp 2010; de Graauw 2016.
38. Fine 2017; Lee and Smith 2019.
39. Gates et al. 2018.
40. Griffith and Gates 2019.
41. Weil 2019, 151.
42. Carré 2015; Doussard 2013; Weil 2014, 2019.
43. Weil 2019, 149.
44. Griffith 2019a.
45. Elmore and Griffith 2021.
46. National Academies of Sciences, Engineering, and Medicine 2020.
47. Bureau of Labor Statistics 2024b.
48. Weil 2019, 151.
49. Batt et al. 2014.
50. Kalleberg 2011.
51. See Bumiller 1992; Hodson 2001; Lamont 2002.
52. Cauthen 2011.
53. Bernhardt et al. 2009; Burnham and Theodore 2012; Jayaraman 2013.
54. Bernhardt et al. 2009.
55. Wage Justice Center, n.d.
56. Rosado Marzán 2017a.
57. Restaurant Opportunities Centers United and Batt 2012.
58. Kundro et al. 2022.
59. Myrlande, interview, New York City, June 1, 2019.
60. Diana, interview, Long Island, August 18, 2020.
61. Bernhardt, Spiller, and Theodore 2013; Bureau of Labor Statistics 2021b.
62. Carmen, interview, Long Island, July 15, 2017.
63. Occupational Safety and Health Administration, n.d.-b.
64. Harold, interview, New Jersey, March 3, 2020.

65. Magalie, interview, New Jersey, February 14, 2020.
66. Benjamin, interview, New Jersey, March 3, 2020.
67. Restaurant Opportunities Center of New York and the New York City Restaurant Industry Coalition 2006.
68. Burnham and Theodore 2012.
69. Clara, interview, New York City, October 12, 2017.
70. Hess and Hegewisch 2019.
71. Maxime, interview, New York City, November 4, 2016.
72. Victoria, interview, New York City, September 30, 2017.
73. Paula, interview, New York City, December 14, 2018.
74. Fabiola, interview, New York City, October 24, 2016.
75. Nelson, interview, Long Island, February 12, 2018.
76. Ruth, interview, New Jersey, October 24, 2020.
77. Kalleberg 2011.
78. Milkman 2018.
79. Neera, interview, New Jersey, February 20, 2020.
80. Magdala, interview, New York City, December 14, 2018.
81. Lucas 2008; Zuberi and Bonilla-Silva 2008.
82. Sprague 2016.
83. Obasogie 2013.
84. Alcidonis 2016; Fisk 2001.
85. Guillermino, interview, Long Island, March 16, 2017.

Chapter 3: Challenging Precarity in the Low-Wage Workplace: Barriers and Pathways

1. Azaroff et al. 2002; Bernhardt et al. 2009; Berrey et al. 2017.
2. The following sources confirm the low overall level of claims-making in civil disputes. Richard Miller and Austin Sarat (1980) find that only 29.4 percent of grievances turn into claims. Using a three-city survey of workers, Charlotte Alexander and Arthi Prasad (2014) find that only 37 percent had advanced a claim about a justiciable problem. Another analysis of the same survey finds that "fully 21.1 percent of the workers in our sample indicated that they did not complain during the past 12 months even though they had experienced a serious problem such as dangerous working conditions, discrimination or not being paid the minimum wage" (Bernhardt, Spiller, and Polson 2013).
3. Lenore Azaroff and her colleagues (2002, 1422) found that "surveys collected from 372 environmental service workers in Baltimore hospitals in 1993 showed that 42 (39 percent) of the 108 workers injured in the previous year had not reported one or more injuries."
4. Alexander and Prasad 2014.
5. Stefano, interview, New Jersey, July 13, 2020.
6. Inari, interview, New Jersey, August 5, 2020.
7. Sexsmith 2016.

8. Windham 2017.
9. Logan 2006.
10. Ana, interview, New Jersey, July 9, 2020.
11. Martha, interview, New Jersey, June 20, 2021.
12. Lina, interview, New Jersey, February 17, 2020.
13. Cherline, interview, New Jersey, March 2, 2020.
14. Jonas, interview, New Jersey, March 1, 2020.
15. Irina, interview, New Jersey, March 3, 2020.
16. Heloise, interview, New York City, July 21, 2016.
17. Griffith 2011a.
18. Patler et al. 2022.
19. Julian, interview, New Jersey, December 7, 2020.
20. Mahalik et al. 2007; Saucedo and Morales 2010.
21. Rosalinda, interview, New Jersey, February 15, 2018.
22. Jeremias, interview, New Jersey, December 15, 2020.
23. Sylvanie, interview, New Jersey, March 1, 2020.
24. Benita, interview, New Jersey, March 3, 2020.
25. Gleeson 2016.
26. Alexander and Prasad 2014.
27. Saskay, interview, New Jersey March 9, 2020.
28. Tiana, interview, New Jersey, June 16, 2020.
29. Wilda, interview, New Jersey, February 20, 2020.
30. Alejandro, interview, Long Island, July 19, 2017.
31. Piore and Schrank 2018, 5.
32. Gleeson 2016.
33. Bernhardt et al. 2008a.
34. Elmore and Griffith 2021; Weil 2014.
35. Griffith 2019b.
36. Samuel, interview, New Jersey, February 13, 2020.
37. Leslie, interview, New Jersey, October 24, 2020.
38. Carré 2015.
39. Juano, interview, New Jersey, December 29, 2020.
40. Linda, interview, New York City, August 27, 2019.
41. Eva, interview, New Jersey, November 18, 2017.
42. Edelman 1992.
43. Salvador, interview, Long Island, June 10, 2017.
44. Rocio, interview, New Jersey, March 3, 2020.
45. Adler et al. 2014; Fine et al. 2018; Milkman et al. 2010.
46. Lesniewski and Gleeson 2022.
47. Fine 2011.
48. Osterman 2018.
49. Raymundo, interview, Long Island, March 18, 2017.
50. Hallett 2018.
51. Alessandra, interview, Long Island, October 20, 2018.

52. Felstiner et al. 1980.
53. Gleeson 2016.
54. Walder, interview, New Jersey, April 24, 2021.
55. Johanne, interview, New York City, August 7, 2016.
56. Gleeson 2021.
57. Gleeson 2010.
58. Javier, interview, New York City, October 3, 2018.
59. Mateo, interview, Long Island, February 17, 2018.
60. Wilmer, interview, Long Island, March 4, 2017.
61. Oscar, interview, Long Island, February 17, 2018.
62. Fine et al. 2018.
63. Griffith and Gates 2019, 232.
64. Fine and Gordon 2010.
65. Glenda, interview, Long Island, August 24, 2017.
66. Cordero-Guzmán 2015; Pinedo-Turnovsky 2019; Valenzuela et al. 2006.
67. Dario, interview, Long Island, February 20, 2018.
68. Batt et al. 2014.
69. Kaitlyn, interview, New Jersey, August 23, 2021.
70. Luna, interview, New Jersey, December 9, 2020.
71. Ajunwa et al. 2017.
72. Bruno, interview, Long Island, August 11, 2018.
73. Guillermo, interview, Long Island, March 16, 2017.
74. Nancy, interview, Long Island, February 12, 2018.
75. Joel, interview, New Jersey, February 16, 2020.
76. Adalie, interview, New York City, October 20, 2016.
77. Dara, interview, New Jersey, June 17, 2020.
78. Gerald, interview, New Jersey, February 19, 2020.
79. Lucas 2017.
80. Fischer-Daly 2021.
81. Lamont 2002.
82. Dodson 2009.
83. Kalleberg 2011.
84. Nadine, interview, New York City, December 19, 2016.
85. Mario, interview, Long Island, March 9, 2017.
86. Sofia, interview, New Jersey, August 26, 2020.
87. Marcello, interview, New Jersey, February 14, 2020.
88. Zach, interview, Long Island, March 20, 2018.
89. Katz et al. 2017.
90. German, interview, New Jersey, May 28, 2021.
91. Moore 2017.
92. Scott 1985.
93. Lord 2022.
94. Ybema and Horvers 2017, 1233.
95. Weeks 2017.

96. Bumiller 1992.
97. Sandrine, interview, New York City, December 17, 2016.
98. Lee 2007, 193–94.

Part 2: An Immigration Regime at Work

1. Browne and Misra 2003; Glenn 1992; HoSang et al. 2012; Roediger 1991.

Chapter 4: How the US Immigration Regime Shapes Worker Precarity

1. Griffith 2011a.
2. Griffith and Gleeson 2017.
3. Fine 2006; Gordon 2011.
4. Wishnie 2008, 1446.
5. Chen 2020. See also work by Cecilia Menjívar (2006), Leisy Abrego and Sarah Lakhani (2015), Miranda Cady Hallett (2014), Jennifer Chacón (2015), and many others.
6. Stumpf 2006.
7. Griffith 2011a.
8. Passel and Krogstad 2024.
9. Krogstad et al. 2020.
10. Chavez 2013; Rumbaut et al. 2019.
11. Marnin 2021.
12. Chen 2020.
13. Lung 2019.
14. Massey 1999.
15. Andreas and Biersteker 2003; Rodriguez 2008.
16. National Conference of State Legislatures 2025.
17. Lee 2009.
18. Lahav 1998, 2000.
19. Calavita 1990; Saucedo 2010.
20. *Sure-Tan Inc. v. National Labor Relations Board*, 467 U.S. 883 (1984).
21. *Hoffman Plastic Compounds, Inc. v. National Labor Relations Board*, 535 U.S. 137 (2002).
22. Bernhardt et al. 2008b.
23. Svajlenka 2020.
24. Fisk and Wishnie 2005; Garcia 2011; Ruiz Cameron 2003.
25. National Employment Law Project 2013; New York State Attorney General 2019.
26. Chavez 1998; Hondagneu-Sotelo 2007.
27. Orrenius et al. 2020.
28. Bernhardt et al. 2009.
29. Michael, interview, New Jersey, February 12, 2020.
30. Griffith 2012.
31. Allison et al. 2018; Choudry and Henaway 2012.
32. Flippen 2012.

33. Holmes 2013; Ribas 2015; Rosales 2014.
34. Durand et al. 2016, 78.
35. Dobbins et al. 2022.
36. Randy, interview, New Jersey, April 29, 2021.
37. Marco, interview, New Jersey, June 7, 2021.
38. Suzette, interview, New Jersey, February 16, 2020.
39. Cavounidis et al. 2024.
40. National Immigration Forum 2024.
41. Warren and Kerwin 2017.
42. Warren and Kerwin 2017.
43. Moslimani 2024; National Immigration Forum 2024.
44. Heeren 2015, 1141, 1119.
45. Griffith and Gleeson 2017; Heeren 2015.
46. Griffith and Gleeson 2017.
47. Menjívar and Abrego 2012.
48. Costa 2017; Griffith et al. 2014; Martin 2017.
49. Motomura 2014; Rabin 2020.
50. Menjívar 2006; see also Abrego and Lakhani 2015; Hallett 2014; Menjívar and Abrego 2012.
51. Cohn et al. 2019.
52. Gleeson and Griffith 2021, 92.
53. Griffith 2011b.
54. Griffith and Gleeson 2017, 134.
55. National Immigration Forum 2024.
56. American Immigration Council 2019; Orrenius and Zavodny 2015b.
57. Hugo, interview, New Jersey, November 30, 2016.
58. Lucrecia, interview, Long Island, August 21, 2017.
59. Lucien, interview, New York City, October 26, 2016.
60. Union leader, interview, September 6, 2018.
61. American Immigration Council 2019.
62. Isaac, interview, New York City, November 3, 2016.
63. Mountz et al. 2002.
64. Manolo, interview, Long Island, August 13, 2017.
65. Gleeson and Griffith 2021.
66. Magdala, interview, New York City, December 14, 2018.
67. Santiago, interview, Long Island, March 6, 2017.
68. Laura, interview, New York City, October 11, 2018.
69. Moslimani and Passel 2024.
70. Bloemraad 2006.
71. De Genova 2005; Ngai 2004.
72. Chen 2020.
73. Szkupinski Quiroga et al. 2014, 1736.
74. Amuedo-Dorantes and Pozo 2019.
75. Flores and Schachter 2019.

76. Abrego et al. 2017.
77. Lenard 2022.
78. Menjívar 2021.
79. Tesfai and Thomas 2020.
80. McKanders 2020.
81. Craemer and Martínez 2021; Jensen and Sousa Dias 2022.
82. Aranda et al. 2014.
83. Capps et al. 2020.
84. Moslimani 2022.
85. López 2021.
86. Abrego 2019.
87. Menjívar et al. 2016.
88. Ramírez and Hinshaw 2022.
89. US Citizenship and Immigration Services 2020, 2021.
90. Walder, interview, New Jersey, April 24, 2021.
91. Kalleberg 2011.
92. Jocelyn, interview, New York City, April 4, 2019.
93. Patricia, interview, New Jersey, February 18, 2020.
94. Bertha, interview, New York City, June 30, 2019.
95. Maribel, interview, New Jersey, April 29, 2021.
96. Anabel, interview, New Jersey, August 10, 2021.
97. Amuedo-Dorantes and Bansak 2011; Lofstrom et al. 2013.
98. Gomberg-Muñoz 2010; Rodriguez 2004; Waldinger and Lichter 2003.
99. Marcello, interview, New Jersey, February 14, 2020.
100. Hall and Greenman 2015, 432.
101. Pascale, interview, New York City, July 6, 2016.
102. Christelle, interview, New York City, April 4, 2019.
103. Marise, interview, New York City, August 22, 2019.

Chapter 5: The US Immigration Regime as Barrier and Pathway to Challenging Precarity

1. Waldinger and Lichter 2003.
2. Pérez 2022.
3. Anis, interview, New York City, December 19, 2016.
4. Lilian, interview, New Jersey, July 13, 2020.
5. Jacinto, interview, New Jersey, November 12, 2017.
6. Abel, interview, New York City, November 3, 2016.
7. US Department of Labor n.d.-b.
8. National Labor Relations Board 2022.
9. Phillips and Massey 1999, 234.
10. Saucedo 2018,
11. Wong et al. 2019.
12. Constantino 2021.

13. Touw et al. 2021.
14. Benner 2020.
15. Dante, interview, New Jersey, February 13, 2020.
16. Adler et al. 2014; Fine et al. 2018; Gordon 2007a.
17. Pallares and Flores-González 2009; Voss and Bloemraad 2011; Zepeda-Millán 2017.
18. Sullivan 2021.
19. Hirschman 1970.
20. Josefina, interview, New Jersey, November 15, 2017.
21. Marisol, interview, New Jersey, February 15, 2018.
22. Ricarda, interview, New Jersey, January 10, 2018.
23. Marco, interview, New Jersey, June 7, 2021.
24. Bada et al. 2018.
25. Milkman 2011, 295.
26. Lee et al. 2022.
27. Goldberg 2024.
28. Germán, interview, New Jersey, May 28, 2021.
29. Fine et al. 2018.
30. Indeed, extant research suggests that education can be an important factor in whether workers make a complaint against their employers. See, for example, Patler et al. 2022.
31. Mateo, interview, Long Island, February 17, 2018.

Part 3: Racisms and Colonial Legacies at Work

1. Golash-Boza 2015.
2. Bonilla-Silva 2001.
3. Grosfoguel 2016, 11.
4. Wingfield and Chavez 2020.

Chapter 6: How Racisms and Colonial Legacies Shape Worker Precarity

1. Gomberg-Muñoz 2012.
2. Hoyt 2016, 39.
3. Alcidonis 2016; Fisk 2001.
4. Johnson 2016; Waters et al. 2014.
5. Herrera 2016, 323; Abrego and Villalpando 2021.
6. Abrego and Menjívar 2023; Abrego and Villalpando 2021.
7. Michener et al. 2022, 154.
8. Rodriguez 2022, 7–8.
9. De Genova 2016a; Mayblin and Turner 2020.
10. Roth and Kim 2013.
11. Abrego and Villalpando 2021; Padilla 2022.
12. Chavez 2013.
13. Rodriguez and Menjívar 2015.

14. Dubuisson 2022b.
15. Jung and Costa Vargas 2021, 7.
16. Bonilla-Silva 2002a.
17. Dubois 2012, 17.
18. Dubois 2012, 18.
19. Obregón 2018.
20. Dubois 2012, 19; see also Trouillot 1982.
21. Obregón 2018, 601; Pressley-Sanon 2017.
22. Hartman 2022.
23. Carbado 2011.
24. Pettit and Sykes 2015.
25. Takeuchi and Williams 2011.
26. Golash-Boza and Oh 2021.
27. Shah and Smith 2021.
28. Oliver and Shapiro 2006.
29. Hunter and Robinson 2016.
30. Kirschenman and Neckerman 1991; Pager et al. 2009.
31. Walter, interview, New Jersey, June 18, 2020.
32. Walter's experience reflects the important role of the public sector for Black worker mobility in the United States. Indeed, US-born Black workers are overrepresented in public-sector jobs; even though these jobs are inaccessible for many noncitizen workers, they have protocols that reduce hiring discrimination (Tesfai and Thomas 2020).
33. Daphnée, interview, New York City, February 11, 2020.
34. Georges, interview, New York City, November 11, 2016.
35. Pager et al. 2009.
36. Juan, interview, New York City, November 1, 2018.
37. Storer et al. 2020, 543.
38. Marise, interview, New York City, August 22, 2019.
39. Matlon 2022; Pager 2009; Wingfield 2007.
40. Fraser 2003.
41. Fisk 2001.
42. Hartman 2022, 757.
43. Suzette, an undocumented worker introduced in chapter 4, felt that anti-Haitianism was most evident when she and workers of other nationalities were applying for the same jobs. For her, the fact that employers saw African and Hispanic immigrants as better hires was clear evidence that the problem was "an injustice against Haitians" in particular.
44. Roselaure, interview, New York City, June 20, 2019.
45. Trouillot 1995, 37.
46. Knight 2005, 392.
47. Dubuisson 2022a.
48. Daut 2024.
49. Daut 2020.

50. Alcenat 2021.
51. Daut 2020.
52. Liberato and St. Jean 2017.
53. Dubois 2012, 8.
54. Solarz 1995, x.
55. Dubois 2012, 8.
56. Sepinwall 2012; Trouillot 1990.
57. Vitali et al. 2018.
58. Dubuisson and Schuller 2024.
59. Peterson, interview, New Jersey, March 1, 2020.
60. Niño-Murcia and Rothman 2008. Indeed, some scholars have argued that Kreyòl and Vodou form the "two pillars of resistance" for Haiti, just as Haitians are also stigmatized for their language and religion (Past 2021).
61. Ulysse 2015.
62. Niño-Murcia and Rothman 2008.
63. Cadeau 2022.
64. Miller 2019.
65. Aparicio 2007; Frasco 2020; Glick-Schiller and Fouron 1998; Lamb and Dundes 2017.
66. López-Sanders 2024; Rosales 2020; Stuesse 2016.
67. Elliott and Smith 2001.
68. López-Sanders 2024.
69. Euraque 2018, 4.
70. Cuéllar 2018, 40.
71. Cuéllar 2018.
72. Ching and Tilley 1998; Martínez Peláez 2009.
73. Venutolo 1996.
74. Hooker 2005; Immerman 1980; Kovalick 2023; Wood 2003.
75. Cuéllar 2018, 50.
76. Bonilla-Silva 2002b; De Genova 1998.
77. Alcenat 2021; Lovato 2018.
78. De Genova 1998, 91.
79. Moslimani and Passel 2024.
80. Campos-Medina 2019; Menjívar 2006.
81. Pirtle 2022.
82. Loza 2016.
83. Orozco 2009.
84. Miller 2019.
85. Armenta 2017, 20.
86. Theodore 2011.
87. Chavez 2013; Osuna 2020.
88. Huber 2016, 23.
89. Abrego and Osuna 2022; Griffith et al. 2020.

90. Huber 2016, 24.
91. Rodriguez and Menjívar 2015.
92. Ngai 2004.
93. De Genova 2005; Paret 2014.
94. Glenn 2015.
95. Calavita 1992; García y Griego 1988; Ngai 2004.
96. Choy-Gómez 2021; De Genova 2016b.
97. Rodriguez and Menjívar 2015.
98. Mora 2014.
99. Neate 2015.
100. Abrego and Osuna 2022; Osuna 2020.
101. Frank-Vitale 2020; Vogt 2017.
102. Rosalina, a Salvadoran worker with permanent status, shared that even though she appeared to be *"blanquita"* (White), she could not "blend" because of her accented English. Workers across occupations experienced this dynamic. "My accent hurts me," Rosalinda explained, "and I hear people outside of my office [at a bank] making fun of me, how I answer the phone." While such behavior was arguably a legally actionable form of hostile environment under discrimination protections, workers pointed to language more generally as a key to mobility and a marker of their worth in the eyes of employers and even coworkers. Rosalina, interview, New Jersey, July 23, 2021.
103. Aparicio 2021; Macedo 2000. Sociologists will note, however, that the well-established premiums for bilingualism (Portes 2002) are generally rendered socially unacceptable in many settings outside of those that elevate perceived class status.
104. Dario, interview, Long Island, February 20, 2018.
105. Rodriguez and Menjívar 2015; Zimmerman et al. 2022.
106. Komisaruk 2009.
107. Arturo, interview, Long Island, February 12, 2018.
108. Bonacich 1972.
109. Alessandro, interview, Long Island, February 12, 2018.
110. Bonilla-Silva 2006; see also Jones 2019.
111. Alejandro, interview, Long Island, July 19, 2017.
112. Gleeson 2015.
113. Lucas 2008, 10.
114. Lucas 2008, 21.
115. Alcorso 2002; Hall et al. 2011; Kreisberg 2019.
116. Doussard 2013.
117. Ribas 2015; Rosales 2020; Stuesse 2016.
118. Robinson 2019.
119. See, for example, Abrego and Menjívar 2023; Trouillot 1995.
120. Herrera 2016, 338.
121. Glenn 2015.

Chapter 7: Racisms and Colonial Legacies as Barriers and Pathways to Challenging Precarity

1. Bonacich 1972.
2. Scott 1985; Vallas and Johnston 2023.
3. Columbia Law School Human Rights Clinic 2014; Sandefur 2019.
4. Weil 2014.
5. Hamburger 2023; Saucedo 2017. Charlotte Alexander (2016, 910) finds that "women and/or people of color are overrepresented in seven of the eight occupations at highest risk for misclassification," and that these same occupations are underrepresented in court challenges related to antidiscrimination law.
6. De Lara et al. 2016; Fine and Lyon 2017.
7. Gleeson 2016.
8. Fine and Gordon 2010.
9. Bernhardt et al. 2008b.
10. Jorge, interview, New Jersey, September 30, 2020.
11. Ribas 2015; Soldatenko 1999.
12. Merlet, interview, New Jersey, February 13, 2020.
13. Pierre-Louis 2021.
14. Miguel, interview, Long Island, August 25, 2017.
15. Mahoney 2001; Paige 1997.
16. Piore 1979.
17. Zavella 2011.
18. Abrego 2014; Menjívar et al. 2016; Schmalzbauer 2006.
19. Baker-Cristales 2009; Gleeson 2010.
20. Gleeson 2015.
21. Gessica, interview, New York City, October 26, 2016.
22. Goldring and Landolt 2011.
23. Saucedo and Morales 2010.
24. Gustavo, interview, New Jersey, January 27, 2018.
25. Jessica, interview, New Jersey, October 4, 2020.
26. Michaelle, interview, New York City, December 14, 2016.
27. New York City elected official, interview, New York City, July 7, 2017.
28. Pierre-Louis 2021.
29. Haitian civil society group representative, interview, New York City, July 26, 2017.
30. Labor union representative, interview, New York City, September 6, 2018.
31. Borger 2018.
32. Belén, interview, New Jersey, January 27, 2018.
33. See, for example, Fink 2003.
34. Benford and Snow 2000.
35. Galanter 1974; Zemans 2006.
36. Nelda, interview, Long Island, January 19, 2018.
37. Milkman 2006.
38. Candelario, interview, Long Island, February 5, 2017.

39. Almeida 2008; Anner 2011; Armbruster-Sandoval 2005.
40. Daut 2024.
41. Jeff, interview, New Jersey, February 24, 2020.
42. Dubuisson 2022a.
43. Immigrant rights group representative, interview, New Jersey, July 9, 2020.
44. Soldatenko 1999.
45. Worker center representative, interview, Florida, July 13, 2021.
46. Zamora 2022.
47. Haitians also traveled through Brazil, a route made possible in part by the government's courting of low-wage labor by relaxing visas for Haitians.
48. See, for example, López-Sanders 2024; Ribas 2015; Rosales 2020.

Chapter 8: Conclusion

1. Osterman 2018.
2. de Graauw, Gleeson, and Bada 2019.
3. Chen 2020.
4. Heeren 2015.
5. Wadhia 2015.
6. Martin 2017; Vosko 2019.
7. de Graauw and Gleeson 2020.
8. Abrego and Villalpando 2021; Oro 2016; Zimmerman et al. 2022.
9. Gomberg-Muñoz 2011; Ribas 2015; Rosales 2020.
10. Bernhardt et al. 2009.
11. Orrenius and Zavodny 2015b.
12. Bernhardt, Spiller, and Polson 2013; Bernhardt, Spiller, and Theodore 2013.
13. Weil 2014.
14. New York State Senate 2023.
15. Griffith 2019a, 173.
16. Zatz 2008.
17. Elmore 2018b; Elmore and Griffith 2021.
18. Weiler 1982.
19. Griffith 2009.
20. Harcourt et al. 2019.
21. Block and Sachs 2020.
22. Andrias 2016.
23. Kochan 2020, 3.
24. Estlund 2002.
25. Qin 2022.
26. Compa 2014.
27. Ginsburg 2017, 502.
28. Hirsch et al. 2024.
29. Gamonal and Marzán 2019.
30. Iafolla 2023.

31. Corbett 2020, 2285.
32. Epp 2010; de Graauw 2016.
33. Fine 2017; Elmore 2018a.
34. Rainey 2023.
35. Berkowitz 2020; Smith and Moreno 2022.
36. Bernhardt et al. 2008b; Gleeson 2016.
37. Weil 2010.
38. Gerstein 2021.
39. Manhattan District Attorney's Office 2023.
40. Elmore and Chishti 2018.
41. Gross 2017.
42. Gordon 2007b.
43. Fine and Gordon 2010; Gleeson 2009.
44. Gleeson 2021.
45. Fine 2006.
46. Gates et al. 2018.
47. Amengual and Fine 2017; Elmore 2018a; Fine and Gordon 2010; Rosado Marzán 2017b.
48. Weil 2010.
49. National Employment Law Project 2018.
50. Sachs 2007, 2692.
51. Elmore and Chishti 2018.
52. Wishnie 2008.
53. Jordan 2023.
54. Gleeson and Griffith 2021.
55. Lahav 1998.
56. Lee 2009.
57. Griffith 2014.
58. Nessel 2016.
59. Menjívar and Abrego 2012.
60. Amuedo-Dorantes and Bansak 2012; Orrenius and Zavodny 2015a.
61. Saucedo and Rodriguez 2022.
62. Lucas 2008.
63. Chetty et al. 2020.
64. López 2015; Ray and Purifoy 2019.
65. Williams 2021; see also Crenshaw 1991.
66. Williams 2021, 51.
67. Lucas 2008.
68. Carbado and Harris 2008.
69. Bartlett 2009.
70. Robinson 2008.
71. McGinley 1999.
72. McGinley 2021.
73. Roy et al. 2023.
74. Stowe 2019.

75. Yamada 2012. Stale Einarsen and his colleagues (2010, 22) define workplace bullying as "harassing, offending, or socially excluding someone or negatively affecting someone's work.... A conflict cannot be called bullying if the incident is an isolated event or if two parties of approximately equal strength are in conflict."
76. Gordon 2007a.
77. Rosado Marzán 2017a, 1211.
78. Rosado Marzán 2017b.
79. Ajunwa et al. 2020.
80. Lee and Tapia 2021.
81. Bussel 2015.
82. Honey 2000; Milkman 2000; Nelson 2002.
83. Mink and Baum 2009.
84. Frank 2024; Jones 2013; Kelley 2015.
85. Watson 2021.
86. AFL-CIO 2017.
87. Frymer and Grumbach 2020.
88. Gleeson and Sampat 2018.
89. Huntington 2004.
90. Gans 2011.
91. Immigrant rights group representative, interview, New Jersey, July 9, 2020.
92. See, for example, Galvin 2024.

Methodological Appendix

1. Bloemraad 2013.
2. Misra et al. 2021.
3. Chen 2020.
4. Loza 2016; Martin 2017; Vosko et al. 2017.
5. Marius 2022; Nicholls 1996.
6. Abrego and Villalpando 2021; López Oro 2021.
7. Kerrissey et al. 2020.
8. Griffith et al. 2020.
9. Collins 1986.
10. Barnes 2016; Obasogie 2013; Parker et al. 2012.
11. Jacobs and Frickel 2009.

REFERENCES

Abrego, Leisy J. 2014. *Sacrificing Families: Navigating Laws, Labor, and Love Across Borders*. Stanford University Press.

Abrego, Leisy J. 2019. "Relational Legal Consciousness of US Citizenship: Privilege, Responsibility, Guilt, and Love in Latino Mixed-Status Families." *Law & Society Review* 53(3): 641–70.

Abrego, Leisy, Mat Coleman, Daniel E. Martínez, Cecilia Menjívar, and Jeremy Slack. 2017. "Making Immigrants into Criminals: Legal Processes of Criminalization in the Post-IIRIRA Era." *Journal on Migration and Human Security* 5(3): 694–715.

Abrego, Leisy J., and Sarah M. Lakhani. 2015. "Incomplete Inclusion: Legal Violence and Immigrants in Liminal Legal Statuses." *Law & Policy* 37(4): 265–93.

Abrego, Leisy J., and Cecilia Menjívar. 2023. "Central American Migration to the United States: Historical Roots and Current Conditions." In *The Routledge History of Modern Latin American Migration*, edited by Andreas E. Feldmann, Xóchitl Bada, Jorge Durand, and Stephanie Schütze. Routledge.

Abrego, Leisy, and Steven Osuna. 2022. "The State of Exception: Gangs as a Neoliberal Scapegoat in El Salvador." *Brown Journal of World Affairs* 29(1): 59–73.

Abrego, Leisy J., and Alejandro Villalpando. 2021. "Racialization of Central Americans in the United States." In *Precarity and Belonging: Labor, Migration, and Noncitizenship*, edited by Catherine S. Ramírez, Sylvanna M. Falcón, Juan Poblete, Steven C. McKay, and Felicity Amaya Schaeffer. Rutgers University Press.

Acharya, Avidit, Matthew Blackwell, and Maya Sen. 2018. *Deep Roots: How Slavery Still Shapes Southern Politics*. Princeton University Press.

Adler, Lee H., Maite Tapia, and Lowell Turner, eds. 2014. *Mobilizing Against Inequality: Unions, Immigrant Workers, and the Crisis of Capitalism*. Cornell University Press.

AFL-CIO. 2017. "AFL-CIO Labor Commission on Racial and Economic Justice Report." January 4. https://s3.amazonaws.com/dev.unionhall.files/img/RaceReport.pdf.

Ajunwa, Ifeoma, Kate Crawford, and Jason Schultz. 2017. "Limitless Worker Surveillance." *California Law Review* 105: 735.

Ajunwa, Ifeoma, Virginia Doellgast, Shannon Gleeson, Kate Griffith, and Verónica Martínez-Matsuda. 2020. "A Call for Radical Labor Solidarity with the #BlackLivesMatter Movement." ILR Worker Institute, June 30. https://www.ilr

.cornell.edu/worker-institute/blog/labor-solidarity-and-racial-injustice/call-radical-labor-solidarity-blacklivesmatter-movement.

Akard, Patrick J. 1992. "Corporate Mobilization and Political Power: The Transformation of US Economic Policy in the 1970s." *American Sociological Review* 57(5): 597–615.

Alcenat, Westenley. 2021. "How US Economic Imperialism Underdeveloped Haiti." *NACLA Report on the Americas* 53(2): 193–201.

Alcidonis, Sendy E. Guerrier. 2016. "The Social Networks of Haitian Immigrants Employed in the Long-Term Care Industry in Metropolitan Philadelphia: Complex Intersections of Race, Nationality, Class, and Gender." PhD diss., Temple University.

Alcorso, Caroline. 2002. "Improving Occupational Health and Safety Information to Immigrant Workers in New South Wales." University of Sydney, Australian Centre for Industrial Relations Research and Training.

Alexander, Charlotte S. 2016. "Misclassification and Antidiscrimination: An Empirical Analysis." *Minnesota Law Review* 101: 907–62.

Alexander, Charlotte S., and Arthi Prasad. 2014. "Bottom-Up Workplace Law Enforcement: An Empirical Analysis." *Indiana Law Journal* 89: 1069–1131.

Allison, Juliann Emmons, Joel S. Herrera, Jason Struna, and Ellen Reese. 2018. "The Matrix of Exploitation and Temporary Employment: Earnings Inequality Among Inland Southern California's Blue-Collar Warehouse Workers." *Journal of Labor and Society* 21(4): 533–60.

Almeida, Paul D. 2008. *Waves of Protest: Popular Struggle in El Salvador, 1925–2005*. University of Minnesota Press.

Amengual, Matthew, and Janice Fine. 2017. "Co-Enforcing Labor Standards: The Unique Contributions of State and Worker Organizations in Argentina and the United States." *Regulation & Governance* 11(2): 129–42.

American Immigration Council. 2019. "Workers with Temporary Protected Status in Key Industries and States." January 7. https://www.americanimmigrationcouncil.org/research/workers-temporary-protected-status-key-industries-and-states.

American Immigration Council. 2023. "The Biden Administration's Humanitarian Parole Program for Cubans, Haitians, Nicaraguans, and Venezuelans: An Overview." October 31. https://www.americanimmigrationcouncil.org/research/biden-administrations-humanitarian-parole-program-cubans-haitians-nicaraguans-and.

Amuedo-Dorantes, Catalina, and Cynthia Bansak. 2011. "The Impact of Amnesty on Labor Market Outcomes: A Panel Study Using the Legalized Population Survey." *Industrial Relations* 50(3): 443–71.

Amuedo-Dorantes, Catalina, and Cynthia Bansak. 2012. "The Labor Market Impact of Mandated Employment Verification Systems." *American Economic Review* 102(3): 543–48.

Amuedo-Dorantes, Catalina, and Susan Pozo. 2019. "The Aftermath of Tougher Immigration Enforcement: E-Verify and Perceptions of Discrimination Among Hispanic Citizens." *American Behavioral Scientist* 63(9): 1299–1330.

Andersen, Margaret L., and Patricia Collins. 2004. "Systems of Power and Inequality." In *Race, Class, and Gender: An Anthology*, edited by Margaret L. Andersen and Patricia Collins. Thomson Wadsworth.

Andreas, Peter, and Thomas J. Biersteker. 2003. *The Rebordering of North America: Integration and Exclusion in a New Security Context*. Routledge.

Andrias, Kate. 2016. "The New Labor Law." *Yale Law Journal* 126(1): 2–100.

Anner, Mark S. 2011. *Solidarity Transformed: Labor Responses to Globalization and Crisis in Latin America*. Cornell University Press.

Aparicio, Ana. 2007. "Contesting Race and Power: Second-Generation Dominican Youth in the New Gotham." *City & Society* 19(2): 179–201.

Aparicio, Frances R. 2021. "Of Spanish Dispossessed." In *Language Ideologies: Critical Perspectives on the Official English Movement*, edited by Roseann Dueñas Gonzalez, with Ildko Melis. Routledge Press.

Aranda, Elizabeth, Cecilia Menjívar, and Katharine M. Donato. 2014. "The Spillover Consequences of an Enforcement-First US Immigration Regime." *American Behavioral Scientist* 58(13): 1687–95.

Armbruster-Sandoval, Ralph. 2005. *Globalization and Cross-Border Labor Solidarity in the Americas: The Anti-Sweatshop Movement and the Struggle for Social Justice*. Routledge.

Armenta, Amada. 2017. *Protect, Serve, and Deport: The Rise of Policing as Immigration Enforcement*. University of California Press.

Azaroff, Lenore S., Charles Levenstein, and David H. Wegman. 2002. "Occupational Injury and Illness Surveillance: Conceptual Filters Explain Underreporting." *American Journal of Public Health* 92(9): 1421–29.

Bada, Xóchitl, Els de Graauw, and Shannon Gleeson. 2018. "Union Organizing, Advocacy, and Services at the Nexus of Immigrant and Labor Rights." In *No One Size Fits All: Worker Organization, Policy, and Movement for a New Economic Age*, edited by Janice Fine, Linda Burnham, Kati Griffith, Minsun Ji, Victor Narro, and Steven Pitts. Labor and Employment Research Association.

Baker-Cristales, Beth. 2009. "Mediated Resistance: The Construction of Neoliberal Citizenship in the Immigrant Rights Movement." *Latino Studies* 7(1): 60–82.

Barnes, Mario L. 2016. "Empirical Methods and Critical Race Theory: A Discourse on Possibilities for a Hybrid Methodology." *Wisconsin Law Review* 2016(3): 443–76.

Bartlett, Katharine T. 2009. "Making Good on Good Intentions: The Critical Role of Motivation in Reducing Implicit Workplace Discrimination." *Virginia Law Review* 95(8): 1893–1972.

Bartley, Tim. 2018. "Transnational Corporations and Global Governance." *Annual Review of Sociology* 44(1): 145–65.

Batt, Rosemary, Jae Eun Lee, and Tashlin Lakhani. 2014. "A National Study of Human Resource Practices, Turnover, and Customer Service in the Restaurant Industry." Restaurant Opportunities Centers United, January. National-Study-of-Human-Resource-Practices-High-Turnover-and-Customer-Service-in-the-Restaurant-Industry.pdf.

Benford, Robert D., and David A. Snow. 2000. "Framing Processes and Social Movements: An Overview and Assessment." *Annual Review of Sociology* 26: 611–39.

Benner, Katie. 2020. "Justice Dept. Establishes Office to Denaturalize Immigrants." *New York Times*, February 26. https://www.nytimes.com/2020/02/26/us/politics/denaturalization-immigrants-justice-department.html.

Berkowitz, Deborah. 2020. "Worker Safety in Crisis: The Cost of a Weakened OSHA." National Employment Law Project, April 28. https://s27147.pcdn.co/wp-content/uploads/Worker-Safety-Crisis-Cost-Weakened-OSHA.pdf.

Bernhardt, Annette, Heather Boushey, Laura Dresser, and Chris Tilly. 2008a. "An Introduction to the Gloves-Off Economy." In *The Gloves-off Economy: Workplace Standards at the Bottom of America's Labor Market*, edited by Annette Bernhardt, Heather Boushey, Laura Dresser, and Chris Tilly. ILR Press.

Bernhardt, Annette, Heather Boushey, Laura Dresser, and Chris Tilly, eds. 2008b. *The Gloves-Off Economy: Workplace Standards at the Bottom of America's Labor Market*. ILR Press.

Bernhardt, Annette, Ruth Milkman, Nik Theodore, et al. 2009. "Broken Laws, Unprotected Workers: Violations of Employment and Labor Laws in America's Cities." Center for Urban Economic Development, National Employment Law Project, and UCLA Institute for Research on Labor and Employment. https://www.nelp.org/app/uploads/2015/03/BrokenLawsReport2009.pdf.

Bernhardt, Annette, Michael W. Spiller, and Diana Polson. 2013. "All Work and No Pay: Violations of Employment and Labor Laws in Chicago, Los Angeles, and New York City." *Social Forces* 91(3): 725–46.

Bernhardt, Annette, Michael Spiller, and Nik Theodore. 2013. "Employers Gone Rogue: Explaining Industry Variation in Violations of Workplace Laws." *ILR Review* 66(4): 808–32.

Berrey, Ellen, Robert L. Nelson, and Laura B. Nielsen. 2017. *Rights on Trial: How Workplace Discrimination Law Perpetuates Inequality*. University of Chicago Press.

Best, Rachel Kahn, Lauren B. Edelman, Linda Hamilton Krieger, and Scott R. Eliason. 2011. "Multiple Disadvantages: An Empirical Test of Intersectionality Theory in EEO Litigation." *Law & Society Review* 45(4): 991–1025.

Block, Sharon, and Benjamin Sachs. 2020. *Clean Slate for Worker Power: Building a Just Economy and Democracy*. Labor and Worklife Program, Harvard Law School. https://clje.law.harvard.edu/app/uploads/2020/0/Clean-Slate-for-Worker-Power.pdf.

Bloemraad, Irene. 2006. *Becoming a Citizen: Incorporating Immigrants and Refugees in the United States and Canada*. University of California Press.

Bloemraad, Irene. 2013. "The Promise and Pitfalls of Comparative Research Design in the Study of Migration." *Migration Studies* 1(1): 27–46.

Bonacich, Edna. 1972. "A Theory of Ethnic Antagonism: The Split Labor Market." *American Sociological Review* 37(5): 547–59.

Bonilla-Silva, Eduardo. 2001. *White Supremacy and Racism in the Post–Civil Rights Era*. Lynne Rienner Publishers.

Bonilla-Silva, Eduardo. 2002a. "The Linguistics of Color Blind Racism: How to Talk Nasty About Blacks Without Sounding 'Racist.'" *Critical Sociology* 28(1/2): 41–64.

Bonilla-Silva, Eduardo. 2002b. "We Are All Americans! The Latin Americanization of Racial Stratification in the USA." *Race and Society* 5(1): 3–16.

Bonilla-Silva, Eduardo. 2006. *Racism Without Racists: Color-Blind Racism and the Persistence of Racial Inequality in the United States.* Rowman & Littlefield.

Bonilla-Silva, Eduardo. 2021. "What Makes Systemic Racism *Systemic*?" *Sociological Inquiry* 91(3): 513–33.

Borger, Julian. 2018. "Fleeing a Hell the US Helped Create: Why Central Americans Journey North." *The Guardian*, December 19. https://www.theguardian.com/us-news/2018/dec/19/central-america-migrants-us-foreign-policy.

Boris, Eileen, and Jennifer Klein. 2015. *Caring for America: Home Health Workers in the Shadow of the Welfare State.* Oxford University Press.

Brookes, Marissa. 2018. "Power Resources in Theory and Practice: Where to Go from Here." *Global Labour Journal* 9(2): 254–57.

Browne, Irene, and Joya Misra. 2003. "The Intersection of Gender and Race in the Labor Market." *Annual Review of Sociology* 29(1): 487–513.

Bumiller, Kristin. 1992. *The Civil Rights Society: The Social Construction of Victims.* John Hopkins University Press.

Bureau of Labor Statistics. 2021a. "Characteristics of Minimum Wage Workers, 2020." BLS Report 1091, February. https://www.bls.gov/opub/reports/minimum-wage/2020/home.htm.

Bureau of Labor Statistics. 2021b. "Injuries, Illnesses, and Fatalities: Table 1: Incidence Rates of Nonfatal Occupational Injuries and Illnesses by Industry and Case Types, 2020." Updated November 3, 2021. Bureau of Labor Statistics. https://www.bls.gov/web/osh/summ1_00.htm.

Bureau of Labor Statistics. 2024a. "Labor Force Characteristics of Foreign-Born Workers Summary: Foreign-Born Workers: Labor Force Characteristics: 2023." US Department of Labor USDL-24-1008. https://www.bls.gov/news.release/pdf/forbrn.pdf.

Bureau of Labor Statistics. 2024b. "Contingent and Alternative Employment Arrangements News Release." USDL-18-0942. https://www.bls.gov/news.release/conemp.htm.

Burnham, Linda, and Nik Theodore. 2012. "Home Economics: The Invisible and Unregulated World of Domestic Work." National Domestic Workers Alliance. https://www.domesticworkers.org/reports-and-publications/home-economics-the-invisible-and-unregulated-world-of-domestic-work.

Bush, Deborah, Shaun Bush, et al. 2019. "Afro-Latino-América: Black and Afro-Descendant Rights and Struggles." In *The Routledge Handbook of Latin American Development*, edited by Julie Cupples, Marcela Palomino-Schalscha, and Manuel Prieto. Routledge.

Bussel, Robert. 2015. *Fighting for Total Person Unionism: Harold Gibbons, Ernest Calloway, and Working-Class Citizenship.* University of Illinois Press.

Cadeau, Sabine F. 2022. *More than a Massacre: Racial Violence and Citizenship in the Haitian-Dominican Borderlands.* Cambridge University Press.

Calavita, Kitty. 1990. "Employer Sanctions Violations: Toward a Dialectical Model of White-Collar Crime." *Law & Society Review* 24(4): 1041–69.

Calavita, Kitty. 1992. *Inside the State: The Bracero Program, Immigration, and the INS*. Routledge.

Calavita, Kitty. 2016. *Invitation to Law and Society: An Introduction to the Study of Real Law*. University of Chicago Press.

Campos-Medina, Patricia. 2019. "Not Legal. Not Illegal. Just TPS. Examining the Integration Experience of Central American Immigrants Living Under a Regime of Long-Term Temporality." PhD diss., Rutgers University.

Campos-Medina, Patricia, Erika Nava, and Sol Aramendi. 2023. "Tandas and Co-operativas: Understanding the Social Economy of Indigenous Mexican Immigrants Settled in Perth Amboy, New Jersey, and Staten Island, New York." In *Beyond Racial Capitalism: Co-operatives in the African Diaspora*, edited by Caroline Shenaz Hossein, Sharon D. Wright Austin, and Kevin Edmonds. Oxford University Press.

Capps, Randy, Julia Gelatt, Ariel G. Ruiz Soto, and Jennifer Van Hook. 2020. "Unauthorized Immigrants in the United States: Stable Numbers, Changing Origins." Migration Policy Institute, December 16. https://www.migrationpolicy.org/research/unauthorized-immigrants-united-states-stable-numbers-changing-origins.

Carbado, Devon W. 2011. "Critical What What?" *Connecticut Law Review* 43(5): 1593–1643.

Carbado, Devon W., and Cheryl I. Harris. 2008. "The New Racial Preferences." *California Law Review* 96(5): 1139–1214.

Carré, Françoise. 2015. "(In)Dependent Contractor Misclassification." Economic Policy Institute, June 8. https://www.epi.org/publication/independent-contractor-misclassification/.

Carré, Françoise, and Chris Tilly. 2017. *Where Bad Jobs Are Better: Retail Jobs Across Countries and Companies*. Russell Sage Foundation.

Cauthen, Nancy K. 2011. "Scheduling Hourly Workers: How Last Minute, Just-in-Time Scheduling Practices Are Bad for Workers, Families, and Business." Dēmos, March 14. https://www.demos.org/publication/scheduling-hourly-workers-how-last-minute-just-time-scheduling-practices-are-bad-workers.

Cavounidis, Costas, Kevin Lang, and Russell Weinstein. 2024. "The Boss Is Watching: How Monitoring Decisions Hurt Black Workers." *Economic Journal* 134(658): 485–514.

Ceron, Ella. 2022. "Federal Minimum Wage: 1 in 3 US Workers Make Less than $15 an Hour." *Bloomberg*, March 22. https://www.bloomberg.com/news/articles/2022-03-22/federal-minimum-wage-1-in-3-us-workers-make-less-than-15-an-hour.

Chacón, Jennifer M. 2015. "Producing Liminal Legality." *Denver University Law Review* 92(4): 709–67.

Chavez, Leo R. 1998. *Shadowed Lives: Undocumented Immigrants in American Society*. Harcourt Brace College.

Chavez, Leo R. 2013. *The Latino Threat: Constructing Immigrants, Citizens, and the Nation*, 2nd ed. Stanford University Press.

Chen, Ming Hsu. 2020. *Pursuing Citizenship in the Enforcement Era*. Stanford University Press.

Chetty, Raj, Nathaniel Hendren, Maggie R. Jones, and Sonya R. Porter. 2020. "Race and Economic Opportunity in the United States: An Intergenerational Perspective." *Quarterly Journal of Economics* 135(2): 711–83.

Ching, Erik, and Virginia Tilley. 1998. "Indians, the Military, and the Rebellion of 1932 in El Salvador." *Journal of Latin American Studies* 30(1): 121–56.

Choudry, Aziz, and Mostafa Henaway. 2012. "Agents of Misfortune: Contextualizing Migrant and Immigrant Workers' Struggles Against Temporary Labour Recruitment Agencies." *Labour, Capital, and Society* 45(1): 36–65.

Choy-Gómez, Jorge. 2021. "Power and Spectacle on Mexico's Southern Border." *NACLA Report on the Americas*, February 18. https://nacla.org/mexico-southern-border-immigration-spectacle.

Cohn, D'Vera, Jeffrey S. Passel, and Kristen Bialik. 2019. "Many Immigrants with Temporary Protected Status Face Uncertain Future in US." Pew Research Center, November 27. https://www.pewresearch.org/fact-tank/2019/11/27/immigrants-temporary-protected-status-in-us/.

Collins, Patricia Hill. 1986. "Learning from the Outsider Within: The Sociological Significance of Black Feminist Thought." *Social Problems* 33(6, special theory issue): S14–32.

Collins, Jane L. 2003. *Threads: Gender, Labor, and Power in the Global Apparel Industry*. University of Chicago Press.

Columbia Law School Human Rights Clinic. 2014. "Access to Justice: Ensuring Meaningful Access to Counsel in Civil Cases: Response to the Fourth Periodic Report of the United States to the United Nations Human Rights Committee." *Syracuse Law Review* 64.

Compa, Lance. 2014. "Not Dead Yet: Preserving Labor Law Strengths While Exploring New Labor Law Strategies." *UC Irvine Law Review* 4(2): 609–24.

Constantino, Annika Kim. 2021. "US Bars Immigration Arrests at Schools, Hospitals, and Other 'Protected Areas.'" CNBC, October 27. https://www.cnbc.com/2021/10/27/us-ends-immigration-arrests-at-schools-hospitals-and-other-protected-areas.html.

Corbett, William R. 2020. "Firing Employment at Will and Discharging Termination Claims from Employment Discrimination: A Cooperative-Federalism Approach to Improve Employment Law." *Cardozo Law Review* 42(6): 2281–2343.

Cordero-Guzmán, Héctor R. 2015. "Worker Centers, Worker Center Networks, and the Promise of Protections for Low-Wage Workers." *WorkingUSA* 18(1): 31–57.

Costa, Daniel. 2017. "Modern-Day Braceros: The United States Has 450,000 Guestworkers in Low-Wage Jobs and Doesn't Need More." Economic Policy Institute, March 31. https://www.epi.org/blog/modern-day-braceros-the-united-states-has-450000-guestworkers-in-low-wage-jobs/.

Craemer, Thomas, and Samuel Martínez. 2021. "Anti-Haitian Stereotypes in Three Dominican Daily Newspapers: A Content Analysis." *Latin American and Caribbean Ethnic Studies* 16(1): 85–107.

Crenshaw, Kimberlé. 1991. "Mapping the Margins: Intersectionality, Identity Politics, and Violence Against Women of Color." *Stanford Law Review* 43(6): 1241–99.

Cuéllar, Jorge E. 2018. "Elimination/Deracination: Colonial Terror, La Matanza, and the 1930s Race Laws in El Salvador." *American Indian Culture and Research Journal* 42(2): 39–56.

Dahl, R. A. 1957. "The Concept of Power." *Behavioral Science* 2(3): 201–15.

Daut, Marlene. 2020. "When France Extorted Haiti—The Greatest Heist in History." *The Conversation*, June 30. https://theconversation.com/when-france-extorted-haiti-the-greatest-heist-in-history-137949.

Daut, Marlene L. 2024. "How Haiti Destroyed Slavery and Led the Way to Freedom Throughout the Atlantic World." *Public Books*, January 9. https://www.publicbooks.org/how-haiti-destroyed-slavery/.

De Genova, Nicholas. 1998. "Race, Space, and the Reinvention of Latin America in Mexican Chicago." *Latin American Perspectives* 25(5): 87–116.

De Genova, Nicholas. 2005. *Working the Boundaries: Race, Space, and "Illegality" in Mexican Chicago*. Duke University Press.

De Genova, Nicholas. 2016a. "The European Question: Migration, Race, and Postcoloniality in Europe." *Social Text* 34 (3 [128]): 75–102.

De Genova, Nicholas. 2016b. "The Incorrigible Subject of the Border Spectacle." In *Public and Political Discourses of Migration: International Perspectives*, edited by Amanda Haynes, Martin J. Power, Eoin Devereux, Aileen Dillane, and James Carr. Rowman & Littlefield.

de Graauw, Els. 2016. *Making Immigrant Rights Real: Nonprofits and the Politics of Integration in San Francisco*. Cornell University Press.

de Graauw, Els, and Shannon Gleeson. 2020. "Metropolitan Context and Immigrant Rights Experiences: DACA Awareness and Support in Houston." *Urban Geography* 42(8): 1119–46.

de Graauw, Els, Shannon Gleeson, and Xóchitl Bada. 2019. "Local Context and Labour-Community Immigrant Rights Coalitions: A Comparison of San Francisco, Chicago, and Houston." *Journal of Ethnic and Migration Studies* 20(4): 728–46.

De Lara, Juan D., Ellen R. Reese, and Jason Struna. 2016. "Organizing Temporary, Subcontracted, and Immigrant Workers: Lessons from Change to Win's Warehouse Workers United Campaign." *Labor Studies Journal* 41(4): 309–32.

Dobbins, James, J. David Goodman, and Edgar Sandoval. 2022. "At Least 46 Migrants Found Dead in San Antonio." *New York Times*, June 28. https://www.nytimes.com/live/2022/06/28/us/migrants-san-antonio-tractor-killed.

Dodson, Lisa. 2009. *The Moral Underground: How Ordinary Americans Subvert an Unfair Economy*. New Press.

Doussard, Marc. 2013. *Degraded Work: The Struggle at the Bottom of the Labor Market*. University of Minnesota Press.

Dreiling, Michael, and Derek Darves. 2011. "Corporate Unity in American Trade Policy: A Network Analysis of Corporate-Dyad Political Action." *American Journal of Sociology* 116(5): 1514–63.

Dubois, Laurent. 2012. *Haiti: The Aftershocks of History*. Metropolitan Books.

Dubuisson, Darlène. 2022a. "Haiti: Black Utopia." Society for Cultural Anthropology, May 3. https://culanth.org/fieldsights/haiti-black-utopia.

Dubuisson, Darlène. 2022b. "The Haitian Zombie Motif: Against the Banality of Antiblack Violence." *Journal of Visual Culture* 21(2): 255–76.

Dubuisson, Darlène, and Mark Schuller. 2024. "Organizing Against Anti-Haitianism Beyond Borders." *NACLA Report on the Americas*, September 30. https://nacla.org/organizing-against-anti-haitianism-beyond-borders.

Dunbar-Ortiz, Roxanne. 2021. *Not "A Nation of Immigrants": Settler Colonialism, White Supremacy, and a History of Erasure and Exclusion*. Beacon Press.

Duncan, Grant. 2003. "Workers' Compensation and the Governance of Pain." *Economy and Society* 32(3): 449–77.

Durand, Jorge, Douglas S. Massey, and Karen A. Pren. 2016. "Double Disadvantage: Unauthorized Mexicans in the US Labor Market." *Annals of the American Academy of Political and Social Science* 666(1): 78–90.

Edelman, Lauren B. 1992. "Legal Ambiguity and Symbolic Structures: Organizational Mediation of Civil Rights Law." *American Journal of Sociology* 97(6): 1531–76.

Einarsen, Stale, Helge Hoel, Dieter Zapf, and Cary Cooper, eds. 2010. *Bullying and Harassment in the Workplace: Developments in Theory, Research, and Practice*, 2nd ed. CRC Press.

Elliott, James R., and Ryan A. Smith. 2001. "Ethnic Matching of Supervisors to Subordinate Work Groups: Findings on 'Bottom-Up' Ascription and Social Closure." *Social Problems* 48(2): 258–76.

Elmore, Andrew. 2018a. "Collaborative Enforcement." *Northeastern University Law Review* 10(1): 72–140.

Elmore, Andrew. 2018b. "Franchise Regulation for the Fissured Economy." *George Washington Law Review* 86(4): 907–65.

Elmore, Andrew, and Muzaffar Chishti. 2018. "Strategic Leverage: Use of State and Local Laws to Enforce Labor Standards in Immigrant-Dense Occupations." Migration Policy Institute, March 13. https://www.migrationpolicy.org/research/strategic-leverage-use-state-and-local-laws-enforce-labor-standards-immigrant.

Elmore, Andrew, and Kati L. Griffith. 2021. "Franchisor Power as Employment Control." *California Law Review* 109(4): 1317–71.

Epp, Charles R. 2010. *Making Rights Real: Activists, Bureaucrats, and the Creation of the Legalistic State*. University of Chicago.

Estlund, Cynthia L. 1995. "Wrongful Discharge Protections in an At-Will World Symposium: The Changing Workplace." *Texas Law Review* 74(7): 1655–92.

Estlund, Cynthia L. 2002. "The Ossification of American Labor Law." *Columbia Law Review* 102(6): 1527–1612.

Euraque, Dario A. 2018. "Political Economy, Race, and National Identity in Central America, 1500–2000." In *Oxford Research Encyclopedia of Latin American History*.

Felstiner, William L. F., Richard L. Abel, and Austin Sarat. 1980. "The Emergence and Transformation of Disputes: Naming, Blaming, Claiming." *Law & Society Review* 15(3/4): 631–54.

Fine, Janice. 2006. *Worker Centers: Organizing Communities at the Edge of the Dream*. ILR Press.

Fine, Janice. 2011. "Worker Centers: Entering a New Stage of Growth and Development." *New Labor Forum* 20(3): 44–53.

Fine, Janice. 2017. "Enforcing Labor Standards in Partnership with Civil Society: Can Co-Enforcement Succeed Where the State Alone Has Failed?" *Politics & Society* 45(3): 359–88.

Fine, Janice, Linda Burnham, Kati Griffith, Minsun Ji, Victor Narro, and Steven C. Pitts, eds. 2018. *No One Size Fits All: Worker Organization, Policy, and Movement in a New Economic Age*. Labor and Employment Relations Association.

Fine, Janice, and Jennifer Gordon. 2010. "Strengthening Labor Standards Enforcement Through Partnerships with Workers' Organizations." *Politics & Society* 38(4): 552–85.

Fine, Janice, and Gregory Lyon. 2017. "Segmentation and the Role of Labor Standards Enforcement in Immigration Reform." *Journal on Migration and Human Security* 5(2): 431–51.

Fink, Leon. 2003. *The Maya of Morganton: Work and Community in the Nuevo New South*. University of North Carolina Press.

Fischer-Daly, Matthew. 2021. "Human Dignity and Power: Worker Struggles Against Precarity in US Agribusiness." *Labor Studies Journal* 46(4): 369–93.

Fisk, Catherine L. 2001. "Humiliation at Work." *William & Mary Journal of Race, Gender, and Social Justice* 8: 73.

Fisk, Catherine L., and Martin H. Malin. 2019. "After Janus." *California Law Review* 107: 1821–76.

Fisk, Catherine L., and Michael J. Wishnie. 2005. "The Story of *Hoffman Plastic Compounds, Inc. v. NLRB*: Labor Rights Without Remedies for Undocumented Immigrants." In *Labor Law Stories*, edited by Laura J. Cooper and Catherine L. Fisk. Foundation Press.

Flippen, Chenoa A. 2012. "Laboring Underground: The Employment Patterns of Hispanic Immigrant Men in Durham, NC." *Social Problems* 59(1): 21–42.

Flores, René D., and Ariela Schachter. 2019. "Examining Americans' Stereotypes About Immigrant Illegality." *Contexts* 18(2): 36–41.

Frank, Dana. 2024. *What Can We Learn from the Great Depression? Stories of Ordinary People and Collective Action in Hard Times*. Beacon Press.

Frank-Vitale, Amelia. 2020. "Stuck in Motion: Inhabiting the Space of Transit in Central American Migration." *Journal of Latin American and Caribbean Anthropology* 25(1): 67–83.

Frasco, Melissa. 2020. "Why There Are No Black Dominicans: How Anti-Haitian Sentiment in the Era of Trujillo and the Deeply Rooted Black History of the Island of Hispaniola Affects How Dominicans Racially Identify in New York Today." Honors thesis, State University of New York at New Paltz, December. https://soar.suny.edu/handle/20.500.12648/1581.

Fraser, Nancy. 2003. "From Discipline to Flexibilization? Rereading Foucault in the Shadow of Globalization." *Constellations* (2): 160–71.
Fritz-Mauer, Matthew. 2020. "The Ragged Edge of Rugged Individualism: Wage Theft and the Personalization of Social Harm." *University of Michigan Journal of Law Reform* 54(3): 735–800.
Frymer, Paul, and Jacob M. Grumbach. 2020. "Labor Unions and White Racial Politics." *American Journal of Political Science* 65(1): 225–40.
Galanter, Marc. 1974. "Why the 'Haves' Come Out Ahead: Speculations on the Limits of Legal Change." *Law & Society Review* 9(1): 95–160.
Galvin, Daniel J. 2016. "Deterring Wage Theft: Alt-Labor, State Politics, and the Policy Determinants of Minimum Wage Compliance." *Perspectives on Politics* 14(2): 324–50.
Galvin, Daniel J. 2024. *Alt-Labor and the New Politics of Workers' Rights*. Russell Sage Foundation.
Gamonal, Sergio, and César F. Rosado Marzán. 2019. *Principled Labor Law: US Labor Law Through a Latin American Method*. Oxford University Press.
Gans, Herbert J. 2011. "The Moynihan Report and Its Aftermaths: A Critical Analysis." *Du Bois Review: Social Science Research on Race* 8(2): 315–27.
Garcia, Ruben J. 2011. "Ten Years After *Hoffman Plastic Compounds, Inc. v. NLRB*: The Power of a Labor Law Symbol." *Cornell Journal of Law and Public Policy* 21: 659.
Garcia, Ruben J. 2012. *Marginal Workers: How Legal Fault Lines Divide Workers and Leave Them Without Protection*. New York University Press.
García y Griego, Manuel. 1988. *The Bracero Policy Experiment: US-Mexican Responses to Mexican Labor Migration, 1942–1955*. University of California.
Gates, Leslie C. 2002. "The Strategic Uses of Gender in Household Negotiations: Women Workers on Mexico's Northern Border." *Bulletin of Latin American Research* 21(4): 507–26.
Gates, Leslie C. 2009. "Theorizing Business Power in the Semiperiphery: Mexico 1970–2000." *Theory and Society* 38(1): 57–95.
Gates, Leslie, Kati L. Griffith, Jonathan Kim, Zane Mokhiber, Joseph C. Bazler, and Austin Case. 2018. "Sizing Up Worker Center Income (2008–2014): A Study of Revenue Size, Stability, and Streams." In *No One Size Fits All: Worker Organization, Policy, and Movement for a New Economic Age*, edited by Janice Fine, Linda Burnham, Kate Griffith, Minsun Ji, Victor Narro, and Steven Pitts. Labor and Employment Research Association.
Gelatt, Julia, Valerie Lacarte, and Joshua Rodriguez. 2022. "A Profile of Low-Income Immigrants in the United States." Migration Policy Institute, November. https://www.migrationpolicy.org/research/low-income-immigrants.
Gerstein, Terri. 2021. "How District Attorneys and State Attorneys General Are Fighting Workplace Abuses." Center for Labor and a Just Economy, Harvard University, May 17. https://clje.law.harvard.edu/how-district-attorneys-and-state-attorneys-general-are-fighting-workplace-abuses/.
Ginsburg, Matthew. 2017. "Nothing New Under the Sun: 'The New Labor Law' Must Still Grapple with the Traditional Challenges of Firm-Based Organizing and

Building Self-Sustainable Worker Organizations." *Yale Law Journal Forum* (April): 488–502.

Gleeson, Shannon. 2009. "From Rights to Claims: The Role of Civil Society in Making Rights Real for Vulnerable Workers." *Law & Society Review* 43(3): 669–700.

Gleeson, Shannon. 2010. "Labor Rights for All? The Role of Undocumented Immigrant Status for Worker Claims-Making." *Law & Social Inquiry* 35(3): 561–602.

Gleeson, Shannon. 2012. *Conflicting Commitments: The Politics of Enforcing Immigrant Worker Rights in San Jose and Houston*. Cornell University Press.

Gleeson, Shannon. 2015. "'They Come Here to Work': An Evaluation of the Economic Argument in Favor of Immigrant Rights." *Citizenship Studies* 19(3/4): 400–420.

Gleeson, Shannon. 2016. *Precarious Claims: The Promise and Failure of Workplace Protections in the United States*. University of California Press.

Gleeson, Shannon. 2021. "Legal Status and Client Satisfaction: The Case of Low-Wage Immigrant Workers." *Law & Social Inquiry* 46(2): 364–90.

Gleeson, Shannon, and Kati L. Griffith. 2021. "Employers as Subjects of the Immigration State: How the State Foments Employment Insecurity for Temporary Immigrant Workers." *Law & Social Inquiry* 46(1): 92–115.

Gleeson, Shannon, and Prerna Sampat. 2018. "Immigrant Resistance in the Age of Trump." *New Labor Forum* 27(1): 86–95.

Glenn, Evelyn Nakano. 1992. "From Servitude to Service Work: Historical Continuities in the Racial Division of Paid Reproductive Labor." *Signs* 18(1): 1–43.

Glenn, Evelyn Nakano. 2015. "Race, Racialization, and Work." In *The SAGE Handbook of the Sociology of Work and Employment*, edited by Stephen Edgell, Heidi Gottfried, and Edward Granter. SAGE Publications.

Glick-Schiller, Nina, and Georges Fouron. 1998. "Transnational Lives and National Identities: The Identity Politics of Haitian Immigrants." In *Transnationalism from Below*, edited by Michael P. Smith and Luis Guarnizo. Transaction.

Golash-Boza, Tanya Maria. 2015. *Race and Racisms: A Critical Approach*. Oxford University Press.

Golash-Boza, Tanya, and Hyunsu Oh. 2021. "Crime and Neighborhood Change in the Nation's Capital: From Disinvestment to Gentrification." *Crime & Delinquency* 67(9): 1267–94.

Goldberg, Mimi. 2024. "Quizás Se Puede: Evaluating Union Success in Incorporating Immigrant Workers." *Harvard Civil Rights--Civil Liberties Law Review* 59(1): 304–24.

Goldring, Luin, and Patricia Landolt. 2011. "Caught in the Work-Citizenship Matrix: The Lasting Effects of Precarious Legal Status on Work for Toronto Immigrants." *Globalizations* 8(3): 325–41.

Gomberg-Muñoz, Ruth. 2010. "Willing to Work: Agency and Vulnerability in an Undocumented Immigrant Network." *American Anthropologist* 112(2): 295–307.

Gomberg-Muñoz, Ruth. 2011. *Labor and Legality: An Ethnography of a Mexican Immigrant Network*. Oxford University Press.

Gomberg-Muñoz, Ruth. 2012. "Inequality in a 'Postracial' Era: Race, Immigration, and Criminalization of Low-Wage Labor." *Du Bois Review: Social Science Research on Race* 9(2): 339–53.

Gordon, Jennifer. 2007a. *Suburban Sweatshops: The Fight for Immigrant Rights*. Belknap Press of Harvard University Press.

Gordon, Jennifer. 2007b. "Transnational Labor Citizenship." *Southern California Law Review* 80: 503–88.

Gordon, Jennifer. 2011. "Tensions in Rhetoric and Reality at the Intersection of Work and Immigration." *UC Irvine Law Review* 2(1): 125–46.

Griffith, David, Diane Austin, Micah N. Bump, Ricardo Contreras, Cindy Hahamovitch, and Elzbieta M. Gozdziak. 2014. *(Mis)Managing Migration: Guestworkers' Experiences with North American Labor Markets*. SAR Press.

Griffith, Kati L. 2009. "The NLRA Defamation Defense: Doomed Dinosaur or Diamond in the Rough?" *American University Law Review* 59(1): 1.

Griffith, Kati L. 2011a. "Discovering 'Immployment' Law: The Constitutionality of Subfederal Immigration Regulation at Work." *Yale Law and Policy Review* 29(2): 389–451.

Griffith, Kati L. 2011b. "ICE Was Not Meant to Be Cold: The Case for Civil Rights Monitoring of Immigration Enforcement at the Workplace." *Arizona Law Review* 53(4): 1137–56.

Griffith, Kati L. 2012. "Undocumented Workers: Crossing the Borders of Immigration and Workplace Law." *Cornell Journal of Law and Public Policy* 21(3): 611–97.

Griffith, Kati L. 2014. "Laborers or Criminals? The Impact of Crimmigration on Labor Standards Enforcement." In *The Criminalization of Immigration: Contexts and Consequences*, edited by Alissa Ackerman and Rich Furman. Carolina Academic Press.

Griffith, Kati L. 2019a. "An Empirical Study of Fast-Food Franchising Contracts: Towards a New Intermediary Theory of Joint Employment." *Washington Law Review* 94(1): 171–216.

Griffith, Kati L. 2019b. "The Fair Labor Standards Act at 80: Everything Old Is New Again." *Cornell Law Review* 104(3): 557–606.

Griffith, Kati L., and Leslie C. Gates. 2019. "Worker Centers: Labor Policy as a Carrot, Not a Stick." *Harvard Law & Policy Review* 14(1): 232–58.

Griffith, Kati L., and Shannon M. Gleeson. 2017. "The Precarity of Temporality: How Law Inhibits Immigrant Worker Claims." *Comparative Labor Law and Policy Journal* 39(1): 111–41.

Griffith, Kati L., Shannon Gleeson, and Vivian Vázquez. 2020. "Immigrants in Shifting Times on Long Island, NY: The Stakes of Losing Temporary Status." *Denver Law Review* 97(4): 743–59.

Grosfoguel, Ramón. 2003. *Colonial Subjects: Puerto Ricans in a Global Perspective*. University of California Press.

Grosfoguel, Ramón. 2016. "What Is Racism?" *Journal of World-Systems Research* 22(1): 9–15.

Gross, James A. 1995. *Broken Promise: The Subversion of US Labor Relations*. Temple University Press.

Gross, James A. 2017. "The Liebman Board: The NLRA, at Its Heart a Human Rights Law." In *Rights, Not Interests: Resolving Value Clashes Under the National Labor Relations Act*, edited by James A. Gross. Cornell University Press.

Guskin, Emily. 2013. "'Illegal,' 'Undocumented,' 'Unauthorized': News Media Shift Language on Immigration." Pew Research Center, June 17. https://www.pewresearch.org/fact-tank/2013/06/17/illegal-undocumented-unauthorized-news-media-shift-language-on-immigration/.

Hall, Matthew, and Emily Greenman. 2015. "The Occupational Cost of Being Illegal in the United States: Legal Status, Job Hazards, and Compensating Differentials." *International Migration Review* 49(2): 406–42.

Hall, Matthew, Emily Greenman, and George Farkas. 2011. "Legal Status and Wage Disparities for Mexican Immigrants." *Social Forces* 89(2): 491–513.

Hallett, Miranda Cady. 2014. "Temporary Protection, Enduring Contradiction: The Contested and Contradictory Meanings of Temporary Immigration Status." *Law & Social Inquiry* 39(3): 621–42.

Hallett, Nicole. 2018. "The Problem of Wage Theft." *Yale Law & Policy Review* 37(1): 93–152.

Hamburger, Jacob. 2023. "Hybrid-Status Immigrant Workers." *Duke Law Journal* 73(4): 737. https://scholarship.law.duke.edu/cgi/viewcontent.cgi?article=4184&context=dlj.

Harcourt, Mark, Gregor Gall, Rinu Vimal Kumar, and Richard Croucher. 2019. "A Union Default: A Policy to Raise Union Membership, Promote the Freedom to Associate, Protect the Freedom Not to Associate, and Progress Union Representation." *Industrial Law Journal* 48(1): 66–97.

Harper, Michael C., Samuel Estreicher, and Kati L. Griffith. 2021. *Labor Law: Cases, Materials, and Problems*, 9th ed. Wolters Kluwer.

Hartman, Saidiya. 2022. *Scenes of Subjection: Terror, Slavery, and Self-Making in Nineteenth-Century America*. W. W. Norton & Co.

Heeren, Geoffrey. 2015. "The Status of Nonstatus." *American University Law Review* 64: 1115–81.

Herrera, Juan. 2016. "Racialized Illegality: The Regulation of Informal Labor and Space." *Latino Studies* 14(3): 320–43.

Hess, Cynthia, and Ariane Hegewisch. 2019. "The Future of Care Work: Improving the Quality of America's Fastest-Growing Jobs." Institute for Women's Policy Research. https://iwpr.org/wp-content/uploads/2020/07/C486_Future-of-Care-Work_final.pdf.

Hill, Herbert. 1985. *Black Labor and the American Legal System: Race, Work, and the Law*. University of Wisconsin Press.

Hirsch, Barry T., David A. Macpherson, and William Even. 2024. "Union Membership, Coverage, and Earnings from the CPS." Updated from the 2023 Current Population Survey completed January 16, 2024. https://www.unionstats.com/.

Hirschman, A. O. 1970. *Exit, Voice, and Loyalty: Responses to Decline in Firms, Organizations, and States*. Harvard University Press.

Hodson, Randy. 2001. *Dignity at Work*. Cambridge University Press.

Holmes, Seth. 2013. *Fresh Fruit, Broken Bodies: Migrant Farmworkers in the United States*. University of California Press.

Hondagneu-Sotelo, Pierrette. 2007. *Doméstica: Immigrant Workers Cleaning and Caring in the Shadows of Affluence*. University of California Press.

Honey, Michael K. 2000. *Black Workers Remember: An Oral History of Segregation, Unionism, and the Freedom Struggle*. University of California Press.

Hooker, Juliet. 2005. "'Beloved Enemies': Race and Official Mestizo Nationalism in Nicaragua." *Latin American Research Review* 40(3): 14–39.

HoSang, Daniel Martinez, Oneka LaBennett, and Laura Pulido, eds. 2012. *Racial Formation in the Twenty-First Century*. University of California Press.

Hoyt, Carlos. 2016. *The Arc of a Bad Idea: Understanding and Transcending Race*. Oxford University Press.

Huber, Lindsay Pérez. 2016. "Constructing 'Deservingness': DREAMers and Central American Unaccompanied Children in the National Immigration Debate." *Association of Mexican American Educators Journal* 9(3). https://journals.coehd.utsa.edu//index.php/AMAE/article/view/180.

Hunter, Marcus Anthony, and Zandria F. Robinson. 2016. "The Sociology of Urban Black America." *Annual Review of Sociology* 42(1): 385–405.

Huntington, Samuel. 2004. "Who Are We? The Challenges to America's National Identity." *Foreign Policy* (March/April): 30–45.

Iafolla, Robert. 2023. "NYC's Protections for Fast-Food Workers Get Second Circuit Test." *Bloomberg Law*, May 18. https://news.bloomberglaw.com/daily-labor-report/nycs-protections-for-fast-food-workers-get-second-circuit-test.

Immerman, Richard H. 1980. "Guatemala as Cold War History." *Political Science Quarterly* 95(4): 629–53.

Jacobs, Jerry A., and Scott Frickel. 2009. "Interdisciplinarity: A Critical Assessment." *Annual Review of Sociology* 35(1): 43–65.

Jayaraman, Saru. 2013. *Behind the Kitchen Door*. Cornell University Press.

Jensen, Katherine, and Lisa M. Sousa Dias. 2022. "Varied Racialization and Legal Inclusion: Haitian, Syrian, and Venezuelan Forced Migrants in Brazil." *American Behavioral Scientist* 66(13).

Jiménez Román, Miriam, and Juan Flores, eds. 2010. *The Afro-Latin@ Reader History and Culture in the United States*. Duke University Press.

Johnson, Violet Showers. 2016. "When Blackness Stings: African and Afro-Caribbean Immigrants, Race, and Racism in Late Twentieth-Century America." *Journal of American Ethnic History* 36(1): 31–62.

Jones, Jennifer A. 2019. *The Browning of the New South*. University of Chicago Press.

Jones, William P. 2013. *The March on Washington: Jobs, Freedom, and the Forgotten History of Civil Rights*. W. W. Norton & Co.

Jordan, Miriam. 2023. "New Florida Immigration Rules Start to Strain Some Businesses." *New York Times*, August 4. https://www.nytimes.com/2023/08/04/us/florida-immigration-law-businesses.html.

Jung, Moon-Kie, and João H. Costa Vargas, eds. 2021. *Antiblackness*. Duke University Press.

Kahn, Jeffrey S. 2018. *Islands of Sovereignty: Haitian Migration and the Borders of Empire*. University of Chicago Press.

Kalleberg, Arne L. 2011. *Good Jobs, Bad Jobs: The Rise of Polarized and Precarious Employment Systems in the United States, 1970s–2000s.* Russell Sage Foundation.

Katz, Harry C., Thomas A. Kochan, and Alexander J. S. Colvin. 2017. *An Introduction to US Collective Bargaining and Labor Relations.* Cornell University Press.

Kelley, Robin D. G. 2015. *Hammer and Hoe: Alabama Communists During the Great Depression.* University of North Carolina Press.

Kerrissey, Jasmine, Eve S. Weinbaum, Clare Hammonds, Tom Juravich, and Dan Clawson, eds. 2020. *Labor in the Time of Trump.* Cornell University Press.

Kessler-Harris, Alice. 2007. *Gendering Labor History.* University of Illinois Press.

Kirschenman, Joleen, and Kathryn M. Neckerman. 1991. "'We'd Love to Hire Them, But . . . ': The Meaning of Race for Employers." In *The Urban Underclass*, edited by Christopher Jencks and Paul E. Peterson. Brookings Institution Press.

Knight, Franklin W. 2005. "The Haitian Revolution and the Notion of Human Rights." *Journal of the Historical Society* 5: 391–416.

Kochan, Thomas A. 2020. "Worker Voice, Representation, and Implications for Public Policies." MIT Task Force on Work of the Future. https://workofthefuture-taskforce.mit.edu/wp-content/uploads/2020/08/WotF-2020-Research-Brief-Kochan_0.pdf.

Komisaruk, Catherine. 2009. "Indigenous Labor as Family Labor: Tributes, Migration, and Hispanicization in Colonial Guatemala." *Labor* 6(4): 41–66.

Kovalick, Daniel. 2023. *Nicaragua: A History of US Intervention and Resistance.* Clarity Press.

Kreisberg, A. Nicole. 2019. "Starting Points: Divergent Trajectories of Labor Market Integration Among US Lawful Permanent Residents." *Social Forces* 98(2): 849–84.

Krogstad, Jens Manuel, Mark Hugo Lopez, and Jeffrey S. Passel. 2020. "A Majority of Americans Say Immigrants Mostly Fill Jobs US Citizens Do Not Want." Pew Research Center, June 10. https://www.pewresearch.org/fact-tank/2020/06/10/a-majority-of-americans-say-immigrants-mostly-fill-jobs-u-s-citizens-do-not-want/.

Kundro, Timothy G., Vanessa Burke, Alicia A. Grandey, and Gordon M. Sayre. 2022. "A Perfect Storm: Customer Sexual Harassment as a Joint Function of Financial Dependence and Emotional Labor." *Journal of Applied Psychology* 107(8): 1385–96.

Lacarte, Valerie. 2022. "Black Immigrants in the United States Face Hurdles, but Outcomes Vary by City." Migration Policy Institute, February 10. https://www.migrationpolicy.org/article/black-immigrants-united-states-hurdles-outcomes-top-cities.

Lahav, Gallya. 1998. "Immigration and the State: The Devolution and Privatisation of Immigration Control in the EU." *Journal of Ethnic and Migration Studies* 24(4): 674–94.

Lahav, Gallya. 2000. "The Rise of Non-State Actors in Migration Regulation in the United States and Europe: Changing the Gatekeepers or 'Bringing Back the State'?" In *Immigration Research for a New Century: Multidisciplinary Perspectives,* edited by Nancy Foner, Rubén G. Rumbaut, and Steven J. Gold. Russell Sage Foundation.

Lamb, Valerie, and Lauren Dundes. 2017. "Not Haitian: Exploring the Roots of Dominican Identity." *Social Sciences* 6(4): 132.

Lamont, Michèle. 2002. *The Dignity of Working Men: Morality and the Boundaries of Gender, Race, and Class*. Harvard University Press.

Lee, Ching Kwan. 2007. *Against the Law: Labor Protests in China's Rustbelt and Sunbelt*. University of California Press.

Lee, Jennifer J., and Annie Smith. 2019. "Regulating Wage Theft." *Washington Law Review* 94(2): 759–822.

Lee, Stephen. 2009. "Private Immigration Screening in the Workplace." *Stanford Law Review* 61(5): 1103–46.

Lee, Tamara L., Sheri Davis-Faulkner, Naomi R. Williams, and Maite Tapia, eds. 2022. *A Racial Reckoning in Industrial Relations: Storytelling as Revolution from Within*. Labor and Employment Research Association.

Lee, Tamara L., and Maite Tapia. 2021. "Confronting Race and Other Social Identity Erasures: The Case for Critical Industrial Relations Theory." *ILR Review* 74(3): 637–62.

Lenard, Patti Tamara. 2022. "Constraining Denaturalization." *Political Studies* 70(2): 367–84.

Leroy, Justin, and Destin Jenkins, eds. 2021. *Histories of Racial Capitalism*. Columbia University Press.

Lesniewski, Jacob, and Shannon Gleeson. 2022. "Mobilizing Worker Rights: The Challenges of Claims-Driven Processes for Re-Regulating the Labor Market." *Labor Studies Journal* 47(3).

Levine, Rhonda F. 1988. *Class Struggle and the New Deal: Industrial Labor, Industrial Capital, and the State*. University Press of Kansas.

Liberato, Ana S. Q., and Yanick St. Jean. 2017. "Systemic Racism and Anti-Haitian Racism: Challenges and Opportunities." In *Systemic Racism: Making Liberty, Justice, and Democracy Real*, edited by Ruth Thompson-Miller and Kimberley Ducey. Palgrave Macmillan US.

Lieberwitz, Risa L. 2022. "Corporatization of Higher Education." In *The Cambridge Handbook of Labor and Democracy*, edited by Angela B. Cornell and Mark Barenberg. Cambridge University Press.

Lipsky, Michael. 2010. *Street-Level Bureaucracy: Dilemmas of the Individual in Public Service*, 30th anniversary ed. Russell Sage Foundation.

Lofstrom, Magnus, Laura Hill, and Joseph Hayes. 2013. "Wage and Mobility Effects of Legalization: Evidence from the New Immigrant Survey." *Journal of Regional Science* 53(1): 171–97.

Logan, John. 2006. "The Union Avoidance Industry in the United States." *British Journal of Industrial Relations* 44(4): 651–75.

López, Ian Haney. 2015. *Dog Whistle Politics: How Coded Racial Appeals Have Reinvented Racism and Wrecked the Middle Class*. Oxford University Press.

López, Jane Lilly. 2021. *Unauthorized Love: Mixed-Citizenship Couples Negotiating Intimacy, Immigration, and the State*. Stanford University Press.

López Oro, Paul Joseph. 2021. "Refashioning Afro-Latinidad Garifuna New Yorkers in Diaspora." In *Critical Dialogues in Latinx Studies: A Reader*, edited by Ana Y. Ramos-Zayas and Mérida M. Rúa. New York University Press.

López-Sanders, Laura. 2024. *The Manufacturing of Job Displacement: How Racial Capitalism Drives Immigrant and Gender Inequality in the Labor Market*. New York University Press.

Lord, Jonathan. 2022. "Quiet Quitting Is a New Name for an Old Method of Industrial Action." *The Conversation*, September 9. https://theconversation.com/quiet-quitting-is-a-new-name-for-an-old-method-of-industrial-action-189752.

Lovato, Roberto. 2018. "El Salvador's Worst Shitholes Are 'Made in America.'" *NACLA Report on the Americas*, January 18. https://nacla.org/news/2018/01/18/el-salvador%E2%80%99s-worst-shitholes-are-%E2%80%98made-america%E2%80%99.

Loza, Mireya. 2016. *Defiant Braceros: How Migrant Workers Fought for Racial, Sexual, and Political Freedom*. University of North Carolina Press.

Lucas, Kristen. 2017. "Workplace Dignity." In *The International Encyclopedia of Organizational Communication*, edited by Craig Scott and Laurie Lewis. John Wiley & Sons.

Lucas, Samuel Roundfield. 2008. *Theorizing Discrimination in an Era of Contested Prejudice: Discrimination in the United States*. Temple University Press.

Lung, Shirley. 2019. "Criminalizing Work and Non-Work: The Disciplining of Immigrant and African American Workers." *University of Massachusetts Law Review* 14: 290–348.

Macedo, Donaldo. 2000. "The Colonialism of the English Only Movement." *Educational Researcher* 29(3): 15–24.

MacKinnon, Catharine A. 1987. *Feminism Unmodified: Discourses on Life and Law*. Harvard University Press.

Mahalik, James R., Shaun M. Burns, and Matthew Syzdek. 2007. "Masculinity and Perceived Normative Health Behaviors as Predictors of Men's Health Behaviors." *Social Science & Medicine* 64(11): 2201–9.

Mahoney, James. 2001. *The Legacies of Liberalism: Path Dependence and Political Regimes in Central America*. Johns Hopkins University Press.

Manhattan District Attorney's Office. 2023. "DA Bragg Announces Creation of Office's First 'Worker Protection Unit' to Combat Wage Theft, Protect New Yorkers from Unsafe Work Conditions." February 16. https://manhattanda.org/d-a-bragg-announces-creation-of-offices-first-worker-protection-unit-to-combat-wage-theft-protect-new-yorkers-from-unsafe-work-conditions/.

Marius, Philippe-Richard. 2022. *The Unexceptional Case of Haiti: Race and Class Privilege in Postcolonial Bourgeois Society*. University Press of Mississippi.

Marnin, Julia. 2021. "Office for Victims of Immigrant Crimes, Opened by Trump, Closed by Biden Administration." *Newsweek*, June 11. https://www.newsweek.com/office-victims-immigrant-crimes-opened-trump-closed-biden-administration-1599936.

Martin, Philip L. 2017. *Merchants of Labor: Recruiters and International Labor Migration*. Oxford University Press.

Martínez Peláez, Severo. 2009. "La Patria Del Criollo: An Interpretation of Colonial Guatemala." In *La Patria Del Criollo*, edited by W. George Lovell and Christopher H. Lutz. Duke University Press.

Massey, Douglas S. 1999. "International Migration at the Dawn of the Twenty-First Century: The Role of the State." *Population and Development Review* 25(2): 303–22.

Matlon, Jordanna C. 2022. *A Man Among Other Men: The Crisis of Black Masculinity in Racial Capitalism*. Cornell University Press.

Mayblin, Lucy, and Joe Turner. 2020. *Migration Studies and Colonialism*. John Wiley & Sons.

McGinley, Ann C. 1999. "¡Viva la Evolución!: Recognizing Unconscious Motive in Title VII." *Cornell Journal of Law and Public Policy* 9(2): 415–92.

McGinley, Ann C. 2021. "Looking South: Toward Principled Protection of US Workers." *Florida International University Law Review* 16(3): 741–80.

McKanders, Karla M. 2020. "Immigration and Racial Justice: Enforcing the Borders of Blackness." *Georgia State University Law Review* 37(4): 1139–76.

Menjívar, Cecilia. 2006. "Liminal Legality: Salvadoran and Guatemalan Immigrants' Lives in the United States." *American Journal of Sociology* 111(4): 999–1037.

Menjívar, Cecilia. 2021. "The Racialization of 'Illegality.'" *Daedalus* 150(2): 91–105.

Menjívar, Cecilia, and Leisy J. Abrego. 2012. "Legal Violence: Immigration Law and the Lives of Central American Immigrants." *American Journal of Sociology* 117(5): 1380–1421.

Menjívar, Cecilia, Leisy J. Abrego, and Leah C. Schmalzbauer. 2016. *Immigrant Families*. John Wiley & Sons.

Michener, Jamila, Mallory SoRelle, and Chloe Thurston. 2022. "From the Margins to the Center: A Bottom-Up Approach to Welfare State Scholarship." *Perspectives on Politics* 20(1): 154–69.

Migration Policy Institute. n.d. "Profile of the Unauthorized Population: US." Migration Policy Institute. https://www.migrationpolicy.org/data/unauthorized-immigrant-population/state/US.

Milkman, Ruth. 2000. *Organizing Immigrants: The Challenge for Unions in Contemporary California*. Cornell University Press.

Milkman, Ruth. 2006. *LA Story: Immigrant Workers and the Future of the US Labor Movement*. Russell Sage Foundation.

Milkman, Ruth. 2011. "Immigrant Workers and the Future of American Labor." *ABA Journal of Labor & Employment Law* 26(2): 295–310.

Milkman, Ruth. 2018. "Making Paid Care Work Visible: Findings from Focus Groups with New York City Home Care Aides, Nannies, and House Cleaners." New York City Department of Consumer Affairs, March. https://www1.nyc.gov/assets/dca/downloads/pdf/workers/Making-Paid-Care-Work-Visible.pdf.

Milkman, Ruth, Joshua Bloom, and Victor Narro. 2010. *Working for Justice: The LA Model of Organizing and Advocacy*. ILR Press.

Milkman, Ruth, and Stephanie Luce. 2021. "The State of the Unions 2021: A Profile of Organized Labor in New York City, New York State, and the United States." CUNY School of Labor and Urban Studies, September. https://slu.cuny.edu/wp-content/uploads/2021/09/Union_Density-2021_D.pdf.

Milkman, Ruth, and Ed Ott, eds. 2014. *New Labor in New York: Precarious Workers and the Future of the Labor Movement.* Cornell University Press.

Miller, Richard E., and Austin Sarat. 1980. "Grievances, Claims, and Disputes: Assessing the Adversary Culture." *Law & Society Review* 15(3/4): 525–66.

Miller, Todd. 2019. *Empire of Borders: How the US Is Exporting Its Border Around the World.* Verso Books.

Mink, Gwendolyn, and Bruce Baum. 2009. "Meat vs. Rice (and Pasta): Samuel Gompers and the Republic of White Labor." In *Racially Writing the Republic: Racists, Race Rebels, and Transformations of American Identity*, edited by Bruce Baum and Duchess Harris. Duke University Press.

Mishel, Lawrence, and Josh Bivens. 2021. "Identifying the Policy Levers Generating Wage Suppression and Wage Inequality." Economic Policy Institute, May 13. https://www.epi.org/unequalpower/publications/wage-suppression-inequality/.

Misra, Joya, Celeste Vaughan Curington, and Venus Mary Green. 2021. "Methods of Intersectional Research." *Sociological Spectrum* 41(1): 9–28.

Moore, Phoebe V. 2017. *The Quantified Self in Precarity: Work, Technology, and What Counts.* Routledge.

Mora, G. Cristina. 2014. *Making Hispanics: How Activists, Bureaucrats, and Media Constructed a New American.* University of Chicago Press.

Moslimani, Mohamad. 2022. "Around Four-in-Ten Latinos in US Worry That They or Someone Close to Them Could Be Deported." Pew Research Center, February 14. https://www.pewresearch.org/fact-tank/2022/02/14/around-four-in-ten-latinos-in-u-s-worry-that-they-or-someone-close-to-them-could-be-deported/.

Moslimani, Mohamad. 2024. "How Temporary Protected Status Has Expanded Under the Biden Administration." Pew Research Center, March 29. https://www.pewresearch.org/short-reads/2024/03/29/biden-administration-further-expands-temporary-protected-status-to-cover-afghanistan-cameroon-ukraine/.

Moslimani, Mohamad, and Jeffrey S. Passel. 2024. "What the Data Says About Immigrants in the US." Pew Research Center, September 27. https://www.pewresearch.org/short-reads/2024/07/22/key-findings-about-us-immigrants/.

Motomura, Hiroshi. 2014. *Immigration Outside the Law.* Oxford University Press.

Mountz, Alison, Richard Wright, Ines Miyares, and Adrian J. Bailey. 2002. "Lives in Limbo: Temporary Protected Status and Immigrant Identities." *Global Networks* 2(4): 335–56.

Munger, Frank, ed. 2002. *Laboring Below the Line: The New Ethnography of Poverty, Low-Wage Work, and Survival in the Global Economy.* Russell Sage Foundation.

National Academies of Sciences, Engineering, and Medicine. 2020. *Measuring Alternative Work Arrangements for Research and Policy.* National Academies Press.

National Conference of State Legislatures. 2025. "Immigration." https://www.ncsl.org/research/immigration/.

National Employment Law Project. 2025. "End Independent Contractor Misclassification." https://www.nelp.org/explore-the-issues/contracted-workers/misclassified-workers/.

National Employment Law Project. 2013. "California's New Worker Protections Against Retaliation." October 31. https://www.nelp.org/insights-research/californias-new-worker-protections-against-retaliation/.

National Employment Law Project. 2018. "California Strategic Enforcement Partnership: A Public Agency-Community Partnership." https://www.nelp.org/app/uploads/2018/11/CA-Enforcement-Document-Letter-11-27-18-1.pdf.

National Immigration Forum. 2024. "Fact Sheet: Temporary Protected Status (TPS)." Updated August 15, 2024. https://immigrationforum.org/article/fact-sheet-temporary-protected-status/.

National Labor Relations Board. 2022. "NLRB General Counsel Issues Memo on Ensuring Access for Immigrant Workers to NLRB Processes." Office of Public Affairs, May 2. https://www.nlrb.gov/news-outreach/news-story/nlrb-general-counsel-issues-memo-on-ensuring-access-for-immigrant-workers.

Neate, Rupert. 2015. "Donald Trump Doubles Down on Mexico 'Rapists' Comments Despite Outrage." *The Guardian*, July 2. https://www.theguardian.com/us-news/2015/jul/02/donald-trump-racist-claims-mexico-rapes.

Nelson, Bruce. 2002. *Divided We Stand: American Workers and the Struggle for Black Equality*. Princeton University Press.

Nessel, Lori A. 2016. "Instilling Fear and Regulating Behavior: Immigration Law as Social Control." *Georgetown Immigration Law Journal* 31(3): 525–59.

Newman, Katherine S. 2009. *No Shame in My Game: The Working Poor in the Inner City*. Knopf Doubleday.

New York State Attorney General. 2019. "AG James: Bill Protecting Immigrant Workers from Workplace Harassment Signed into Law." July 29. https://ag.ny.gov/press-release/2019/ag-james-bill-protecting-immigrant-workers-workplace-harassment-signed-law.

New York State Senate. 2023. "Senate Bill S3155." January 30. https://www.nysenate.gov/legislation/bills/2023/s3155.

Ngai, Mae M. 2004. *Impossible Subjects: Illegal Aliens and the Making of Modern America*. Princeton University Press.

Nicholls, David. 1996. *From Dessalines to Duvalier: Race, Colour, and National Independence in Haiti*. Rutgers University Press.

Niño-Murcia, Mercedes, and Jason Rothman. 2008. *Bilingualism and Identity: Spanish at the Crossroads with Other Languages*. John Benjamins Publishing.

Obasogie, Osagie K. 2013. "Foreword: Critical Race Theory and Empirical Methods." *UC Irvine Law Review* 3: 183.

Obregón, Liliana. 2018. "Empire, Racial Capitalism, and International Law: The Case of Manumitted Haiti and the Recognition Debt." *Leiden Journal of International Law* 31(3): 597–615.

Occupational Safety and Health Administration. n.d.-a. "Industry-Specific Resources." https://www.osha.gov/complianceassistance/industry.

Occupational Safety and Health Administration. n.d.-b. "OSHA Quick Card: Top Four Construction Hazards." OSHA 3216-6N-06. Occupational Safety and Health

Administration. https://www.osha.gov/sites/default/files/publications/construction_hazards_qc.pdf.

Oliver, Melvin L., and Thomas M. Shapiro. 2006. *Black Wealth/White Wealth: A New Perspective on Racial Inequality*. Routledge.

Olsen-Medina, Kira, and Jeanne Batalova. 2020. "Haitian Immigrants in the United States." Migration Policy Institute, August 12. https://www.migrationpolicy.org/article/haitian-immigrants-united-states-2018.

Oro, Paul Joseph López. 2016. "'Ni de Aquí, Ni de Allá': Garífuna Subjectivities and the Politics of Diasporic Belonging." In *Afro-Latin@s in Movement: Critical Approaches to Blackness and Transnationalism in the Americas*, edited by Petra R. Rivera-Rideau. Springer.

Orozco, Cynthia E. 2009. *No Mexicans, Women, or Dogs Allowed: The Rise of the Mexican American Civil Rights Movement*. University of Texas Press.

Orrenius, Pia M., and Madeline Zavodny. 2015a. "The Impact of E-Verify Mandates on Labor Market Outcomes." *Southern Economic Journal* 81(4): 947–59.

Orrenius, Pia M., and Madeline Zavodny. 2015b. "The Impact of Temporary Protected Status on Immigrants' Labor Market Outcomes." *American Economic Review* 105(5): 576–80.

Orrenius, Pia M., Madeline Zavodny, and Sarah Greer. 2020. "Who Signs Up for E-Verify? Insights from DHS Enrollment Records." *International Migration Review* 54(4): 1184–1211.

Osterman, Paul. 2018. "In Search of the High Road: Meaning and Evidence." *ILR Review* 71(1): 3–34.

Osuna, Steven. 2020. "Transnational Moral Panic: Neoliberalism and the Spectre of MS-13." *Race & Class* 61(4): 3–28.

Oswalt, Michael M., and César F. Rosado Marzán. 2018. "Organizing the State: The 'New Labor Law' Seen from the Bottom-Up." *Berkeley Journal of Employment & Labor Law* 39(2): 415–80.

Padilla, Yajaira M. 2022. *From Threatening Guerrillas to Forever Illegals: US Central Americans and the Cultural Politics of Non-Belonging*. University of Texas Press.

Pager, Devah. 2009. *Marked: Race, Crime, and Finding Work in an Era of Mass Incarceration*. University of Chicago Press.

Pager, Devah, Bruce Western, and David Padulla. 2009. "Employment Discrimination and the Changing Landscape of Low-Wage Labor Markets." *University of Chicago Legal Forum* 2009(1): 317–44.

Paige, Jeffery M. 1997. *Coffee and Power: Revolution and the Rise of Democracy in Central America*. Harvard University Press.

Pallares, Amalia, and Nilda Flores-González. 2009. *¡Marcha! Latino Chicago and the Immigrant Rights Movement*. University of Illinois Press.

Paret, Marcel. 2014. "Legality and Exploitation: Immigration Enforcement and the US Migrant Labor System." *Latino Studies* 12(4): 503–26.

Parker, Joe, Ranu Samantrai, and Mary Romero. 2012. *Interdisciplinarity and Social Justice: Revisioning Academic Accountability*. State University of New York Press.

Passel, Jeffrey S., and Jens Manuel Krogstad. 2024. "What We Know About Unauthorized Immigrants Living in the US." Pew Research Center, July 22. https://www.pewresearch.org/short-reads/2023/11/16/what-we-know-about-unauthorized-immigrants-living-in-the-us/.

Past, Mariana. 2021. "Twin Pillars of Resistance: Vodou and Haitian Kreyòl in Michel-Rolph Trouillot's *Ti Difé Boulé Sou Istoua Ayiti* [*Stirring the Pot of Haitian History*]." *Latin American Literary Review* 48(97): 39–49. https://doi.org/10.26824/lalr.218/.

Patler, Caitlin, Shannon Gleeson, and Matthias Schonlau. 2022. "Contesting Inequality: The Impact of Immigrant Legal Status and Education on Legal Knowledge and Claims-Making in Low-Wage Labor Markets." *Social Problems* 69(2): 356–79.

Perea, Juan F. 2011. "The Echoes of Slavery: Recognizing the Racist Origins of the Agricultural and Domestic Worker Exclusion from the National Labor Relations Act." *Ohio State Law Journal* 72(1): 95–138.

Pérez, David Marcial. 2022. "Four Hours Inside a Sweltering Truck: The Migrant Dream That Ended in Tragedy." *El País*, July 4. https://english.elpais.com/usa/2022-07-04/four-hours-inside-a-sweltering-truck-the-migrant-dream-that-ended-in-tragedy.html.

Pettit, Becky, and Bryan L. Sykes. 2015. "Civil Rights Legislation and Legalized Exclusion: Mass Incarceration and the Masking of Inequality." *Sociological Forum* 30(S1): 589–611.

Phillips, Julie A., and Douglas S. Massey. 1999. "The New Labor Market: Immigrants and Wages After IRCA." *Demography* 36(2): 233–46.

Pierre-Louis, Francois, Jr. 2021. "Coalition Building in the Making of the Haitian Community in Queens." In *Immigrant Crossroads: Globalization, Incorporation, and Placemaking in Queens, New York*, edited by Tarry Hum, Francois Pierre-Louis Jr., and Michael Alan Krasner. Temple University Press.

Pinedo-Turnovsky, Carolyn. 2019. *Daily Labors: Marketing Identity and Bodies on a New York City Street Corner*. Temple University Press.

Piore, Michael J. 1979. *Birds of Passage: Migrant Labor and Industrial Societies*. Cambridge University Press.

Piore, Michael J., and Andrew Schrank. 2018. *Root-Cause Regulation: Protecting Work and Workers in the Twenty-First Century*. Harvard University Press.

Pirtle, Whitney N. Laster. 2022. "'White People Still Come Out on Top': The Persistence of White Supremacy in Shaping Coloured South Africans' Perceptions of Racial Hierarchy and Experiences of Racism in Post-Apartheid South Africa." *Social Sciences* 11(2): 70.

Piven, Frances Fox. 2008. "Can Power from Below Change the World?" *American Sociological Review* 73(1): 1–14.

Population Reference Bureau. 2023. "2022 World Population Data Sheet." https://www.prb.org/international/.

Portes, Alejandro. 2002. "English-Only Triumphs, but the Costs Are High." *Contexts* 1(1): 10–15.

Prechel, Harland. 1990. "Steel and the State: Industry Politics and Business Policy Formation, 1940–1989." *American Sociological Review* 55(5): 648–68.

Prechel, Harland. 2000. *Big Business and the State: Historical Transitions and Corporate Transformations, 1880s–1990s.* State University of New York Press.

Prechel, Harland. 2003. "Historical Contingency Theory, Policy Paradigm Shifts, and Corporate Malfeasance at the Turn of the 21st Century." *Research in Political Sociology* 12 (31): 313–42.

Pressley-Sanon, Toni. 2017. *Istwa Across the Water: Haitian History, Memory, and the Cultural Imagination.* University Press of Florida.

Qin, Amy. 2022. "New York and California Experiment with Giving Workers a Say in Industry Standards." *In These Times,* May 1. https://inthesetimes.com/article/worker-council-sectoral-bargaining-fast-food-workers-nail-salon-workers-extension-provisions.

Rabin, Nina. 2020. "Legal Limbo as Subordination: Immigrants, Caste, and the Precarity of Liminal Status in the Trump Era." *Georgetown Immigration Law Journal* 35(2): 567–613.

Racabi, Gali. 2022. "Abolish the Employer Prerogative, Unleash Work Law." *Berkeley Journal of Employment and Labor Law* 43(1): 79–138.

Rainey, Rebecca. 2022. "Wage-Hour Investigator Hiring Plans Signal DOL Enforcement Drive." *Bloomberg Law,* January 28. https://news.bloomberglaw.com/daily-labor-report/wage-hour-investigator-hiring-plans-signal-dol-enforcement-drive.

Rainey, Rebecca. 2023. "Wage and Hour Staff Crunch May Hinder DOL Child Labor Crackdown." April 11. https://news.bloomberglaw.com/daily-labor-report/wage-and-hour-staff-crunch-may-hinder-dol-child-labor-crackdown.

Ramírez, Mónica, and Catherine Hinshaw. 2022. "Changemakers: Latinas Working to Close the Pay Gap." Justice for Migrant Women. https://img1.wsimg.com/blobby/go/c5bcf997-5277-4c09-9674-defec462dc86/J4MW%202022%20CHANGEMAKERS%20REPORT.pdf.

Ray, Victor. 2019. "A Theory of Racialized Organizations." *American Sociological Review* 84(1): 26–53.

Ray, Victor, and Danielle Purifoy. 2019. "The Colorblind Organization." In *Race, Organizations, and the Organizing Process,* edited by Melissa E. Wooten. Emerald Publishing.

Restaurant Opportunities Center of New York and the New York City Restaurant Industry Coalition. 2006. "Dining Out, Dining Healthy: The Link Between Public Health and Working Conditions in New York City's Restaurant Industry." April. https://workercenterlibrary.org/wp-content/uploads/2021/08/2006_Dining-Out-Dining-Healthy-The-Link-Between-Public-Health-and-Working-Conditions-in-New-York-Citys-Restaurant-Industry.pdf.

Restaurant Opportunities Centers United and Rosemary Batt. 2012. "Taking the High Road: A How-To Guide for Successful Restaurant Employers." January. https://workercenterlibrary.org/resources/taking-the-high-road-a-how-to-guide-for-successful-restaurant-employers/.

Rhomberg, Chris. 2012. *The Broken Table: The Detroit Newspaper Strike and the State of American Labor*. Russell Sage Foundation.

Rhomberg, Chris, and Steven Lopez. 2021. "Understanding Strikes in the 21st Century: Perspectives from the United States." In *Power and Protest*, edited by Lisa Leitz. Emerald Publishing.

Ribas, Vanesa. 2015. *On the Line: Slaughterhouse Lives and the Making of the New South*. University of California Press.

Ritchie, Kathryn, Johnnie Kallas, and Deepa Kylasam Iyer. 2023. "Labor Action Tracker: Annual Report 2023." Cornell University ILR School and University of Illinois LER School. https://www.ilr.cornell.edu/faculty-and-research/labor-action-tracker/annual-report-2023.

Robinson, Cedric J. 2019. *Cedric J. Robinson: On Racial Capitalism, Black Internationalism, and Cultures of Resistance*, edited by H.L.T. Quan. London: Pluto Press.

Robinson, Russell K. 2008. "Perceptual Segregation." *Columbia Law Review* 108: 1093–1180.

Rodriguez, Nestor. 2004. "Workers Wanted." *Work and Occupations* 31(4): 453–73.

Rodriguez, Nestor P., and Cecilia Menjívar. 2015. "Central American Immigrants and Racialization in a Post–Civil Rights Era." In *How the United States Racializes Latinos: White Hegemony and Its Consequences*, edited by José A. Cobas, Jorge Duany, and Joe R. Feagin. Taylor & Francis.

Rodriguez, Robyn M. 2008. "(Dis)Unity and Diversity in Post-9/11 America." *Sociological Forum* 23(2): 379–89.

Rodriguez, Robyn Magalit. 2022. "Introduction." In *Race, Gender, and Contemporary International Labor Migration Regimes: 21st-Century Coolies?*, edited by Leticia Saucedo and Robyn Magalit Rodriguez. Edward Elgar Publishing.

Roediger, David R. 1991. *The Wages of Whiteness: Race and the Making of the American Working Class*. Verso.

Rosado Marzán, César. 2017a. "Dignity Takings and Wage Theft." *Chicago-Kent Law Review* 92(3): 1203–23.

Rosado Marzán, César. 2017b. "Worker Centers and the Moral Economy: Disrupting Through Brokerage, Prestige, and Moral Framing Law and the Disruptive Workplace." *University of Chicago Legal Forum* 2017(1): 409–34.

Rosales, Rocío. 2014. "Stagnant Immigrant Social Networks and Cycles of Exploitation." *Ethnic and Racial Studies* 37(14): 2564–79.

Rosales, Rocío. 2020. *Fruteros: Street Vending, Illegality, and Ethnic Community in Los Angeles*. University of California Press.

Rosenfeld, Jake. 2014. *What Unions No Longer Do*. Harvard University Press.

Roth, Wendy D., and Nadia Y. Kim. 2013. "Relocating Prejudice: A Transnational Approach to Understanding Immigrants' Racial Attitudes." *International Migration Review* 47(2): 330–73.

Roy, Reena, Emily Lippiello, Osej Serratos, and Ivan Pereira. 2023. "Inside the Movement to Ban Caste Discrimination Across the US." *ABC News*, May 31. https://abcnews.go.com/US/inside-movement-ban-caste-discrimination-us/story?id=99694302.

Ruiz Cameron, Christopher David. 2003. "Borderline Decisions: Hoffman Plastic Compounds, the New Bracero Program, and the Supreme Court's Role in Making Federal Labor Policy." *UCLA Law Review* 51(1): 1–34.

Rumbaut, Rubén G., Katie Dingeman, and Anthony Robles. 2019. "Immigration and Crime and the Criminalization of Immigration." In *The Routledge International Handbook of Migration Studies*, 2nd ed., edited by Steven J. Gold and Stephanie J. Nawyn. Routledge.

Sachs, Benjamin I. 2007. "Employment Law as Labor Law." *Cardozo Law Review* 29(6): 2685–2748.

Sandefur, Rebecca L. 2019. "Access to What?" *Daedalus* 148(1): 49–55.

Saucedo, Leticia M. 2010. "Immigration Enforcement Versus Employment Law Enforcement: The Case for Integrated Protections in the Immigrant Workplace." *Fordham Urban Law Journal* 38(1): 303–25.

Saucedo, Leticia M. 2017. "The Legacy of the Immigrant Workplace: Lessons for the 21st Century Economy." *Thomas Jefferson Law Review* 40(1): 1–21.

Saucedo, Leticia. 2018. "The Parallel Worlds of Guest Work and Gig Work." *Saint Louis University Law Journal* 63(1). https://scholarship.law.slu.edu/lj/vol63/iss1/8.

Saucedo, Leticia M., and Maria Cristina Morales. 2010. "Masculinities Narratives and Latino Immigrant Workers: A Case Study of the Las Vegas Residential Construction Trades." *Harvard Journal of Law & Gender* 33(2): 625–87.

Saucedo, Leticia, and Robyn Magalit Rodriguez, eds. 2022. *Race, Gender, and Contemporary International Labor Migration Regimes: 21st-Century Coolies?* Edward Elgar.

Schmalzbauer, Leah. 2006. *Striving and Surviving: A Daily Life Analysis of Honduran Transnational Families*. Routledge.

Scott, James C. 1985. *Weapons of the Weak: Everyday Forms of Peasant Resistance*. Yale University Press.

Sepinwall, Alyssa Goldstein. 2012. *Haitian History: New Perspectives*. Routledge.

Sexsmith, Kathleen. 2016. "Exit, Voice, Constrained Loyalty, and Entrapment: Migrant Farmworkers and the Expression of Discontent on New York Dairy Farms." *Citizenship Studies* 20(3/4): 1–15.

Shah, Paru, and Robert S. Smith. 2021. "Legacies of Segregation and Disenfranchisement: The Road from *Plessy* to *Frank* and Voter ID Laws in the United States." *RSF: The Russell Sage Foundation Journal of the Social Sciences* 7(1): 134–46. https://doi.org/10.7758/RSF.2021.7.1.08.

Sherman, Rachel. 2007. *Class Acts: Service and Inequality in Luxury Hotels*. University of California Press.

Shrider, Em. 2023. "Black Individuals Had Record Low Official Poverty Rate in 2022." US Census Bureau, September 12. https://www.census.gov/library/stories/2023/09/black-poverty-rate.html.

Smith, Paige, and J. Edward Moreno. 2022. "State Anti-Bias Agency, EEOC Budgets Shift as Workloads Persist." *Bloomberg Law*, September 1. https://news.bloomberglaw.com/daily-labor-report/state-anti-bias-agency-eeoc-budgets-shift-as-workloads-persist.

Solarz, Stephen. 1995. "Foreword." In Hans Schmidt, *The United States Occupation of Haiti, 1915–1954.* Rutgers University Press.

Soldatenko, Maria Angelina. 1999. "Made in the USA: Latinas/os?, Garment Work, and Ethnic Conflict in Los Angeles' Sweat Shops." *Cultural Studies* 13(2): 319–34.

Sprague, Joey. 2016. "How Feminists Count: Critical Strategies for Quantitative Methods." In Sprague, *Feminist Methodologies for Critical Researchers: Bridging Differences.* Rowman & Littlefield.

Stainback, Kevin, and Donald Tomaskovic-Devey. 2012. *Documenting Desegregation: Racial and Gender Segregation in Private-Sector Employment Since the Civil Rights Act.* Russell Sage Foundation.

Storer, Adam, Daniel Schneider, and Kristen Harknett. 2020. "What Explains Racial/Ethnic Inequality in Job Quality in the Service Sector?" *American Sociological Review* 85(4): 537–72.

Stowe, Stacey. 2019. "New York City to Ban Discrimination Based on Hair." *New York Times*, February 18. https://www.nytimes.com/2019/02/18/style/hair-discrimination-new-york-city.html.

Stuesse, Angela. 2016. *Scratching Out a Living: Latinos, Race, and Work in the Deep South.* University of California Press.

Stumpf, Juliet P. 2006. "The Crimmigration Crisis: Immigrants, Crime, and Sovereign Power." *American University Law Review* 56(2): 367–419.

Sullivan, Michael. 2021. "Labor Citizenship for the Twenty-First Century." *Seattle Journal for Social Justice* 19(3): 809–40.

Svajlenka, Nicole Prchal. 2020. "Protecting Undocumented Workers on the Pandemic's Front Lines." Center for American Progress, December 2. https://www.americanprogress.org/article/protecting-undocumented-workers-pandemics-front-lines-2/.

Szkupinski Quiroga, Seline, Dulce M. Medina, and Jennifer Glick. 2014. "In the Belly of the Beast: Effects of Anti-Immigration Policy on Latino Community Members." *American Behavioral Scientist* 58(13): 1723–42.

Takeuchi, David T., and David R. Williams. 2011. "Past Insights, Future Promises: Race and Health in the Twenty-First Century." *Du Bois Review: Social Science Research on Race* 8(1): 1–3.

Tesfai, Rebbeca, and Kevin J. A. Thomas. 2020. "Dimensions of Inequality: Black Immigrants' Occupational Segregation in the United States." *Sociology of Race and Ethnicity* 6(1): 1–21.

Theodore, Nik. 2011. "Policing Borders: Unauthorized Immigration and the Pernicious Politics of Attrition." *Social Justice* 38(1/2): 90–106.

Tomassetti, Julia. 2022. "The Powerful Role of Unproven Economic Assumptions in Work Law." *Journal of Law and Political Economy* 3(1): 49–71.

Touw, Sharon, Grace McCormack, David U. Himmelstein, Steffie Woolhandler, and Leah Zallman. 2021. "Immigrant Essential Workers Likely Avoided Medicaid and SNAP Because of a Change to the Public Charge Rule." *Health Affairs* 40(7): 1090–98.

Trouillot, Michel-Rolph. 1982. "Motion in the System: Coffee, Color, and Slavery in Eighteenth-Century Saint-Domingue." *Review* (Fernand Braudel Center) 5(3): 331–88.

Trouillot, Michel-Rolph. 1990. *Haiti, State Against Nation: The Origins and Legacy of Duvalierism*. New York University Press.

Trouillot, Michel-Rolph. 1995. *Silencing the Past: Power and the Production of History*. Beacon Press.

Troy, Leo. 2000. "US and Canadian Industrial Relations: Convergent or Divergent?" *Industrial Relations: A Journal of Economy and Society* 39(4): 695–713.

Ulysse, Gina Athena. 2015. *Why Haiti Needs New Narratives: A Post-Quake Chronicle*. Wesleyan University Press.

US Citizenship and Immigration Services. 2021. "Form I-9 Acceptable Documents." January 14. https://www.uscis.gov/i-9-central/form-i-9-acceptable-documents.

US Citizenship and Immigration Services. 2020. "Form I-9 Verification of Lawful Permanent Residents." May 13. https://www.uscis.gov/i-9-central/form-i-9-related-news/form-i-9-verification-of-lawful-permanent-residents.

US Department of Labor. n.d.-a. "Fair Labor Standards Act." Wage and Hour Division. https://www.dol.gov/sites/dolgov/files/WHD/legacy/files/comprehensive.ppt.

US Department of Labor. n.d.-b. "Frequently Asked Questions: Complaints and the Investigation Process." https://www.dol.gov/agencies/whd/faq/workers.

US Department of Labor. n.d.-c. "US Department of Labor Organizational Chart." https://www.dol.gov/general/aboutdol/orgchart.

Valenzuela, Abel, Jr., Nik Theodore, Edwin Meléndez, and Ana Luz Gonzalez. 2006. "On the Corner: Day Labor in the United States." UCLA Center for the Study of Urban Poverty, January. https://nlg-laboremploy-comm.org/media/documents/nlg-laboremploy-comm.org_32.pdf.

Vallas, Steven Peter, and Hannah Johnston. 2023. "Labor Unbound? Assessing the Current Surge in Labor Activism." *Work and Occupations* 50(3): 376–84.

Venutolo, Ana Patricia Alvarenga. 1996. *Cultura y ética de la violencia: El Salvador, 1880–1932*. EDUCA.

Vitali, Ali, Kasie Hunt, and Frank Thorp V. 2018. "Trump Referred to Haiti and African Nations as 'Shithole' Countries." *NBC News*, January 11. https://www.nbcnews.com/politics/white-house/trump-referred-haiti-african-countries-shithole-nations-n836946.

Vogt, Wendy. 2017. "The Arterial Border: Negotiating Economies of Risk and Violence in Mexico's Security Regime." *International Journal of Migration and Border Studies* 3(2/3): 192–207.

Vogt, Wendy A. 2018. *Lives in Transit: Violence and Intimacy on the Migrant Journey*. University of California Press.

Vosko, Leah F. 2019. *Disrupting Deportability: Transnational Workers Organize*. ILR Press.

Voss, Kim, and Irene Bloemraad, eds. 2011. *Rallying for Immigrant Rights: The Fight for Inclusion in 21st Century America*. University of California Press.

Vosko, Leah F., Valerie Preston, and Robert Latham. 2017. *Liberating Temporariness? Migration, Work, and Citizenship in an Age of Insecurity*. McGill-Queen's University Press.

Wadhia, Shoba Sivaprasad. 2015. *Beyond Deportation: The Role of Prosecutorial Discretion in Immigration Cases.* New York University Press.

Wage Justice Center. n.d. "Wage Theft Facts." https://www.wagejustice.org/wage-theft-facts.

Waldinger, Roger D., and Michael I. Lichter. 2003. "What Employers Want." In Waldinger and Lichter, *How the Other Half Works: Immigration and the Social Organization of Labor.* University of California Press.

Ward, Nicole, and Jeanne Batalova. 2023. "Central American Immigrants in the United States." Migration Policy Institute, May 10. https://www.migrationpolicy.org/article/central-american-immigrants-united-states.

Warren, Robert, and Donald Kerwin. 2017. "A Statistical and Demographic Profile of the US Temporary Protected Status Populations from El Salvador, Honduras, and Haiti." *Journal on Migration and Human Security* 5(3): 577–92.

Waters, Mary C., Philip Kasinitz, and Asad L. Asad. 2014. "Immigrants and African Americans." *Annual Review of Sociology* 40(1): 369–90.

Watson, Travis. 2021. "Union Construction's Racial Equity and Inclusion Charade." *Stanford Social Innovation Review*, June 14. https://ssir.org/articles/entry/union_constructions_racial_equity_and_inclusion_charade.

Weeks, Kathi. 2017. "Down with Love: Feminist Critique and the New Ideologies of Work." *WSQ: Women's Studies Quarterly* 45(3/4): 37–58.

Weil, David. 2010. *Improving Workplace Conditions Through Strategic Enforcement: A Report to the Wage and Hour Division.* Boston University School of Management Research Paper No. 2010-20. Last revised March 27, 2012. https://papers.ssrn.com/sol3/papers.cfm?abstract_id=1623390.

Weil, David. 2014. *The Fissured Workplace: Why Work Became So Bad for So Many and What Can Be Done to Improve It.* Harvard University Press.

Weil, David. 2019. "Understanding the Present and Future of Work in the Fissured Workplace Context." *RSF: The Russell Sage Foundation Journal of the Social Sciences* 5(5): 147–65. https://doi.org/10.7758/RSF.2019.5.5.08.

Weiler, Paul. 1982. "Promises to Keep: Securing Workers' Rights to Self-Organization Under the NLRA." *Harvard Law Review* 96: 1769–1827.

Williams, Jamillah Bowman. 2021. "Beyond Sex-Plus: Acknowledging Black Women in Employment Law and Policy." *Employee Rights and Employment Policy Journal* 25(1): 13–51.

Windham, Lane. 2017. *Knocking on Labor's Door: Union Organizing in the 1970s and the Roots of a New Economic Divide.* University of North Carolina Press.

Wingfield, Adia Harvey. 2007. "The Modern Mammy and the Angry Black Man: African American Professionals' Experiences with Gendered Racism in the Workplace." *Race, Gender, & Class* 14(1/2): 196–212.

Wingfield, Adia Harvey, and Koji Chavez. 2020. "Getting In, Getting Hired, Getting Sideways Looks: Organizational Hierarchy and Perceptions of Racial Discrimination." *American Sociological Review* 85(1): 31–57.

Wishnie, Michael J. 2008. "Labor Law After Legalization." *Minnesota Law Review* 92(5): 1446–61.

Wong, Tom K., Karina Shklyan, Andrea Silva, and Josefina Espino. 2019. "Fractured Immigration Federalism: How Dissonant Immigration Enforcement Policies

Affect Undocumented Immigrants." University of California–San Diego, US Immigration Policy Center, April 3. https://usipc.ucsd.edu/publications/Fractured-Immigration-Federalism-.pdf.

Wood, Elisabeth Jean. 2003. *Insurgent Collective Action and Civil War in El Salvador.* Cambridge University Press.

Wright, Erik Olin. 2000. "Working-Class Power, Capitalist-Class Interests, and Class Compromise." *American Journal of Sociology* 105(4): 957–1002.

Yamada, David C. 2012. "Emerging American Legal Responses to Workplace Bullying." *Temple Political & Civil Rights Law Review* 22(2): 329–54.

Yates, Caitlyn. 2021. "Haitian Migration Through the Americas: A Decade in the Making." Migration Policy Institute, September 30. https://www.migrationpolicy.org/article/haitian-migration-through-americas.

Ybema, Sierk, and Martha Horvers. 2017. "Resistance Through Compliance: The Strategic and Subversive Potential of Frontstage and Backstage Resistance." *Organization Studies* 38(9): 1233–51.

Zamora, Sylvia. 2022. *Racial Baggage: Mexican Immigrants and Race Across the Border.* Stanford University Press.

Zatz, Noah D. 2008. "Working Beyond the Reach or Grasp of Employment Law." In *The Gloves-Off Economy: Workplace Standards at the Bottom of America's Labor Market*, edited by Annette Bernhardt, Heather Boushey, Laura Dresser, and Chris Tilly. ILR Press.

Zavella, Patricia. 2011. *I'm Neither Here nor There: Mexicans' Quotidian Struggles with Migration and Poverty.* Duke University Press.

Zemans, Frances Kahn. 2006. "Framework for Analysis of Legal Mobilization: A Decision-Making Model." *Law & Social Inquiry* 7(4): 989–1071.

Zepeda-Millán, Chris. 2017. *Latino Mass Mobilization: Immigration, Racialization, and Activism.* Cambridge University Press.

Zimmerman, Arely, Joanna Perez, and Leisy J. Abrego. 2022. "Complexities of Belonging: Compounded Foreignness and Racial Cover Among Undocumented Central American Youth." *Ethnicities* 23(6): 822–42.

Zuberi, Tukufu, and Eduardo Bonilla-Silva. 2008. *White Logic, White Methods: Racism and Methodology.* Rowman & Littlefield.

INDEX

Tables are listed in **boldface**.

Abruzzo, Jennifer, 103
abuses of low-wage workers: dangerous conditions, 34–36; deflecting with humor, 60; discrimination and demeaning treatment, 37–38; disrespect, 2, 5, 34; precarity and, 38–39; typical abusive practices, 1–2, 24, 31; ubiquity of, 39; underpayment of wages and overtime (wage theft), 33–34. *See also* discrimination; improvements in low-wage work
Acharya, Avidit, 6
AFL. *See* American Federation of Labor (AFL)
AFL-CIO, and reform agenda, 181–82
Alexander, Charlotte, 41, 46, 187n2, 208n5
American Community Survey, 168
American Federation of Labor (AFL), 181
Amuedo-Dorantes, Catalina, 89
Antiterrorism and Effective Death Penalty Act of 1996 (AEDPA), 14, 72
Azaroff, Lenore, 187n3

Bernhardt, Annette, 168
Black diaspora, animosity between groups in, 151
Black Lives Matter movement, 181

Bonilla-Silva, Eduardo, 141
Bracero Program, 136
Brown, Mike, 182
Bumiller, Kristin, 64–65

California, immigrant rights in, 74, 104–5, 169, 175–76, 180
care and home-health workers, dangers faced by, 35–36
Central America: colonial exploitation and violence, effects of, 16–17, 132–33, 156–57; definition of, 194n32; history of collective organizing, 157; US imperialism in, ongoing effects of, 133–36
Central American immigrants: animosity between national groups, 151–52, 161; asylum protections and, 134; large number of, 18, 134; long period of temporary protected status, 134; racism as barrier to seeking job improvements, 149–50; respondents' demographics and immigration status, 8, **8**, 9, **9**, 189, 194–95nn33–35; and TPS, 79, 194n33; in US, areas of concentration, 194n32. *See also* discrimination against Central American workers

Chen, Ming Hsu, 69, 167
Chetty, Raj, 178
Civil Rights Act of 1964, 16, 178–79
civil rights laws: ineffectiveness against racialized labor hierarchies, 6, 16, 22, 178; necessary reforms of, 19, 178–80; persistence of racism despite, 142–43; state and local action on, 179–80
Collins, Patricia Hill, 191
colonial exploitation: animosity within ethnicities and, 150, 152, 161; in Central America, ongoing effects of, 16–17, 132–33, 156–57; as driver of worker migration, 6; in Haiti, ongoing effects of, 16–17, 125–26, 155; impact on low-wage immigrants' experience, 163; legacy of, as barrier to demands for job improvements, 145–46, 155; ongoing effects of, 164, 178; origin-country realities as inspiration for resistance, 158–60, 162
community organizations, and worker protections, 28, 55–56, 147
COVID-19 pandemic, 191
critical race theory, 4
Cuéllar, Jorge, 133

Deferred Action for Childhood Arrivals (DACA), 167
Department of Labor (DOL): immigrants' lack of information on, 46–47; and immigration status in labor law, 103; and worker protections, 26–27, 48, 55, 57, 101–2, 106, 108, 110, 174
Dessalines, Jean-Jacques, 159–60
dignity and respect: achievement of, as type of power, 5; as beyond legal requirements, 61, 123; civil rights legislation to project, 180, 211n75; demands for, **53**, 61–63; desire for, 24, 31, 35, 37–38, 61; finding despite conditions, 5, 42; humiliation as employer control strategy, 123; origin-country experiences as source of, 159–60; quiet resistance and, **53**, 64–65; racial discrimination and demeaning treatment and, 116, 143
discrimination: intersectionality of, 4, 121, 123; persistence despite civil rights laws, 142–43. *See also* gender discrimination; racial discrimination; racism
discrimination against Central American workers, 18, 131–42; anti-Latino bias, 116, 117–18, 135–36; colonial exploitation, ongoing effects of, 132–33; denigration by Whites, 140; homogenization as Latino/Hispanic, 131, 134, 135, 136–39; language-based bias, 116, 138–39; policies enforcing inequality, 134; racialized labor hierarchies and, 135–36, 137; racist border policies and, 134–35; stereotypes and, 117–18, 135, 137; US imperialism, ongoing effects of, 133–36; work assignments vs. peers, 140–42. *See also* racism, anti-Latino
discrimination against Haitian workers, 17–18, 118–31; anti-Blackness, 116, 117, 118–23; anti-Haitian racism, 116, 117, 124–28; as barrier to seeking job improvements, 149; and criminality, assumptions about, 121, 123; degrading "slave-like" treatment, 122–23; in hiring, 120–21, 205n43; by Hispanic workers, 128–31, 149, 161; intersectionality of, 121, 122–23; language-based bias, 127, 149, 207nn102–3; pay disparities, 121; schedule disparities, 121–22
Durand, Jorge, 77
Duvalier, "Papa Doc" and "Baby Doc," 125–26, 155

EADs. *See* employment authorization documents
Einarsen, Stale, 211n75

INDEX | 245

employers: control of low-wage work experience, 11–12, 15, 23–24, 25; ease of manipulating undocumented workers, 94, 98–99, 100–101; exploitation of poor labor law enforcement, 54; immigration enforcement by, as barrier to worker rights, 3–4, 14, 18, 164, 176–77; limited communication to workers about rights, 47; and temporarily authorized workers, extra work and risk of, 15, 70, 81–82, 85, 101, 176–77; use of race to divide workers, 148, 159, 182; voluntary measure to improve low-wage labor, 165–66. *See also* intermediary employers

employers' power to terminate workers (at-will employment): amplification by immigration policies, 97, 98–102, 111, 164; as barrier to worker rights, 3, 42–44, 65, 171; and employer control over work, 11–12, 15, 25; legally-protected exceptions, 11–12, 163–64; legislation to remedy, 173; as leverage to divide workers, 145; *vs.* other countries, 12; temporarily authorized workers and, 82, 96; unions as protection against, 63, 172

employment authorization documents (EADs) (work permits): delays in extension or receipt of, 70, 85–86; employers' leverage over, 70; extra work and risk for employers, 15, 70, 81–82, 85, 101, 176–77. *See also* temporary protected status (TPS) workers

enforcement of workers' rights law: fragmented jurisdictions and, 47–48, 174; lack of resources for, 26, 173–74; necessary reforms in, 18, 173–76; need for brokers to advance workers' complaints, 55–57, 175; need for coordination of federal, state, and local agencies, 176; need for robust damages, 176; need for strategic enforcement efforts, 174, 175–76; reliance on worker-initiated complaints, 42, 44–48, 164, 173; under-enforcement, 21, 24, 25, 26–27, 163–64; weak, employers' exploitation of, 54

Fair Labor Standards Act (FLSA), 21, 25–26
Fanon, Franz, 97, 111
fissuring, 29–30, 170
Floyd, George, 182, 190
FLSA. *See* Fair Labor Standards Act

gender discrimination: and demeaning treatment, 37–38, 168; intersection with other biases, 4, 121, 123
Gomberg-Muñoz, Ruth, 168
Gompers, Samuel, 181
government regulation: inability to stop racial discrimination, 146–47, 150; inadequacies of, 3–4. *See also* immigration regime; workers' rights law
Greenman, Emily, 94–95

Haiti: Kreyòl and Vodou as forms of resistance in, 124, 206n60; Kreyòl-speakers, discrimination against, 127; revolutionary legacy in, as inspiration, 159–60
Haiti, history of, 118–20, 124–28; and anti-Haitian racism, 117, 124–28, 155; conflict with Dominican Republic, 128; effects of colonial exploitation, 16–17, 125–26, 155
Haitian immigrants: areas of concentration in US, 194n31; conditions in Haiti, and fear of deportation, 154–55; Kreyòl-speaking, discrimination against, 127; as relatively new arrivals in New York, 155; respondents' demographics and immigration status, 7–8, **8**, 9, **9**, 189,

194n31, 195n35; and TPS, 79; unstable immigration regime and, 195–96n51; xenophobia and racism experienced by, 89–90. *See also* discrimination against Haitian workers
Hall, Matthew, 94–95
Hartman, Saidiya, 123
Harvard Law School Labor and Worklife Program, 171
health and safety standards: employers' ignoring of, 142; under-enforcement of, 34–35
Heeren, Geoffrey, 79–80
Hernández Martínez, Maximiliano, 132
Hispanic workers: creation of category, 136–37; discrimination against Haitian workers, 128–31, 149, 161; homogenization as Latino/Hispanic (erasure of national-origin), 131, 134, 135, 136–39; stereotyping as invasion force, 135
Hoffman Plastics decision (2002), 73–74, 103, 178
human resource offices (HR), complaints to, 51–53, 60–61

Illegal Immigration Reform and Immigrant Responsibility Act of 1996 (IIRAIRA), 14, 72
Immigration and Customs Enforcement, US (ICE): immigrants' fear of, 92; state and local law cooperation with, 14, 88–89
Immigration Reform and Control Act of 1986 (IRCA), 14, 72, 73–74, 181
immigration regime: anti-Latino racism of, 134–35; disempowerment of low-wage immigrant workers, 164; exacerbation of immigrant precarity, 97, 111; immigrants' fear of interaction with, 156–57, 167; necessary reforms of, 18, 176–78; need for decriminalization of infractions, 177; need for universal path to citizenship, 18; and precarity of immigrant life, 13–14; racialized labor hierarchy and, 67; reform, failures of, 69; stratifying of workers by immigration status, 13, 67, 96; undermining of workers' rights by, 69; unstable, impact of, 195–96n51; vulnerability of undocumented workers, 3–4
immigration status: precarious, psychological effects of, 153–54, 177; presumption of illegality for immigrants of color, 14, 88–90; of respondents, **8**, **9**, 9–10, 194–95nn33–35; terminology for, 194n30. *See also* permanently authorized workers; temporary protected status (TPS) workers; undocumented (unauthorized) workers
improvements in low-wage work: employers' lack of incentive for, 148; formal complaints, rarity of, 40, 55, 187nn2–3; improved immigration status and, 98, 108–9; successful efforts by workers, 40, 41. *See also* enforcement of workers' rights law
improvements in low-wage work, barriers to workers' action, 2, 13, 40, 41–53, 65, 153; fear of deportation as, 97, 99–100, 105–6, 153–57, 177; fear of government interaction as, 104–5, 153, 155, 167, 177; fear of losing job as, 41–44, 97, 98–102, 171; fragmented jurisdictions of enforcement agencies as, 47–48; futile internal complaint processes as, 51–53; hope of acceptance through hard work as, 153; immigration enforcement by employers as, 3–4, 14, 18, 164, 176–77; intermediary companies as, 12–13, 42, 48–51, 103–4, 147; lack of access to support as, 147; lack of knowledge about rights as, 42, 44–46, 97, 102–5; lack of knowledge about where and

how to complain as, 42, 46–48; lack of worker solidarity as, 97, 105–6, 145, 150–52, 182–83; language barrier as, 47, 56, 147, 151; obligation to support family as, 152–53, 154, 162; poor conditions in home country as, 153–57; punishment for attempting change as, 54, 62; US system's reliance on worker-initiated complaints as, 42, 44–48, 164, 173; weak labor unions as, 51–52; workers' acceptance of abuses as, 41–42. *See also* racism as barrier to seeking job improvements

improvements in low-wage work, pathways to, **53**, 53–65, 165–66; avenues other than formal complaints, 41; brokers' assisting with complaints, 55–57, 175; demands beyond legal requirements, **53**, 61–63; formal complaints, **53**, 54–58, 60–61, 165; immigration advocacy groups and, 98, 110–11, 204n30; informal collectives and, 62–63; informal negotiations with supervisors, 58–60, 165; labor unions and, 63, 98, 109–10; move to new job, 62, 108–9; origin country realities as inspiration for resistance, 162, 158–60; quiet resistance as, **53**, 64–65; range of, 146; recommendations for improving, 65–66; solidarity as, 54, 97–98, 107–8, 160–61, 165, 182–83

independent contractors, lack of recourse for, 36

Indigenous peoples of Central America, colonial efforts to commit genocide, 17, 132–33

intermediary employers: difficulty of addressing rights violations by, 42, 48–51, 103–4; exploitation of undocumented immigrants, 103–4; fees charged by, 101; misclassification of workers, 104, 169, 208n5; needed reforms, 170; number of contingent workers nationally, 30; recognition of joint employer status as remedy for, 12, 49–50, 170; as strategy to circumvent workers' rights law, 12–13, 24, 29–31, 42, 48–51, 103–4, 147; workers' confusion about employer and employment status and, 48–51

IRCA. *See* Immigration Reform and Control Act of 1986

Janus v. AFSCME (2018), 27–28
Jim Crow era, 120
Jung, Moon-Kie, 118

Kalleberg, Arne, 37

labor laws. *See* workers' rights law
labor unions: access barriers for low-wage workers, 2, 3, 28–29, 51–52; assistance with formal complaints, 55; constraints on, in current labor law, 171; decline in membership, 12, 24, 27; demands beyond legal requirements and, 63; history of racism and nativism, 181; immigrants' bad experience with, 157; improvements in low-wage work and, 98, 109–10; insufficient legal protections for, 26; as key check on employer power, 24, 27, 28; low coverage in low-wage jobs, 24; need for strengthening of, 172; political and judicial assaults on, 27–28; proposal for unionized workplace as default status, 171; push to expand low-wage worker protections, 169; recent upsurge in, 27; role in advancing reform agenda, 181–82; and total person unionism, 181

lawful permanent residents (LPRs), 87. *See also* permanently authorized workers

lawyers, assistance with formal complaints, 55

Lee, Ching Kwan, 66

Legal Services Corporation (LSC) program, 175
low-wage work: employers' control of, 11–12, 15, 23–24, 25; overrepresentation of immigrants in, 1; types of jobs, 10, 31, **32**, 195n36; workers' desire for acknowledgment, 37; workers' desire for autonomy and empowerment, 31
LSC. *See* Legal Services Corporation (LSC) program
Lucas, Samuel, 142

MacKinnon, Catharine, 4
methodology: advantages of New York region for, 166–67, 187–88; analysis of legal and policy landscape, 11; bottom-up epistemologies, 7. 166, 186–87; comparative design, 187–88; goals, 185–86; inductive method, 7; multidisciplinary approach, 185–86, 191–92; and objective *vs.* subjective view, 191–92; project timing and cultural environment, 190–91; qualitative work, benefits of, 168; sample and interviews, 1, 7–10, **8, 9**, 166, 187, 189–90, 191, 196n59; worker-centered approach, 166–69
Mexican-American War, 133
Mexico, Bracero Program and, 136
Miller, Richard, 187n2

National Domestic Workers Alliance, 169
National Labor Relations Act (NLRA): gendered and racial exclusions, 12; minimal worker protections under, 26, 170–71; proposed revisions of, 171–72; racist foundations of, 21, 26
National Labor Relations Board, 103, 174–75
New York City reputation as immigrant haven, 127, 139
New York State: laws against immigration retaliation, 74, 104–5;

Nail Salon Minimum Standards Act, 171–72
NLRA. *See* National Labor Relations Act

Occupational Safety and Health Act of 1970, 26
Occupational Safety and Health Administration, 26–27
organizing to advance reform agenda, 19, 180–83

people of color: as immigrants, and presumption of illegality, 14, 88–90; lesser access to job complaint supports, 147; overrepresentation in low-wage work, 1
permanently authorized workers: anti-immigrant sentiment and, 88–90; factors not improved by permanent status, 93; freedom to travel, 93; improved opportunities, 71, 87, 88, 91–93; and inequitable resource distribution, 90; obstacles to finding work, 93–95; poor English skills as handicap, 94–95; vast majority of immigrants as, 87; vulnerability of undocumented family and friends and, 90; work experience of, 70, **70**, 87–95; xenophobia and racial discrimination and, 14, 71, 87, 88, 89, 94–95, 96
Piore, Michael, 47, 152
Piven, Frances Fox, 4
police brutality, 181, 190
policy recommendations, 169–80; civil rights law reforms, 19, 178–80; immigration regime reforms, 18, 176–78; labor law reforms, 18, 169–76; organizing to advance reform agenda, 19, 180–83; strengthening of rights enforcement, 18, 173–76
Pozo, Susan, 89
Prasad, Arthi, 41, 46, 187n2

pride in work: as capitalist tool of worker control, 64–65; as form of quiet resistance, 64–65
Protecting the Right to Organize Act of 2021, 170
public sector work, and Black advancement, 121, 205n32

Quiroga, Seline Szkupinski, 88–89

race: racial caste system as legacy of slavery, 119; solidarity across races, resistance enabled by, 160–61, 165, 182–83
racial discrimination, 37–38; bias against Haitian workers and, 116, 117, 118–23; bias against Latin Americans and, 128–30; Black men and, 123; difficulty of documenting, 38; as fifth step of racialization, 115; need for revaluation of, 143; as often not actionable, 116; ongoing failure to address, 66; as ongoing problem, 14, 16, 71, 87, 88, 89, 94–95, 96, 178–79; persistence despite "race-neutral" legal environment, 22, 117, 142–43, 145, 164, 179; radical transformation required to eliminate, 178; range of types and severity, 115, 116, 118, 131, 143; respondents' verification of theorists' work, 117, 123; scholarship on, 118, 122, 127
racialization: five steps of process, 115; and power relations, 140; as strategy to fragment working class, 140, 141, 142
racialized labor hierarchies: Central American workers in, 140–41; government's failure to address, 3, 4; historical roots of, 5–6, 164; history of, in Central America, 132–33; immigration regime and, 67; ineffectiveness of civil rights laws against, 6, 22; Latino/Hispanic workers and, 135–36, 137–38; other stratifying factors and, 4; reforms to end, 176; workers' performance of racial identity and, 141
racism: Afro- and Indigenous Latinos and, 116–17; disproportionate impact on Black migrants, 116; multiple forms of, 116, 131; as obstacle to worker solidarity, 105; as systemic, 131, 145, 162. *See also* discrimination
racism, anti-Latino: homogenization of Latino/Hispanic workers and, 131, 134, 135, 136–39; Latino migrants as threatening invaders and, 135; migrant labor policies and, 135–36; racialized labor hierarchies and, 135–36, 137–38; and stereotype of Latinos as criminals, 135, 137; in US border policies, 134–35
racism as barrier to seeking job improvements: discrimination by non-Whites, 148; inadequacy of legal protections, 146–47; lack of solidarity for collective resistance, 150–52; racist supervisors and, 147–50; types of barriers, 145–46, 164–65
reform agenda, organizing to advance, 19, 180–83
research, future avenues for, 166–69
Ribas, Vanesa, 168
Rosado Marzán, César, 33, 180
Rosales, Rocío, 168
Rosenfeld, Jake, 28
Ryswick, Treaty of (1697), 128

Sachs, Benjamin, 176
Sarat, Austin, 187n2
Schrank, Andrew, 47
September 11th terrorist attacks, and immigration law, 72–73
service workers, demeaning treatment of, 38

Sexsmith, Kathleen, 42
slavery: history of, 118–20; ongoing effects of, 6, 117, 120, 164, 178
Storer, Adam, 122
Supreme Court: and labor unions, 27–28; on protections for undocumented workers, 73–74
Sure-Tan Inc. v. National Labor Relations Board (1984), 73

Taft-Hartley amendments, 28
temporary H-2A/H-2B seasonal workers, 80
temporary protected status (TPS) workers: benefits of status, 80, 82–83; Central American immigrants and, 194n33; fees paid by, 85; goals of program, 79; groups for future research, 166; liminality of, 9; limited rights of, 79; necessary reforms for, 18, 176–77; number of, 79; relegation to bottom-of-the-barrel jobs, 70; respondents with TPS status, **8**, 9, **9**; risk inherent in registration with government, 15, 84, 167; work experience of, 70, **70**, 79–87. *See also* employment authorization documents (EADs) (work permits)
temporary protected status (TPS) workers, precarity of: hazy legal status and, 14, 79–81, 96; lack of pathway to permanent status, 86; renewal or revocation of TPS, uncertainty of, 14, 15, 79, 81–82, 84–87; temporary status as employment handicap, 81–82; Trump administration and, 81, 84, 86; uncertainty of TPS renewal or revocation, 14, 15, 70, 79, 81–82, 84–87, 167, 177
TPS. *See* temporary protected status
Trump, Donald: denigration of Haitians, 126; and immigrant insecurity, 95, 104–5, 190; and precarity of temporarily authorized workers, 81, 84, 86; stereotyping of immigrants, 72, 86, 135

Ulysse, Gina, 127
undocumented (unauthorized) workers: criminalization of work, and precarity, 70, 72–73, 95–96; E-Verify and, 74, 176; fraudulent work documents and, 72, 75, 76; harrowing journeys to US, 77, 99; intermediary companies' exploitation of, 103–4; intersectionality of disempowerment, 122–23; investment in travel to US as reason for staying, 153, 154, 155–56, 158–59; labor brokers and, 76; lack of knowledge about rights, 102–3; large number of, 71; limited access to worker protections, 14, 73–74; mental health effects of precarity, 90; need for laws recognizing rights of, 178; racial discrimination and, 72–73, 78–79; relegation to bottom-of-the-barrel jobs, 70, 74–75, 76–79; stereotyping as outsiders and criminals, 14, 72; work experience of, 70, **70**, 71–79; work for cash in informal economy, 75–76, 104
United States: dominance in Latin America, and White privilege, 117; exploitation of Haiti, 125–26; imperialism, ongoing effects of, 6, 133–36, 193n22; slavery and anti-Black racism in, 120. *See also* colonial exploitation

Vargas, João Costa, 118

Wadhia, Shoba, 167
Weil, David, 29–30, 170
White privilege/supremacy: ongoing effects of, 117, 119, 140, 162; understanding, as key to addressing racism, 143
Williams, Jamillah Bowman, 179
Wishnie, Michael, 69

work permits. *See* employment authorization documents (EADs)
work slowdowns (quiet quitting), 64, 146
worker centers: financial support for, 175; and improvements in low-wage work, 109–10, 204n30; support for worker protections, 28–29, 57–58, 169, 175
worker empowerment: definition and types of, 4–5; quiet resistance and, 64–65
workers' rights law: barriers to workers' use of, 26–27; basic protections of, 163; employers' political action to affect, 24–25; immigration status as irrelevant in, 102–3; limited protections in, 11–12, 25–26; as limited to employees, 25, 169; privileging of employers' interests, 163, 170–71; racist and sexist foundations of, 12, 21; radical reform as necessary but insufficient, 180–1; routine violation in some industries, 164; state level reforms, 170; violations, difficulty of proving, 25, 26, 164; weak protections in, 3, 21, 23–24, 161; worker organizations' and, 28–29. *See also* intermediary employers
workers' rights law, necessary reforms in, 18, 169–76; expansion of number of protected workers, 18, 169–70; increased volume of workers' rights, 170–73; need for public education on, 174–75; protections from unwarranted firing, 18, 171, 172–73; revisions to NLRA, 171–72; state and local reforms, 171–72; strengthening of labor unions, 172

Yamada, David, 180